T0251416

INTELLIGENT DATA WAREHOUSING

From Data Preparation to Data Mining

Zhengxin Chen

CRC PRESS

Boca Raton   London   New York   Washington, D.C.

Library of Congress Cataloging-in-Publication Data

Chen, Zhengxin.
    Intelligent data warehousing : from data preparation to data mining / Zhengxin Chen.
        p. cm.
    Includes bibliographical references and index.
    ISBN 0-8493-1204-3 (alk. paper)
    1. Database design. 2. Data warehousing. I. Title.

QA76.9.D26 C46 2001
005.74—dc21
                                                        2001043272
                                                         CIP

Visit the CRC Press Web site at www.crcpress.com

© 2002 by CRC Press LLC

No claim to original U.S. Government works
International Standard Book Number 0-8493-1204-3
Library of Congress Card Number 2001043272
Printed in the United States of America 1 2 3 4 5 6 7 8 9 0
Printed on acid-free paper

About the author

Zhengxin Chen earned his Ph.D. from Louisiana State University. He currently is professor of computer science at the University of Nebraska at Omaha. Professor Chen teaches courses in artificial intelligence and database management systems. His research involves building intelligent information systems using integrated approaches and systematic thinking.

Contents

Part I

Chapter 1   Introduction 3
  1.1   Why this book is needed..3
  1.2   Features of the book...5
  1.3   Why intelligent data warehousing 5
  1.4   Organization of the book 6
  1.5   How to use this book...7
  References...8

Chapter 2   Enterprise intelligence and artificial intelligence.................11
  2.1   Overview..11
  2.2   Data warehousing and enterprise intelligence............11
  2.3   Historical development of data warehousing 12
    2.3.1   Prehistory..12
    2.3.2   Stage 1: early 1990s 13
    2.3.3   Stage 2: mid-1990s...14
    2.3.4   Stage 3: toward business intelligence 14
  2.4   Basic elements of data warehousing 14
  2.5   Databases and the Web...15
    2.5.1   World Wide Web and e-commerce...................15
    2.5.2   Data Webhouse 17
    2.5.3   Ontologies and semantic Web.........................20
  2.6   Basics of artificial intelligence and machine learning 21
    2.6.1   Artificial intelligence as construction of intelligent
      agents...21
    2.6.2   State space search and knowledge representation 22
    2.6.3   Knowledge-based systems................................24
    2.6.4   Symbol-based machine learning......................24
    2.6.5   Genetic algorithms 25
  2.7   Data warehousing with intelligent agents 26
    2.7.1   Integration of database and knowledge-based
      systems..26
    2.7.2   The role of AI in warehousing.........................27
    2.7.3   Java and agent technology...............................28

2.8   Data mining, CRM, Web mining, and clickstream 29
        2.8.1   What can be analyzed using intelligent data
                 analysis 29
        2.8.2   From data mining to Web mining 30
                 2.8.2.1   Background 30
                 2.8.2.2   Creating and enhancing Web data 31
                 2.8.2.3   Mining Web data 31
                 2.8.2.4   Other issues of Web mining 32
                 2.8.2.5   Approaches for Web mining 33
        2.8.3   Clickstream analysis 33
                 2.8.3.1   Components of clickstream analysis 33
                 2.8.3.2   Clickstream data mart 33
2.9   The future of data warehouses 34
2.10   Summary 35
References 36

Chapter 3   From DBMS to data warehousing 39
3.1   Overview 39
3.2   An overview of database management systems 39
        3.2.1   Data modeling 39
        3.2.2   Relational data model 40
        3.2.3   Integrity constraints 42
        3.2.4   Normalization and normal forms 43
        3.2.5   Basics of query processing 43
        3.2.6   Basics of transaction processing 44
3.3   Advances in DBMS 46
        3.3.1   Basics of deductive databases 46
        3.3.2   Object-relational and object-oriented databases 47
        3.3.3   Distributed and parallel databases 47
        3.3.4   Motivations of data warehousing: a technical
                 examination 48
3.4   Architecture and design of data warehouses 52
        3.4.1   Operational systems and warehouse data 52
        3.4.2   Data warehouse components 53
        3.4.3   Data warehouse design 54
3.5   Data Marts 55
        3.5.1   Why data marts 55
        3.5.2   Types of data marts 56
        3.5.3   Multiple data marts 57
        3.5.4   Networked data marts 57
3.6   Metadata 58
3.7   Data warehousing and materialized views 60
        3.7.1   Materialized views 60
        3.7.2   Indexing techniques 62
        3.7.3   Indexing using metadata 62

3.8   Data warehouse performance.......................................64
     3.8.1   Measuring data warehouse performance.................64
     3.8.2   Performance and warehousing activities................65
3.9   Data warehousing and OLAP...................................66
     3.9.1   Basics of OLAP...66
     3.9.2   Relationship between data warehousing and
             OLAP..67
3.10 Summary...68
References...68

Part II

Chapter 4 Data preparation and preprocessing 73
4.1   Overview..73
4.2   Schema and data integration.................................73
4.3   Data pumping 75
4.4   Middleware...76
4.5   Data quality 77
4.6   Data cleansing 78
     4.6.1   General aspects of data cleansing.....................78
     4.6.2   Data cleansing methods 79
          4.6.2.1   Domain relevance 79
          4.6.2.2   Sorted neighborhood duplicate detection
                  method.......................................80
          4.6.2.3   Multi-pass sorted neighborhood duplicate
                  detection method 80
          4.6.2.4   Transitive closure 81
          4.6.2.5   Union-find algorithms 81
          4.6.2.6   K-way sorting method....................82
4.7   Dealing with data inconsistency in multidatabase systems......83
4.8   Data reduction...84
4.9   Case study: data preparation for stock food chain analysis......85
     4.9.1   Overview...85
     4.9.2   Preparing the data....................................87
          4.9.2.1   Data integration 88
          4.9.2.2   Data cleaning............................88
          4.9.2.3   Data transformation 89
          4.9.2.4   Data reduction...........................89
          4.9.2.5   SQL query examples 89
     4.9.3   Building the hierarchies 91
     4.9.4   Resulting data 91
4.10 Web log file preparation.......................................93
4.11 Summary...96
References...96

Chapter 5   Building data warehouses...**97**
   5.1   Overview...97
   5.2   Conceptual data modeling..97
       5.2.1   Entity-relationship (ER) modeling...............................97
       5.2.2   Dimension modeling 99
   5.3   Data warehouse design using ER approach.........................100
       5.3.1   An example 100
       5.3.2   Steps in using ER model for warehousing conceptual
              modeling...102
       5.3.3   Research work on conceptual modeling 104
   5.4   Aspects of building data warehouses..................................105
       5.4.1   Physical design 105
       5.4.2   Using functional dependencies.....................................106
       5.4.3   Loading the warehouse...107
       5.4.4   Metadata management..107
       5.4.5   Operation phase 108
       5.4.6   Using data warehouse tools 108
       5.4.7   User behavior modeling for warehouse design............109
       5.4.8   Coherent management of warehouses for security......110
       5.4.9   Prototyping data warehouses...110
   5.5   Data cubes...111
   5.6   Summary...113
   References..113

Chapter 6   Basics of materialized views...**117**
   6.1   Overview...117
   6.2   Data cubes...118
       6.2.1   Materialization of data cubes...118
       6.2.2   Using the lattice...121
            6.2.2.1   Hierarchies in lattice..............................121
            6.2.2.2   Composite lattices for multiple, hierarchical
                     dimensions.......................................122
            6.2.2.3   The cost analysis.....................................123
   6.3   Using a simple optimization algorithm to select views..........125
   6.4   Aggregate calculation using preconstructed data structures
       in data cubes...127
       6.4.1   Preliminaries of aggregation functions.........................127
       6.4.2   Aggregation operations defined on data cubes............128
            6.4.2.1   Calculating SUM on data cube using
                     PRE_SUM cube 128
            6.4.2.2   Calculating COUNT................................129
            6.4.2.3   Calculating MAX by constructing PRE-MAX
                     tree...130
   6.5   Case study: view selection for a human service data
       warehouse 130
       6.5.1   Overview of the case study...132

	6.5.2	Background information	133
	6.5.3	Data model	133
	6.5.4	Queries selected	134
	6.5.5	Development of the OR view graph	134
	6.5.6	Implementation	135
		6.5.6.1 Genetic algorithm description	136
		6.5.6.2 Solution encoding, reproduction, and mutation	136
		6.5.6.3 Description of the fitness function	137
		6.5.6.4 Query benefit function	138
		6.5.6.5 Penalty function	138
		6.5.6.6 Total query cost and maintenance cost calculation example	139
		6.5.6.7 Genetic algorithm implementation	139
	6.5.7	Resulting views	139
		6.5.7.1 Small OR view graph	139
		6.5.7.2 Results from a small view graph	141
		6.5.7.3 Complete OR view graph	142
		6.5.7.4 Results from a complete view graph	143
	6.5.8	Summary of the case study	144
6.6	Summary		145
References			145
Chapter 7	**Advances in materialized views**		**147**
7.1	Overview		147
7.2	Data warehouse design through materialized views		148
	7.2.1	Data warehouse design	148
	7.2.2	View selection problem	148
	7.2.3	View data lineage problem	150
7.3	Maintenance of materialized views		151
	7.3.1	Snapshot differential problem	151
	7.3.2	Using full and partial information for view maintenance	151
	7.3.3	Using incremental techniques	152
	7.3.4	Using auxiliary data and auxiliary views	153
	7.3.5	Dealing with irrelevant update	154
	7.3.6	Incremental maintenance of materialized views with duplicates	154
	7.3.7	Externally materialized views	155
	7.3.8	Views and queries	155
	7.3.9	Unified view selection and maintenance	156
	7.3.10	Other work	157
7.4	Consistency in view maintenance		157
	7.4.1	Immediate and deferred view maintenance	157
	7.4.2	Dealing with anomalies in view maintenance	159
	7.4.3	Concurrent updates in distributed environment	162

7.5 Integrity constraints and active databases 163
     7.5.1 Integrity constraints 163
     7.5.2 Active databases 164
7.6 Dynamic warehouse design 165
     7.6.1 Dynamicity of warehouse design 165
     7.6.2 Warehouse evolution 165
     7.6.3 From static to dynamic warehouse design 166
     7.6.4 View redefinition and adaptation 167
7.7 Implementation issues and online updates 168
     7.7.1 Physical implementation 168
     7.7.2 Indexing techniques 168
     7.7.3 Online updates 168
7.8 Data cubes 169
7.9 Materialized views in advanced database systems 173
     7.9.1 Materialized views and deductive databases 173
     7.9.2 Materialized views in object-oriented databases 174
7.10 Relationship with mobile databases 175
7.11 Other issues 175
     7.11.1 Temporal view self-maintenance 175
     7.11.2 Real-time warehousing 176
     7.11.3 Materialized views in Oracle 176
7.12 Summary 177
References 177

Part III

Chapter 8 Intelligent data analysis 187
8.1 Overview 187
8.2 Basics of data mining 188
     8.2.1 Categories of data mining 188
     8.2.2 Association rule mining 189
     8.2.3 Data classification and characterization 191
8.3 Case study: stock food chain analysis 192
     8.3.1 Overview of the case study 192
     8.3.2 Implementing the Apriori algorithm 192
     8.3.3 Graphical user interface 193
     8.3.4 Analysis 194
8.4 Case study: rough set data analysis 195
     8.4.1 Basics of rough set theory 195
     8.4.2 Applying RSDA methodology for bankruptcy
            analysis 199
            8.4.2.1 Description of the RSDA methodology 199
            8.4.2.2 Source data used in the case study 199
            8.4.2.3 Applying RSDA on sample data 203

8.5   Recent progress of data mining 204
        8.5.1   Mining the metadata..205
        8.5.2   User expectations...205
        8.5.3   Discovery of low-support rules 205
        8.5.4   Dynamics of data mining...205
8.6   Summary 206
References...206

Chapter 9   Toward integrated OLAP and data mining............................209
9.1   Overview..209
9.2   Integration of OLAP and data mining..209
9.3   Influential association rules 210
9.4   Significance of influential association rules 212
9.5   Reviews of algorithms for discovery of conventional
        association rules..214
9.6   Discovery of influential association rules 216
        9.6.1   The IARM algorithm...216
        9.6.2   Support counting of condition part item set.................217
        9.6.3   Categorization and support counting of a numeric
                    measure 217
        9.6.4   Mining candidate influential association rules 218
        9.6.5   Pruning and refining candidate influential
                    association rules...218
        9.6.6   Problems of the IARM algorithm 219
9.7   Bitmap indexing and influential association rules 220
        9.7.1   Basic idea of bitmap indexing..220
        9.7.2   Bitmap indexing in data warehouses 221
9.8   Mining influential association rules using bitmap indexing
        (IARMBM) 223
9.9   Summary..226
References...226

Index 229

Part I

chapter one

Introduction

1.1 Why this book is needed

Decision support systems (DSSs) are rapidly becoming a key to gaining competitive advantage for businesses. DSSs allow businesses to retrieve data locked away in operational databases and transform that data into useful information or knowledge. Many corporations have built or are building unified decision-support databases, usually referred to as data warehouses, on which intelligent data analysis can be carried out. According to a popular definition, a data warehouse is a "subject-oriented, integrated, time-varying, nonvolatile collection of data that is used primarily in organizational decision making" (Inmon, 1996). Data warehousing provides an effective approach to dealing with complex decision support queries over data from multiple sites.

Data warehousing and related techniques used for analyzing data stored in data warehouses (including data mining) are rooted in database management systems (DBMSs) and artificial intelligence (AI). In this book we examine the application of intelligent techniques in various stages of data warehousing. The book presents the state of the art, as well as some original work in this active area. A popular misconception is that data warehousing is a discipline "within" management information systems (MISs). In fact, much research work has been done from a computer science perspective as well. This book integrates theoretical and practical studies related to data warehousing from both computer science and MIS perspectives.

There are numerous books on data warehousing. However, all of the existing data warehousing books are mainly business-oriented. Research work from a computer science perspective mainly consists of research papers on materialized views; in fact, a nice collection of recent research papers has been edited by Gupta and Mumick (1998). However, so far no single monograph on data warehousing addresses major concerns from a computer science perspective. There is a need to bridge the gap between such theoretical research and business applications; this book is trying to fill this gap. It covers aspects related to various stages involved in data warehousing, such as how to prepare data, how to store data in data warehouses, and how to analyze data stored in data warehouses using data mining techniques, as well as other issues. Methodology discussed in this book employs artificial intelligence techniques. The book can also be compared with data mining books because it addresses data mining but, unlike many data mining books, this book discusses intelligent data analysis in the context of data warehouses.

There is a wide gap between research and practice in data warehousing. The term data warehouse was invented by business-driven consultants and practitioners, rather than database researchers. Nevertheless, a broad variety of data warehouse research projects started in the last decade has addressed specific technical issues related to managing data warehouses. Although many approaches for interesting problems of building data warehouses were developed, combining these partial and often very abstract and formal solutions with an overall design and warehousing strategy is still left to the practitioners. In addition, the influence of research results on the commercial stream of data warehouse products is very limited because the commercial data warehouse business has overrun and mostly ignored data warehouse research (Gatziu et al., 2000). Therefore, there is an urgent need for narrowing the gap between these two communities. This book is intended as an effort to narrow this gap. It summarizes main ideas behind recent research development in data warehousing, rather than the technical detail itself. Business people should know what kind of research work has been done in the database research community and computer science people should know what business people need to be told, so that the gap between research and business communities can be effectively reduced. This book contains that information.

Aside from its wide applications, intelligent data warehousing is an interesting topic due to the extremely rich methodologies used. This is an interesting issue that, so far, has not received enough attention. Although most problems investigated in data warehousing are rooted in various applications, research methods can be quite theoretical. First of all, data warehousing is about integration — integration of data, integration of data with knowledge, integration of various methods applied on the data for analysis. The complexity of data warehousing techniques thus has created a tremendous opportunity for studying the nature of integration, a key element in the study of system theory (Klir, 1985). Various optimization issues related to warehouse design bring mathematical beauty into the field of data warehousing. The structural properties of data warehousing encourage examination from a system-theoretic perspective; for example, the practice of data warehousing contributes to the theory concerning parts and whole (here parts could be data marts or materialized views, while the whole refers to the data warehousing). In addition, metadata, and various "meta" issues related to data warehousing and data mining, stimulate in-depth examination of various ontology issues at different knowledge levels. Although this book does not directly address these issues, materials presented here can be used for this type of research.

1.2 Features of the book

The following are some important features of this book:

- The book provides state-of-the-art data warehousing research and practice from an integrated business and computer science perspective.
- This book discusses intelligent data analysis techniques (i.e., data mining) in the context of data warehousing. Therefore, it has a broader scope than books dealing only with data mining.
- The book presents recent work from existing literature (previously scattered in various papers), as well as original research results, illustrated by examples and case studies.
- Intelligent techniques are applied to the entire process of data warehousing: preparing data, building data warehousing (by selecting and maintaining materialized views), and analyzing data stored in data warehouses using data mining techniques.
- The book presents main ideas of methods developed, research directions, and state-of-the-art related topics, thus serving as a roadmap for studying intelligent data warehousing.
- The book is designed for different levels of readers. For readers who need general information, the text itself suffices. On the other hand, readers who want to learn more technical details should find the references listed at the end of each chapter helpful.

1.3 Why intelligent data warehousing

A data warehouse is a database that collects and stores integrated data from several databases, usually integrating data from multiple sources and providing a different way of looking at the data than do the databases being integrated (Gupta and Mumick, 1998). Before we present the actual materials covered in this book, we first briefly describe what we mean by intelligent data warehousing, as well as important things one should know about intelligent data warehousing.

First, we want to point out that data warehousing extends traditional interests of database management systems. Therefore, knowledge of data modeling, relational algebra, query processing, transaction processing, advanced database architecture (including distributed and parallel database systems), etc., are all prerequisites of data warehousing techniques. The success or failure of data warehousing is closely related to the historical development of database management systems (DBMSs). In a sense, data warehousing has offered an alternative approach to traditional DBMSs and has also raised many challenging issues for the database community. For convenience of reading, in this book we have included a brief review of these related materials. However, for a better understanding of these materials, readers should refer to the reference lists.

Another important aspect is related to artificial intelligence. This book is titled *Intelligent Data Warehousing* because we want to emphasize all aspects of intelligence related to data warehousing:

- We start with a discussion from the perspective of business intelligence, which brought to us exciting and challenging issues on the manipulation of huge amounts of data, the meaning of such data, the implications of these data, and the methodology used to analyze them, as well as on the other aspects related to data.
- We also want to emphasize that building data warehousing is an intelligent process. For example, we need to decide what kind of data should be included in a data warehouse. Artificial intelligence (AI) techniques, including heuristic search methods and various learning methods (such as genetic algorithms), can aid these tasks. In addition, computational methods other than those in classical AI can also contribute to intelligent data warehousing. For example, Web-enabling techniques may significantly enhance warehouse construction and enrich data warehousing functionality. Another interesting sample issue of intelligent data warehousing is modeling user behavior for warehouse design.
- Data warehousing facilitates analysis of stored data and can effectively handle on-line analytical processing (OLAP) for decision support queries in many business applications. Data warehousing can also serve as an enabling technique of data mining; an integration of OLAP and data mining is also emerging. In addition, data warehouses can also hold science and engineering data, so their impact goes far beyond business applications.

Integrating artificial intelligence techniques into data warehousing or, more generally, combining artificial intelligence with business intelligence, is not an easy task. Efforts to integrate knowledge-based approaches or other AI-based techniques into database techniques have lasted several decades, but many problems still remain, including how to scale up AI algorithms for huge amounts of data, how to deal with mismatches between reasoning and database computation, etc. Intelligent data warehousing is a continuation of this challenging direction of research.

1.4   Organization of the book

Part I of this book presents an overview. Chapter 1 contains an introduction and provides state-of-the-art ideas behind data mining, with an emphasis on integrated data, as well as an integrated methodology rooted largely in artificial intelligence. Chapter 2 discusses business intelligence and artificial intelligence. This chapter starts with an examination of the driving forces of data warehousing, mainly from a business-oriented perspective. The remaining part of this chapter addresses issues related to incorporating artificial intelligence techniques into business intelligence. Chapter 3 covers the basics of data warehousing by examining its relationship with traditional DBMS and describes its basic architecture. We also discuss a related issue, namely, on-line analytical processing (OLAP). A sketch of viewing data warehousing as materialized views is also provided.

Part II presents core materials on data warehousing. Chapter 4 is on data preparation and preprocessing. Starting with an examination of the overall data warehousing lifecycle, this chapter addresses various issues for data preprocessing such as data cleansing, data integration, data categorization, and Web data handling, as well as other related topics. Chapter 5 examines issues related to building data warehouses. This chapter summarizes existing approaches to building data warehouses, mainly from a business perspective. Both entity-relationship (ER) and dimensional modeling approaches are discussed. From a computer science perspective, a data warehouse (built using relational techniques) is a collection of materialized views (MVs) derived from base relations that may not reside at the warehouse. Chapters 6 and 7 are devoted to materialized views. Chapter 6 examines this perspective using simple examples; continuing the discussion in Chapter 6, Chapter 7 summarizes advanced work related to MVs and addresses various aspects related to MVs, including algorithms related to view selection and maintenance.

Part III addresses data analysis and knowledge discovery in the data warehousing environment. Chapter 8 is on data mining techniques, discussing how to perform intelligent data analysis in the data-warehousing environment. A concise description of several selected data analysis techniques (such as rough set theory) is provided and illustrated by case studies. We also summarize several typical data mining functionalities (such as clustering, classification, and association) conducted in the data warehousing environment; these functionalities are illustrated by examples and case studies. Chapter 9 covers discovery of influential association patterns. As a concrete example of performing combined data mining/OLAP in the data warehousing environment, we describe a new development of data mining: influential association rule mining combines basics of association rule mining and OLAP.

1.5   How to use this book

Companion books from the same author are *Computational Intelligence for Decision Support* and *Data Mining and Uncertain Reasoning: An Integrated Approach*. The first book contains background information and covers a wide range of topics related to decision support, including data warehousing and data mining. The second discusses data mining techniques, with a particular emphasis on the relationship between data mining and uncertain reasoning. Since data mining is a complex topic and since this current book covers the topic only briefly, the latter book will provide concrete information for readers interested in data mining.

This book has been written based on the assumption that readers have basic knowledge about database management systems (DBMSs), including conceptual and logical data modeling, basic knowledge of relational databases, basic database programming using SQL, basic knowledge of implementing a DBMS (including query processing and transaction processing), basics of distributed and parallel databases, etc. These are the fundamentals for implementing a data warehouse. In order to make this book self-contained, we have included a very brief review on these topics. Readers should consult DBMS books (Silberschatz et al., 2001; Elmasri and Navathe, 2000) for more detail.

Most existing books on data warehousing (including Kimball et al. 1998; Kimball and Merz, 2000) are from an MIS perspective. Nevertheless, research progress from a computer science perspective can be accessed from the Stanford University Web site http://www-db.stanford.edu/. Readers are encouraged to check this site frequently. In particular, recent research publications are available at http://dbpubs.stanford.edu:8090/aux/index-en.html. These research papers are an important source for recent development of data warehousing research. Much information is available from various other Web sites. For example, for progress in data mining, the Web pages at http://www.kdnuggets.com/ should be very helpful.

Han and Kamber (2000) have recently written a book covering data mining in detail that also contains a brief discussion on data warehousing. Tutorial sections of this book can be found at http://www.cs.sfu.ca/~han/dmbook. Publications from this authors' research group can be found at the home page: http://db.cs.sfu.ca/sections/publication/kdd/kdd.html. Other useful materials for data mining can be found in Fayyad et al. (1996) and Cios et al. (1998). A discussion of practical data mining with Java implementations can be found in Witten and Frank (1999).

References

Chen, Z., *Computational Intelligence for Decision Support,* CRC Press, Boca Raton, FL, 1999.

Chen, Z., *Data Mining and Uncertain Reasoning: An Integrated Approach,* Wiley Inter-science, New York, 2001.

Cios, K. J., W. Pedrycz, and R. Swiniarski, *Data Mining Methods for Knowledge Discovery,* Kluwer Academic Publishers, Boston, 1998.

Elmasri, R. and S. B. Navathe, *Fundamentals of Database Systems,* Addison-Wesley, Reading, MA, 2000.

Fayyad, U. M., G. Piatetsky-Shapiro, P. Smyth, and R. Uturusamy (Eds.), *Advances in Knowledge Discovery and Data Mining,* AAAI/MIT Press, Cambridge, MA, 1996.

Gatziu, S., M. Jeusfeld, M. Staudt, and Y. Vassiliou, Design and management of data warehouses (Report on the DMDW'99 workshop), *SIGMOD Rec.,* 28(4), 5–8, 1999.

Gupta, A. and I. S. Mumick, *Materialized Views: Techniques, Implementations, and Applications,* MIT Press, Cambridge, MA, 1998.

Han, J. and M. Kamber, *Data Mining: Concepts and Techniques*, Morgan Kaufmann, San Francisco, CA, 2000.

Inmon, W. H., *Building the Data Warehouse*, John Wiley & Sons, New York, 1996.

Kimball, R., L. Reeves, M. Ross, and W. Thornthwaite, *The Data Warehouse Lifecycle Toolkit*, John Wiley & Sons, New York, 1998.

Kimball, R. and R. Merz, *The Data Webhouse Toolkit: Building the Web-Enabled Data Warehouse*, John Wiley & Sons, New York, 2000.

Klir, G., *Architecture of Systems Problem Solving*, Plenum Press, New York, 1985.

Mattison, R. and B. Kilger-Mattison (Eds.), *Web Warehousing and Knowledge Management* (Enterprise Computing Series), McGraw-Hill, New York, 1999.

Silberschatz, A., H. F. Korth, and S. Sudarshan, *Database System Concepts*, 4th ed., McGraw-Hill, New York, 2001.

Witten, I. H. and E. Frank, *Data Mining: Practical Machine Learning Tools and Techniques with Java Implementations*, Morgan Kaufmann Publishers, San Francisco, 1999.

chapter two

Enterprise intelligence and artificial intelligence

2.1 Overview

Over the past several years, the data warehouse has evolved into a necessary foundation for the successful trend of decision-support system (DSS) development environments. This chapter begins with an examination of the driving forces of data warehousing, mainly from a business-oriented perspective, as well as a brief review of the historical development of data warehousing. The basic components of data warehousing are then described. A discussion on the Web-enabled data warehouse, or Webhouse, leads to a review of agent-based artificial intelligence (AI) techniques, as well as the notions of ontology and semantic Webs. Intelligent data analysis in the data warehousing environment, including data mining, Web mining, and clickstream analysis, is also examined.

2.2 Data warehousing and enterprise intelligence

A data warehouse is a structure for organizing information systems using all possible data available in the enterprise to create one integrated view of the entire business. Data warehouses facilitate analysis on the integrated data, including on-line analytical processing (OLAP) and data mining tasks (discussed later in this book). Advantages to a well-constructed data warehouse include better data quality, accurate trend analysis, efficient access to data, uniform data, and decision support. With the advent of large scale e-commerce initiatives by many companies, the ability to integrate high volumes of real-time sales and customer data with legacy enterprise data is another compelling reason to build a data warehouse (No, 2000).

From the perspective of enterprise intelligence, data warehousing is also important to the success of an e-business initiative (No, 2000). E-business is a topic related to Web-enabling techniques, which will be discussed in a later section. Data warehousing is important to e-business because accurate information and seamlessly tied systems may be the most critical components for excelling in e-business. Without them, the integrity of shared data is compromised and systems are inefficient. Data warehousing enables the consolidation of data from product, manufacturing, and customer databases into operational data stores. This gives delivery channel applications, such as customer relationship management (CRM) systems, access to suppliers, products, inventory, and customer data. By opening warehouse access via the Web to suppliers and customers, relationships along the supply chain are strengthened and greater value is realized. Online ordering saves both cost and time — two of the greatest value propositions for any organization. Time is money in the new economy. An effective e-business strategy supported by tightly integrated systems can make the supply chain more efficient, as well as provide the ability to track transactions throughout the supply chain, understand customer behavior, craft more accurately targeted sales and marketing efforts, and automate processes across the enterprise and with external vendors and partners. The sharing of accurate data among involved parties strengthens relations between customer and supplier as well.

According to data quoted in Vassiliadis (2000), the average time for the construction of a data warehouse is 12 to 36 months, and the average cost for its implementation is between \$1 and \$1.5 million. The design costs consist of disk storage (30%), processor costs (20%), integration and transformation (15%), DBMS (10%), network (10%), access analysis tools (6%), and metadata design (5%), as well as other factors.

To determine if an organization's data warehouse return on investment (ROI) is satisfactory, one first needs to identify measures for success and failure; these should be mapped to goals and objectives. There are a few key ways to measure the success (or failure) of one's data warehouse: 1. a successful data warehouse shows a profitable return of investment (ROI), 2. the warehouse is used, 3. the initial data warehousing project is delivered on time and within budget, 4. there are requests for additional functionality from the data warehouse, 5. business problems are solved and, most importantly, 6. business opportunities are realized. On the other hand, a data warehouse project is heading toward failure if funding has dried up, only a small percentage of users actually use the data warehouse and are unhappy with the quality of the data, and the data warehouse is unable to expand, with poor performance a result.

2.3 Historical development of data warehousing

2.3.1 Prehistory

Data warehousing was motivated by serious problems with the legacy environment in the 1980s. According to a retrospective review from Inmon (2001), most serious problems included legacy applications that

- solved yesterday's business problems and could not be changed or replaced;
- looked at current data, which represents only one aspect of information, but not at historical data;
- were not integrated collectively at all; (unfortunately, modern corporations needed integrated information in order to look at the entire corporation);
- were built on older technology, and moving away from that technology was difficult; and
- were designed to collect and store information efficiently — not to allow data to be easily and elegantly accessed.

In the late 1980s and early 1990s, something had to be done to address the growing level of discomfort with legacy applications. Thus, the concept of the data warehouse — a database that stored detailed, integrated, current, and historical data — was born.

The data warehouse was built from the detailed transaction data generated by and aggregated in the legacy applications. One of the major tasks of the data warehouse developer was to go back into the legacy systems environment to find, convert, and reformat legacy data. The task of integrating legacy data never designed for integration was daunting and dirty. Yet, it was one of the cornerstones of the success of data warehousing.

Major milestones in data warehousing can be summarized in three stages (Hwang and Woerner, 1998), as discussed below.

2.3.2   Stage 1: early 1990s

Open systems data warehousing started with a new form of presenting information from transaction data. Two major technological factors contributed to its success in the early 1990s:

1. Smart query generation positioning: the query engine outside the traditional database engine can generate better sequences of queries. In a way, relational database management system (RDBMS) technology and the structured query language (SQL) model are not very good for data warehousing.
2. Multidimensional visual presentation of information: just as the spreadsheet was a milestone in data presentation, new tools provided graphic and n-dimension information presentation — a milestone for the interpretation of data.

During this stage, no leading hardware or software companies produced OLAP tools. Data warehouses in this period were like islands of information for decision support or marketing.

2.3.3   Stage 2: mid-1990s

In the mid-1990s, through product improvement and corporate in-house system integration, building islands of information in OLAP systems became feasible. OLAP differs from traditional OLTP (on-line transaction processing) in that, unlike an OLTP query which simply retrieves data from the database, an OLAP query is intended to analyze data for decision support. From a business perspective, OLAP sits in the middle of the business intelligence architecture, bridging the gap between the warehouse storage and the presentation layer. During this period, collecting and moving data became a constant battle in the warehouse environment, so another group of vendors came to this arena to address those needs. However, in this stage, there were still no leading hardware or software companies playing a role here. Through the struggle of moving and changing data, the need for metadata became inevitable in corporate data warehousing.

2.3.4   Stage 3: toward business intelligence

With growing maturity brought about through earlier stages and emerging new distributed enterprise computing needs, data warehousing evolved to respond to the needs of a broader infrastructure. Business knowledge could be built into the system and larger user populations could have adequate access to the system to facilitate decision making. Nevertheless, problems still existed. In particular, when business rules changed (such as product dimension), it became very difficult to change and maintain the data warehouse because it was somewhat hard-coded to the vendors' point solutions. More advanced, flexible structure was needed.

Making a reality of bringing business intelligence into data warehousing is the task of intelligent data warehousing.

2.4   Basic elements of data warehousing

This section offers a brief overview of basic elements of data warehousing, mainly from a business perspective (Kimball and Merz, 2000).

First, there are backend components, including the source system (which could be a legacy system), operational data store (ODS, which keeps a diverse and incompatible set of business requirements), and data staging area (which is everything between the source system and the data presentation server). At the heart of data warehousing is the dimensional model, which contains the same information as an entity-relationship (ER) model, but packages the data in a symmetric format whose design goals are user understandability, query performance, and resilience to change. The main components of a dimensional model are fact tables and dimension tables (to be further discussed in Chapters 3 and 5). A fact table is the primary table in each dimensional model meant to contain measurements of the business; the most useful facts are numeric and additive. Every fact table represents a many-to-many relationship and contains a set of two or more foreign keys that join to their respective dimension tables. On the other hand, a dimension table is one of a set of companion tables to a fact table. Each dimension is defined by its primary key, which serves as the basis for referential integrity with any given fact table to which it is joined.

A logical subset of the complete data warehouse is called a data mart, which is a complete "pie wedge" of the overall data warehouse pie. A data mart can be viewed as a departmental data warehouse. A data warehouse is made up of the union of all its data marts. The extreme top-down perspective is that a completely centralized, tightly designed master database must be completed before parts of it are summarized and published as individual data marts. The extreme bottom-up perspective is that an enterprise data warehouse can be assembled from disparate and unrelated data marts. However, the only workable solution is a blend of the two approaches.

When all the pieces of all the data marts are broken down to individual physical tables on various database servers, as they must ultimately be, then the only physical way to combine the data from these separate tables and achieve an integrated enterprise data warehouse is to make sure that the dimensions of the data mean the same thing across these tables. These are called conformed dimensions. Data marts are based on granular data and may or may not contain performance enhancing summaries.

Kimball termed the queryable source of data as a data warehouse, which is simply the union of all the constituent data marts. A data warehouse is fed from the data staging area. The data warehouse manager is responsible for both the data warehouse and the data staging area. The data warehouse data are also assisted by metadata, which are data about data, or what the warehouse looks like (rather than warehouse data themselves).

At the front end, various facilities are concerned with data analysis, such as the presentation server (which is the target physical machine on which the data warehouse data are organized and stored for direct querying by end users, report writers, and other applications), end user data access tool (which is a client of the data warehouse), and ad hoc query tool.

The architecture of data warehouses will be revisited in Chapter 3, in terms more familiar to the database research community.

2.5   Databases and the Web

2.5.1   World Wide Web and e-commerce

At the beginning of this chapter business intelligence from the e-business perspective was discussed. It is now necessary to take a closer look at the issue of databases and the Web (Ramakrishnam, 2000; Silberschatz et al., 2001). The Web makes it possible to access a file (identified by a universal resource locator, or URL) anywhere on the Internet. The file is a document formatted using hypertext markup language (HTML) and contains links to other files. The formatting commands are interpreted by a Web browser to display the document, and users can navigate to other related documents by choosing links. A collection of such documents at a Web site is managed using a program called a Web server, which accepts URLs and returns the corresponding documents. The World Wide Web (WWW) is the collection of Web sites accessible over the Internet.

An HTML link contains a URL, which identifies the site containing the linked file. When a user clicks on a link, the Web browser connects to the Web server at the destination Web site using a connection protocol called HTTP and submits the link's URL. When the browser receives a file from a Web server, it checks the file type by examining the extension of the file name. HTML is a simple language used to describe a document. It is a markup language because HTML works by augmenting regular text with "marks" that hold special meaning for a Web browser handling the document.

The Web is the cornerstone of electronic commerce. The use of a Web browser to invoke a program at a remote site leads to the role of database on the Web: the invoked program can generate a request to a database system. This capability allows easy placement of a database on a computer network, and makes services that rely upon database access available over the Web. This leads to a new and rapidly growing source of concurrent requests to a DBMS. The diversity of information on the Web, its distributed nature, and the new uses that it is put to lead to challenges for DBMSs that go beyond simply improved performance in traditional functionality. In addition, the emergence of the extensible markup language (XML) standard for describing data leads to challenges in managing and querying XML data.

To execute a program at the Web server's site, the server creates a new process and communicates with this process using the common gateway interface (CGI) protocol. The results of the program can be used to create an HTML document that is returned to the requestor. For example, Perl is an interpreted language often used for CGI scripting and many Perl libraries called modules provide high-level interfaces to the CGI protocol. Two such libraries are DBI and CGI. DBI is a database-independent Application Programming Interface (API) for Perl that allows one to abstract from the DBMS used. Note that DBI plays the same role for Perl as Java Database Connection (JDBC) plays for Java.

CGI protocol is used to dynamically assemble Web pages whose content is computed on demand. However, since each page request results in the creation of a new process, this solution does not scale well to a large number of simultaneous requests. This performance problem led to the development of specialized programs called application servers. An application server has preforked threads or processes and thus avoids the startup cost of creating a new process for each request. Application servers have evolved into flexible middle tier packages that provide many different functions in addition to eliminating the process-creation overhead, such as integration of heterogeneous data sources, transactions involving several data sources in e-commerce, security, etc. A process structure in the application server architecture can be described as follows. The client (i.e., a Web browser) interacts with the Web server through the HTTP protocol. The Web server delivers static (i.e., existing) HTML or XML pages directly to the client. In order to assemble dynamic pages (which are computed by executing a program using CGI), the Web server sends a request to the application server. The application server contacts one or more data sources to retrieve necessary data or sends update requests to the data sources. After the interaction with the data sources is completed, the application server assembles the Web page and reports the result to the Web server, which retrieves the page and delivers it to the client.

The execution of business logic at the Web server's site, or server-side processing, has become a standard model for implementing more complicated business processes on the Internet. One technology for server-side processing is Java Servlet API, which allows Web developers to extend the functionality of a Web server by using small Java programs called servlets that interact with the Web server through a well-defined API. A servlet consists of mostly business logic and routines to format relatively small datasets into HTML. Java servlets are executed in their own threads.

Server-side applications can also be written using JavaBeans (which are reusable software components) and Java Server Pages (JSPs, which can also be used for generating dynamic content on the server side).

While HTML is adequate to represent the structure of documents for display purposes, the features of the language are not sufficient to represent the structure of data within a document for more general applications than a simple display as mentioned earlier. Extensible markup language (XML) is an improved markup language. In contrast to a fixed set of tags whose meaning is fixed by the language (as in HTML), XML allows the user to define new collections of tags that can then be used to structure any type of data or document the user wishes to transmit. XML is an important bridge between the document-oriented view of data implicit in HTML and the schema-oriented view of data central to a DBMS. It has the potential to make database systems more tightly integrated into Web applications than ever before.

The availability of portable computers and wireless communications has created a new breed of nomadic database users. Users may simply access a database through a network that is similar to distributed DBMSs. However, at a more sophisticated level, the network as well as data and user characteristics may have novel properties, which affect basic assumptions in many components of DBMS processing.

2.5.2   Data Webhouse

As to be discussed further in consecutive sections, today's data warehouses are the critical hubs of such burgeoning strategic initiatives as e-commerce, knowledge management, database marketing, and customer relationship management (CRM). Given this, a working knowledge of the fundamentals of data warehousing is essential for today's executives, managers, and other professionals who must maximize the power of data warehousing in both existing business contexts and future strategic initiatives.

Kimball (1999) noted that the Web is pummeling the data warehouse marketplace on all sides. The Web's presence is changing clients' and servers' architecture by forcing the front-end tool vendors to move the bulk of their technologies toward the server. This shift is taking place because vendors can no longer control software content and because everyone is demanding that a Web browser, not a dedicated application, paint the bits on the screen.

End-user application developers are increasingly building applications around Web pages. The user interface development environment of choice is now a Web page development environment. The vendor can simply set up a Web page and embed various data-aware objects in it. Endow the Web page's user interface with a few data warehouse gestures, and a sophisticated drag-and-drop, drill-up-and-down, pivoting application is created. An interesting side effect of this forced migration of user interfaces to Web technology is that it is as easy to deliver an application over the Web as it is to deliver one to a dedicated single user.

Kimball coined the term data Webhouses to refer to Web-enabling data warehouses. The medium is not only the delivery vehicle, but the business itself. Increasingly, the fundamental business content of what is sold is mixed with Web services and capabilities. Issues related to Web-enabling data warehouses include (No, 2000):

- Web users want personalized information.
- The number of data warehouse users can escalate sharply. More users mean more data. There is a need for understanding the notion of data inflation.
- Customers demand robust data warehouse support. An important concern for effectiveness is continuously updating the information in an organization's warehouse while keeping it available without interruption.

A related issue is e-catalog. As noted in Baron et al. (2000), Web-based catalogs provide the main entry point for business-to-business e-commerce and will fundamentally transform supply-chain relationships. In the broadest sense, e-catalogs are electronic representations of information about the products and/or services of an organization. A company's Web page providing a short list of its products can be viewed as an example of static, passive, and dumb e-catalog. Such e-catalogs are not able to learn from experience. In contrast to these, intelligent catalogs are dynamic, active, and capable of learning. Virtual catalogs are defined as those which dynamically retrieve information from multiple smart catalogs and present these data in a unified manner with their own look and feel, not that of the source smart catalogs. E-catalogs can drastically reduce the cost of coordination, data gathering, and analysis. The integrity of an organization's data is at least as important as safeguarding traditional assets like cash. The use of e-catalogs creates an interorganizational information system allowing two or more organizations to exchange information in an automated and electronic form. In addition, Dyché (2000) coined the term e-data, which refers to any data that have been refined and stored in a data warehouse, whether Internet-related or not.

The Internet, intranet, and World Wide Web, have become an appropriate platform for building data warehouses and for broader deployment of OLAP is the Internet/intranet/World Wide Web, because of the following reasons (Singh, 1999):

- The Web provides complete platform independence and easy maintenance.
- Skills, techniques used to navigate and select information, and browser interface are the same as those for all other Web-based applications.
- With increased security, the Internet can be used as an inexpensive wide area network for decision support and OLAP applications.

Web-enabled data warehouses deliver the broadest access to decision support. In order to understand how to create a Web-based data warehouse architecture for maximum growth and flexibility, it is necessary to take a look at issues related to the Internet, as well as intranets. Web-enabled OLAP can be achieved through various approaches:

- Through static HTML reports (created off-line), data can be pulled from off-line OLAP engines, creating static HTML reports from HTML templates.
- The OLAP server populates HTML templates with data on the fly.
- The Java or ActiveX components feeding the browser use Java applets and ActiveX controls to minimize communication between browser and Web server, and to enhance the user experience through improvements to the interface.

The Internet has opened up tremendous business opportunities needing nontraditional categories of information and has emerged as the largest database. The true promise of the Internet is in making OLAP a mainstream technology, that is, moving OLAP from the domain of analysts to that of consumers. E-commerce has emerged as one of the largest applications of the Internet in decision support. The basic concepts of data warehousing and aggregation have naturally made their way onto the web. In fact, some of the most popular Web sites on the Internet are basically databases.

Intranets are essentially secure mini-internets implemented within organizations. An intranet can offer a single point of entry into a corporate world of information and applications. Intranets provide a powerful solution for data warehousing. A key benefit of intranet technology is the ability to provide up-to-date information quickly and cost effectively. Some advantages are listed below (Singh, 1999):

- Intranets allow the integration of information, making it easy to access, maintain, and update. Data warehouses can be made available worldwide on public or private networks at much lower cost. Web browsers can provide a universal application delivery platform for any data mart or data warehouse user. As a result, the enterprise can create, integrate, or deploy new, more robust applications quickly and economically. Use of intranets enables the integration of a diverse computing environment into a cohesive information network.

- Information disseminated on an intranet enables a high degree of coherence for the entire enterprise (whether the data content comes from data marts or a central data warehouse) because the communications, report formats, and interfaces are consistent. An intranet provides a flexible and scalable nonproprietary solution for a data warehouse implementation. The intuitive nature of the browser interface also reduces user support and training requirements.
- The Internet can be easily extended into wide area networks (WANs) or extranets that serve remote company locations, business partners, and customers. External users can access internal data, drill through, or print reports through secure proxy servers that reside outside the firewall.

Many of the activities in relational databases (constructed as relational data models described in Section 3.2.2) for the Web are in the following categories (Malaika, 1998):

- Store and manage Web resources in relational databases: storing Web-related information (such as hypertext documents and hypertext links) in relational databases, and then making this information accessible through the Web;
- Query and access Web resources using relational database techniques: making Web resources resemble structured data, often by augmenting them with metadata or by building indices, and then querying, searching, or mining the data using database query languages which can operate in conjunction with query optimizers;
- Store and manage relational data on the Web: transforming tabular data in relational databases into formats immediately accessible on the Web and managing the transformed relational data in caches and data stores around the network;
- Query and access relational data using Web techniques: accessing tablular data in relational databases from Web clients via server gateways or through software which are running in the clients.

2.5.3   Ontologies and semantic Web

The Web does not just provide a set of useful mechanisms for accessing information. As envisioned by Berners-Lee (1989), a semantic Web provides automated information access based on machine-processable semantics of data and heuristics that use these metadata. The explicit representation of the semantics of data, accompanied with domain theories (that is, ontologies), will enable a Web that provides a qualitatively new level of service (Fensel and Musen, 2001). This will eventually result in the creation of an extremely knowledgeable system with various specialized reasoning services that will significantly enhance the status of knowledge acquisition, as well as knowledge representation.

The preceding discussion brings the important issue of artificial intelligence (AI) to front stage. In AI, the notion of ontology is usually the specification of a conceptualization, namely, defined terms and relationships between them, usually in some formal and preferably machine-readable manner. Hendler (2001) defines ontology as a set of knowledge terms, including vocabulary, semantic interconnections, and some simple rules of inference and logic for some particular topic. It has been envisioned that a great number of small ontological components consist largely of pointers to each other. Agent-based computing (to be summarized in the next section) will play a crucial rule in the infrastructure of the knowledge Web. The integration of agent technology and ontologies could significantly affect the use of Web services and the ability to extend programs to perform tasks for users more efficieintly and with less human intervention. Ontologies serve as metadata schemas, providing a controlled vocabulary of concepts, each with explicitly defined and machine-processable semantics. By defining shared and common domain theories, ontologies help people and machines to communicate concisely because they support semantics exchange, not just syntax (Maedche and Staab, 2001).

Semantic Web also marks the transition of pull technology to push technology. The current pull technology in information dissemination assumes that the individual user knows which data sources are available, how frequently to search these data sources for appropriate information or potential updates, and how to further filter the information gathered from these data sources after all the processing is done by the underlying information gathering tools. This leaves the burden of information access to the user. In contrast, using the push technology, the system is able to deliver the needed information to the user at the appropriate time. The user is a direct consumer of information, and the information is delivered automatically. Agent-based AI techniques will make significant contributions to changing this.

2.6   Basics of artificial intelligence and machine learning

In this section some basic concepts in artificial intelligence that influence all aspects of intelligent data warehousing are described.

2.6.1   Artificial intelligence as construction of intelligent agents

Artificial intelligence (AI), as the science of "making machines do things that would require intelligence if done by men," has introduced a new discipline for contemporary thinking, research, and practice in all walks of life.

Artificial intelligence is now defined as the study and construction of intelligent agents. The 18th century philosopher Gottfried Leibniz, best known as the inventor of integral calculus and methods of symbolic logic, developed the concept of the agent to a deep level. What is new are the implementations. Before silicon tools to automate computing methods existed, Leibniz found agents in nature and called them monads. An agent is something that perceives and acts. The following important aspects of the concept of intelligent software agent should be emphasized (Bradshaw, 1997):

- Agents are (semi)autonomous. Each agent has certain responsibilities in problem solving with little or no knowledge of what other agents do or how they do it. Mobile agent lets the agent move from computer to computer across a network in order to perform its task.
- Agents are "situated." Each agent is sensitive to its own surrounding environment and usually has no knowledge of the full domain of all agents.
- Agents are interactional and the society of agents is structured. Agents cooperate on a particular task. Within a single environment or across different environments, knowledge transfer among agents or groups of agents will exponentially add power to agent intellect. This capability lets agents collaborate on tasks or problems. It also lets agents enable other agents to perform tasks on their behalf.
- The phenomenon of intelligence in this environment is "emergent." The overall cooperative result of the society of agents can be viewed as greater than the sum of its individual contributors.

Roughly speaking, these features indicate that an intelligent software agent is able to conduct reasoning (namely, to derive conclusions and make decisions in its environment), adaptation, learning (to improve its performance), and communication (with other agents) for decision making and problem solving.

As noted in Case et al. (2001), intelligent agents offer an ideal technology platform for providing data sharing, personalized services, and pooled knowledge while maintaining user privacy and promoting interaction in e-communities.

2.6.2   *State space search and knowledge representation*

In order to employ AI techniques for problem solving, an intelligent agent conducts searches for solutions to problems represented in certain knowledge representation schemes. A main knowledge representation scheme takes a logic-based perspective, which is based on the assumption of physical symbolism and representation. This assumption states that intelligent actions are demonstrated based on physical symbols. In the context of AI, a symbol is just a token to denote a thing which has a well-defined meaning. For example, "student" is a symbol denoting a concrete thing (an object), "thought" is a symbol denoting an abstract object, and "take" is a symbol denoting an activity. The use of symbols facilitates problem solving through state space search. A state space consists of states; intuitively, a state is represented by a set of related variables along with their values. Usually, a state space can be modeled as a directed acyclic graph (DAG), which consists of nodes representing states and directed edges indicating the search direction (Weiss, 1998). However, in order to make searches more effective and more efficient, it would be beneficial to develop some criteria to evaluate the "goodness" of each state. This is where heuristic search comes from. A heuristic is a rule of thumb; it may provide useful insight for problem solving, but it is fallible. Heuristics can be used to prune the search space so that the search can be conducted in a more efficient fashion.

A specific version of this algorithm is generally referred to as the A* algorithm. This algorithm requires the evaluation function to take a specific form. For any state on the search path from the start state to the goal state, its goodness is measured by two parts: the actually incurred cost from the start state of search to this state and an estimated cost from this state to reach the goal state. As mentioned in Section 7.2.3, the A* algorithm (sketched below) has been proven very useful in data warehouse design.

A* algorithm

In best first search algorithm with evaluation function

$$f(n) = g(n) + h(n)$$

where

n is any state encountered in the search,
$g(n)$ is the cost of n from the start state,
$h(n)$ is the heuristic estimate of the cost of going from n to a goal,
  and
$h(n)$ is less than or equal to the cost of the minimal path from n
  to the goal.

In order to reduce computations involved in the search, one needs knowledge. In order to represent knowledge, one needs knowledge representation schemes. In fact, without an effective way of representing knowledge involved in any specific problem to be solved, state space search cannot be conducted.

Due to different needs in problem solving, various knowledge representation schemes (or methods) have been developed. One of the most fundamental is predicate logic, which employs deductive reasoning techniques. Other forms of reasoning also exist. For example, induction refers to inference from the specific case to the general. The following is a simple example of induction: suppose one has observed facts: $p(a) \rightarrow q(a)$, $p(b) \rightarrow q(b)$, and so on; one may attempt to conclude $\forall X, p(X) \rightarrow q(X)$.

Although predicate logic has served as theoretical foundation for mainstream AI, production systems provide a useful alternative for knowledge representation and reasoning in real-world problem solving. The knowledge base of a production system consists of production rules of the form "IF (premise or antecedent), THEN (conclusion or consequent)." Production systems have been found very useful in building knowledge-rich expert systems in many application domains. In a rule-based expert system, the execution of production rules is handled by an inference engine.

Both predicate logic and production systems support modularity because both predicates and production rules represent a piece of knowledge. On the other hand, in many other applications it is desirable to make use of structured knowledge representation and reasoning schemes, such as conceptual graphs and frame systems. In these knowledge representation schemes, relevant knowledge is grouped together as a unit.

2.6.3 *Knowledge-based systems*

There are many successful stories of AI, ranging from toy problems such as puzzles and games (particularly in the early history of AI) to large scale, real-world applications. One of the most successful areas of AI application is expert systems or, more generally, knowledge-based systems. The rationale behind knowledge-based systems can be briefly explained as follows. Earlier, the importance of search in AI was emphasized because many AI problems are not well defined. In order to solve such problems, one must resort to search because there are no alternatives. On the other hand, if there is plenty of knowledge with which to start, this situation could be changed. Indeed, the more knowledge obtained, the less search is needed. From this consideration, knowledge-based systems have been developed. A knowledge-based system contains a knowledge base that stores knowledge in the form of IF/THEN rules (or some other form) that is controlled by an inference engine. In particular, expert systems are able to demonstrate expertise (i.e., the expert level of knowledge) in a narrow, specific knowledge domains (such as disease diagnosis or car trouble-shooting) and solve problems in these specific domains for consultation. Knowledge-based systems provide a viable approach complementary to database management systems.

2.6.4 *Symbol-based machine learning*

Although knowledge-based systems are powerful, such knowledge is usually static, and the systems are usually not able to acquire new knowledge or improve their behavior. This is not an ideal situation, because an intelligent agent should possess the ability to learn. Machine learning is the field of AI dealing with these kinds of problems, and machine learning techniques can be incorporated into knowledge-based systems. (An interesting note: the relationship between machine learning and knowledge-based approaches is mutually beneficial, because knowledge-based approaches can also be used to aid machine learning, as well as data mining.) Roughly speaking, learning refers to positive changes toward improved performance. When symbol-based machine learning is used, a learner must search the concept space to find the desired concept. Learning programs must commit to a direction and order of search, as well as to the use of available training data and heuristics to search efficiently.

The basic idea of machine learning can be demonstrated through inductive reasoning, which refers to the process of deriving conclusions from given facts (usually the facts are referred to as samples, or the training set). For example, if one has observed that a friend has a Toyota, an uncle has a Toyota, and a colleague at work also drives a Toyota, one may tend to think everybody drives a Toyota. This is a simple, but typical example of induction: one has learned that "everybody drives a Toyota." Of course induction is not sound because it does not guarantee the correctness of the conclusion. Nevertheless, induction is a useful approach to derive new conclusions from the given facts. An important form of performing inductive reasoning is through generalization. Many machine learning algorithms (such as ID3) have been developed. Machine learning algorithms have a close relationship with data mining, related algorithms will be discussed in Chapter 8 when data mining.

Non-symbolic reasoning approaches, such as various artificial neural networks (ANNs, also called connectionist networks) have also made important contributions in many applications.

2.6.5   Genetic algorithms

To illustrate the diversity of machine learning algorithms, it is now necessary to turn to genetic algorithms, which are general-purpose search algorithms using principles inspired by natural genetic populations to evolve solutions to problems. The basic idea is to maintain a population of knowledge structures that evolves over time through a process of competition and controlled variation. Each structure in the population represents a candidate solution to the concrete problem and has an associated fitness to determine which structures are used to form new ones in the competition process. The new ones are created using genetic operators such as crossover and mutation. Genetic algorithms have had a great measure of success in search and optimization problems, in great part because of their ability to exploit information accumulated about an initially unknown search space in order to bias subsequent searches into useful subspaces, i.e., their robustness. Offering a valid approach to problems requiring efficient and effective search techniques is their key feature, particularly in large, complex, and poorly understood search spaces, where classical search tools, such as enumerative or heuristic methods, are inappropriate. Genetic algorithms are most appropriate for optimization type problems.

Generic algorithms are an iterative procedure that consists of a constant-sized population of individuals, each one represented by a finite linear string of symbols, known as the genome, encoding a possible solution in a given problem space. This space, referred to as the GA search space, comprises all possible solutions to the optimization problem at hand. Standard genetic algorithms are implemented where the initial population of individuals is generated at random. At every evolutionary step, also known as generation, the individuals in the current population are decoded and evaluated according to a fitness function set for a given problem. The expected number of times an individual is chosen is approximately proportional to its relative performance in the population. Crossover is performed between two selected individuals by exchanging part of their genomes to form new individuals. The mutation operator is introduced to prevent premature convergence. Further discussion on this topic, along with a case study using genetic algorithms, is presented in Chapter 6.

2.7   Data warehousing with intelligent agents

2.7.1   Integration of database and knowledge-based systems

Historically, intelligent database systems have been developed along two major directions: efforts originated in a prevailing database (DB) or AI context. Efforts originated in a prevailing DB context include nested and semantic data models (which have eventually lead to object-oriented DB systems), object-oriented DB systems, and active DB systems. On the other hand, efforts toward intelligent databases originated in prevailing AI context are largely related to knowledge-based systems, the resolution principle in deductive reasoning, and inference by inheritance (as discussed in object-oriented approaches). These efforts include deductive DB systems (particularly using the Datalog model), coupling knowledge-based systems (KBSs) with conventional DBMSs, as well as other advanced solutions for integration. More recent developments include temporal databases, ontologies, multimedia databases dealing with semistructured data, use of multiagent systems, as well as others (Bertino et al., 2000). One challenge faced in the integration of AI techniques and DBMS techniques is the mismatch of the scalability in these two problem domains.

Integration of database and knowledge-based systems can be significantly promoted through knowledge management (KM), which is the formal management of knowledge for facilitating creation, access, and reuse of knowledge stored in various knowledge bases, typically using advanced technology. Typical KM tools include the World Wide Web, Lotus notes, the Internet, and intranets. A recent discussion on knowledge management can be found in O'Leary and Studer (2001).

Agent-based AI techniques have opened tremendous opportunities for data warehousing. With a well-developed data warehouse in place, one can see every aspect of every imaginable business circumstance (Gannon and

Bragger, 1998). OLAP tools provide advanced functionality, allowing users to do multidimensional data analysis. They also offer the ability to page, rotate, and aggregate warehouse data to provide a real-life view of the business situation for advanced analytical purposes. Nevertheless, in many organizations, a dilemma ultimately arises. Because this type of decision support system (DSS) implementation has never been done before, most organizations continue to use traditional means to develop DSSs within these advanced arenas and miss out on key opportunities. Intelligent agent solutions in a data warehouse environment maximize the warehouse investment and enable business intelligence software solutions in ways never before attainable. The key to implementing these advanced DSS solutions is to start small, deliver fast, and build incrementally. Intelligent agents play a big role in this scenario.

2.7.2   The role of AI in warehousing

The use of intelligent agent techniques in warehousing is a continuation of integration of AI and database management (DBM) techniques started decades ago. Because of their autonomy, agents can work independently of their users. The potential uses of agents are quite diverse. They can be used to automate the maintenance of data warehouses or marts by controlling data loads or monitoring the application's performance. One of the most attractive uses for intelligent agents is for customizing user interfaces based on perceived or stated user preferences. The browser provides a highly attractive medium for applications that uses a thin-client approach and has a high level of malleability. Agents can be used to alter the interface automatically based on perceived preferences.

As an example of collaborative work of agents, consider updating a data mart (Agosta, 1998; Grannon and Bragger, 1998). A data mart is typically made up of a number of data sources, so updates will need to be coordinated (A more detailed discussion of data marts is found in Chapter 3). There can be a load scheduling agent controlling which data sources are loaded and when. It may take into account system use, historical load times, priorities, and the data source pipeline. It should use any knowledge that it has at its disposal to make such scheduling decisions. The goal of this agent is to maximize data throughput and satisfy user demands. This agent can empower another agent designed to track the arrival of new data sources. This track agent tracks source availability and preprocessing time. The agent estimates and monitors the availability of data sources and reports its findings to the load scheduling agent. In addition the monitoring agent may report back the current status of data sources: for example, that the first data source is available for loading, while the second data source is currently being processed with an estimated completion time of 2 hours. Depending on the length of time needed to load the given data sources, the load scheduling agent may decide whether it is better to wait for the second data source to complete before proceeding with loading the first. If the estimated arrival time of the second data source is two days, the scheduling agent may decide to go ahead with the load of the first data source.

Agents range in their complexity, depending on their task or responsibility. All agents have basic characteristics, but not all require such features as advanced data gathering capabilities. Agents can be simple reactive agents or more complex, goal-oriented agents. A reactive agent does not have a goal or a plan in mind when it is instantiated. Its job is to react to events that occur around it in a rational manner, such as notifying a user of important e-mail. The goal-oriented agent must have more advanced characteristics such as advanced planning.

2.7.3   *Java and agent technology*

One of the things making the Web come alive and creating interaction is Java (Agosta, 1998; Ritter, 1999), which provides a breakthrough to Web-based business initiatives in securely connecting to enterprise data about products, customers, and history. In a sense, the Web is the ultimate database, whose defining schema, however, is constantly being transformed by a loosely coupled network of servers constantly entering and exiting. In the context of the vast distributed computing landscape of the Internet, clients may not always be able to rely on the convenience of executable content or the pre-established harmony of push technology's publish-and-subscribe model.

The idea of an agent-based approach implemented in frameworks using Java can be briefly described as follows: The network orientation of Java includes downloading executable code in a manner that is machine independent. Executable content points in the direction of increasing agency. So it is no accident that leading agent frameworks (called ontologies since they bring agents into being) are all written in Java.

What agents in all of these systems have in common is that they can do the following:

- Require a mechanism capable of moving code from one server to another;
- Include class libraries for communicating with remote agents as they migrate from one location to another on the network;
- Provide a way of simulating the transportation of program state from one location to another; and
- Provide an agent server and the equivalent of an agent sandbox.

Recent progress has extended the applet metaphor in the direction of agents by introducing the "aglet." Instead of virtual references, an agent transfer protocol (atp) is invoked to move code between contexts. The atp demon is the server that listens for incoming aglets over the network. The server context provides all aglets with a uniform environment within which initialization and execution of the code base occurs. Special functions invoked when the agent "wakes up" at the remote location are used to determine the initial and continuing state based on the messaging and retrieval of auxiliary variables. The code base provides the base URL of the directory that contains the aglet's compiled class code.

With the release of Oracle8*i*, IBM's DB2 Universal Database, and similar products, a user can easily treat his/her database server as an application server. All major relational database vendors now support the use of Java for stored procedures. Using Java, one can put robust business logic straight into the database server, perhaps skipping the middleware issue altogether. (Nevertheless, the concept of middleware is still very important and will be briefly discussed in Chapter 3).

2.8   Data mining, CRM, Web mining, and clickstream

2.8.1   What can be analyzed using intelligent data analysis

The discussion in the previous section indicates that agent-based artificial intelligence techniques have made important contributions to data warehousing. The availability of data warehousing provides various intelligent aspects. For example, intelligent data analysis can be conducted on the warehouse data. Data mining techniques play a very important role in intelligent data analysis. Data mining is an important component of customer relationship management (CRM). Data mining, also referred to as knowledge discovery in databases (KDD) (Fayyad et al., 1996), is the nontrivial extraction of implicit, previously unknown, interesting, and potentially useful information (usually in the form of knowledge patterns or models) from data. The extracted knowledge is used to describe the hidden regularity of data, to make predictions, or to aid human users in other ways. It is concerned with mining the data stored in the warehouse.

Although data mining may not necessarily use database or data warehousing techniques, in general, it is believed that data warehousing provides an ideal environment for data mining. However, Parsaye (1999) argued that the content of the data in the miner is often different from that of the data in the warehouse because it is often enriched by additional external data not found within the warehouse. Parsaye further distinguished three cases in regard to data warehousing and data mining:

1. *Data mining is above the warehouse, as a set of conceptual views.* Data mining above the warehouse provides a minimal architecture for discovery and analysis. It is suitable only in cases where data mining is not a key objective for the warehouse.
2. *The data mining is beside the warehouse, as a separate repository.* The major advantage of this separation is that data mining can be effectively performed beside the warehouse, with data structures that lend themselves to detailed analyses.
3. *Data mining is within the warehouse, as a distinct set of resources.* In some cases where the warehouse is a very large, massively parallel process-

ing (MPP) computer, the data mine may actually reside as a separate repository within the large warehouse. This is very similar to a data miner beside the warehouse, where the miner uses a portion of the physical warehouse, but is independent of the warehouse structures.

In this book, the perspective taken is that of viewing data warehousing as an enabling technique of data mining, and data mining will be examined mainly in the data warehousing environment.

Another important aspect of intelligent data analysis in the warehouse is how the data are used. Particularly, when the warehouse is actually a Webhouse, Web mining, which is a version of data mining in the Web environment, can take place. The enthusiasm of this direction is reflected in a study of the so called clicksteam. According to Goldman (2000), the idea behind clickstream analysis is similar to attaching a video camera to someone's head while he is reading a magazine. By recording and analyzing the articles selected, the advertisements scanned, and the speed at which the eyes track across the page, an in-depth understanding of the reader's interests could be developed. With this information, the magazine could be customized to cater to the reader's individual preferences.

Technical issues related to data mining will be examined in Chapter 8. In the rest of this section, issues related to applying data mining concepts to the Web, as well as clickstream analysis, will be examined.

2.8.2   From data mining to Web mining

2.8.2.1   Background

Web mining is an important asset of enterprise intelligence. It can be defined as the discovery and analysis of useful information from the World Wide Web. Recent work has shown that the analysis needs of Web usage data have much in common with those of data warehouses, and hence OLAP techniques are quite applicable. Web mining demonstrates many basic features of data mining as discussed so far, but with special concern for the Internet. This section presents some additional concerns related to Web mining.

Before an organization starts to mine data, one must define the objective and what information is needed to achieve the objective. For example, the Web master in an organization may need to issue visitor identification cookies when visitors complete registration forms at its Web site. This will enable the organization to match the information captured from various forms, such as the visitor's ZIP code, with the transaction information generated from the cookies. It will also allow the organization to merge its cookie information, which will provide details of the locations visited, with specific visitor attributes like age and gender, from the forms owned by the organization. In addition, a ZIP code or visitor address will allow the Web master to match the company's cookie and form data with demographics and household information matched from third-party data resellers.

One will likely need to scrub and prepare the data from the Web site before beginning any sort of data mining analysis. Log files, for example, can be fairly redundant since a single "hit" generates a record not only of that HTML but also of every graphic on that page. However, once a template, script, or procedure has been developed for generating the proper recording of a single visit, the data can be input into a database format from which additional manipulations and refinements can take place. If a site traffic analyzer tool is used, these data may already be format-ready for additional mining analysis (Mena, 1999).

2.8.2.2   Creating and enhancing Web data

Web data are diverse and voluminous. In order to analyze e-commerce data one must assemble the divergent data components captured via server log files, and then form databases and e-mails generated by visitors into a cohesive, integrated, and comprehensive view. This requires careful planning.

Server log files provide domain types, time of access, keywords, and search engine used by visitors and can provide some insight into how a visitor arrived at a website and what keywords he or she used to locate it. Cookies dispensed from the server can track browser visits and pages viewed and provide some insight into how often this visitor has been to the site and into what sections he or she wandered.

All of this internal and external information can be implemented using a database management product such as Oracle, or using a flat file, which then can be linked or imported into a data mining tool. These include automated tools, which have principally been used in data warehouses to extract patterns, trends, and relationships and new easy-to-use data mining tools with GUI interfaces designed for business and marketing personnel. These data mining analyses can provide actionable solutions in many formats, which can be shared with those individuals responsible for the design, maintenance, and marketing of an e-commerce site.

2.8.2.3   Mining Web data

Various data mining techniques can be used for Web mining. For example, by using a data mining tool incorporating a machine-learning algorithm, a Website database can be segmented into unique groups of visitors, each with individual behavior. These same tools perform statistical tests on the data and partition them into multiple market segments independent of the analyst or marketer. These types of data mining tools can autonomously identify key intervals and ranges in the data, which distinguish the good from the bad prospect, and can generally output their results in the form of graphical decision trees or IF/THEN rules. This type of Web mining allows a merchant to make some projections about the profitability potential of its visitors in the form of business rules, which can be extracted directly from the Web data:

IF search keywords are "e-commerce" and "B2B"
AND search engine YAHOO
AND subdomain .AOL
AND gender male
AND age 25–34,
THEN average projected sale amount is $1000 → High.

On the other hand, predicting customer propensity to purchase can also be done using a data mining tool incorporating a back-propagation neural network. Neural networks can be used to construct customer behavior models that can predict who will buy, or how much a prospect is likely to buy. The ability to learn is one of the features of neural networks.

2.8.2.4   Other issues of Web mining

There are some additional issues after Web mining proper is carried out. The following are some sample issues.

Acting on mining solutions. Most likely one will need to do Web mining on a separate server dedicated to analysis. After the analysis one will need to validate the results through some sort of mechanism such as a test marketing e-mail campaign. Web mining is not an isolated process carried out in a vacuum; it must be integrated into the entire electronic retailing and marketing process. Electronic retailing not only changes the distribution and marketing of products but, more importantly, also alters the process of consumption and the related transactions of buying and selling.

Web marketing, mining, and messaging. An organization should use segmentation analysis to stratify its e-mail offers to prospects it has identified via the mining analysis, use targeted e-mail to provide incentives only to those individuals likely to be interested in its products or services, and use Web mining analysis to discover customer demographics, as well as consumer preferences, values, and lifestyles. It then needs to incorporate such knowledge about customers in the tone, manner, and method by which the company would communicate with them. The company can also track advertising efforts to know what works and why. It is of paramount importance that retailers in a networked economy be adaptive and receptive to the needs of their customers. In this expansive, competitive, and volatile environment Web mining will be a critical process impacting every retailer's long-term success, where failure to react, adapt, and evolve quickly can translate into customer "churn" with the click of a mouse.

Web trackers fine-tune mining consumer interests. Various techniques can be used; many of them put an emphasis on personalization. The personalization industry can be divided into three camps. One is the platforms, the software applications that Web publishers and marketers use to create their sites and campaigns. Another is the companies that make analysis and reporting tools, and the third is composed of those who enable marketers to take actions such as sending e-mail or serving up dynamic content. Of course, some vendors might dispute that breakdown or argue over into which group they fit.

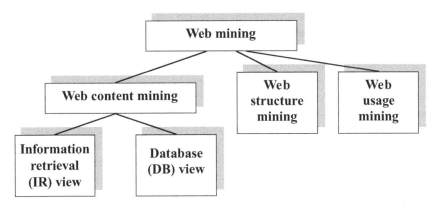

Figure 2.1 Web mining categories.

2.8.2.5 *Approaches for Web mining*

According to Kosala and Blackeel (2000), Web mining can be categorized into three areas of interest based on which part of the Web to mine: 1. Web content mining, which describes the discovery of useful information from Web contents, Web data, or Web documents; 2. Web structure mining, discovers the model underlying the link structures of the Web; and 3. Web usage mining, which discovers regularity of the data generated by the Web user's sessions or behaviors.

In addition, there are two ways of viewing Web content mining from an information retrieval (IR) view where Web documents are treated as unstructured documents, or from a database view where Web documents are treated as semistructured documents stored at various Web sites (which are viewed as databases). Web mining categories are summarized in Figure 2.1 (Cooley, Srivastava, and Mobasher, 1997).

2.8.3 *Clickstream analysis*

2.8.3.1 *Components of clickstream analysis*

Clickstream analysis exemplifies the importance of Web mining in enterprise intelligence. There are three key components to clickstream analysis: 1. Referral analysis looks at how a visitor arrives at a given Web site. This is most relevant in tracking the use of outside links to a site; 2. Repeat visitor analysis tracks how and when visitors return to a Web site; and 3. The path to the purchase analyzes how customers come to place an order (or when they abandon an order).

2.8.3.2 *Clickstream data mart*

An interesting part of the emerging data Webhouse is the data mart that stores and presents Web activity for later analysis. It is desirable to build a comprehensible view of the immense stream of clicks arriving at sites, whether one is dealing with intranet users or with customers on the public

Web site. Kimball (1999) coined the term clickstream data mart to refer to this aspect of a data Webhouse and, according to him, the clickstream data mart can reveal a great deal about detailed customer behavior. If there is information on customers' every click, gesture, and trajectory through a Web site, it should be possible to answer such questions as which parts of a certain Web site get the most visitors or can be associated most frequently with actual sales, or which are superfluous or visited infrequently, or even "session killers," where the remote user stops the session and leaves. One can also learn about user profiles, such as profiles of the new-visitor click profile on a certain site, and the click profiles of an existing customer, a profitable customer, or a complaining customer that all too frequently returns the product. The click profile of a customer about to cancel the service can also be ascertained.

It is important to characterize customer behaviors from the start, instead of trying to recreate the user's thought processes from abstract clickstreams. By formulating views of customer actions and properly logging these actions, data can be accumulated with a value exceeding the demographics on which traditional businesses rely. Within the Web-enabled environment, this knowledge is referred to as e-business intelligence (E-BI) (Loshin, 2000). Its attendant benefits include understanding who users are and what they like to do, enabling creation of a better customized user experience, increasing revenue through personalized one-to-one marketing, enhancing product branding and customer loyalty, locating and drawing potential customers to the Web site, etc.

Actions are activities a user can perform while navigating a Web site. Tracking user behavior involves more than just collecting server log files. Instead of relying on the traditional server log data, it is necessary to incorporate a more meaningful characterization of user activity.

After customer actions are captured for a period of time, the information in the user activity table will represent a collection of time series of the ways that all e-commerce business visitors browse through the site. Several frameworks have been developed. For example, one analysis framework presumes a desired outcome and looks for patterns that lead to that outcome, while a different analysis framework looks for behaviors that are not known *a priori*.

2.9   The future of data warehouses

Although the area of data warehousing thrives and the potential for further growth is promising, a data warehouse project could be a great risk and is endangered by several factors. The reasons for the failure of a data warehousing project can be grouped into four categories (Vassiliadis, 2000): 1. design factors, such as lack of metadata management or unrealistic schema design, 2. technical factors, such as lack of study of hardware/software selection for the warehouse environment, or lack of study in volume of queries, data sets, and network traffic, 3. procedural factors, which involve reasons for deficiencies concerning the deployment of the data warehouse, and 4. sociotechnical issues, such as problems due to data ownership and access. Several desirable features for future data warehousing development are now described.

Distributed data marts. Continuing the notion of data warehousing as the union of data marts, Inmon (2001) envisioned the future of data warehousing as modular, cost effective, incrementally designed, distributed data marts. The data warehouse technology will be a rich mixture of large monolithic machines that grind through massive data sets with parallel processing, together with many separate small machines nibbling away on individual data sets that may be granular, mildly aggregated, or highly aggregated. The separate machines will be tied together with navigator software that will serve as switchboards for dispatching queries to the servers best able to respond.

Metadata. The next generation of data warehousing solutions will have all types of metadata (technical, operational, business) and will have business intelligence built in, which will require vertical industry knowledge to be incorporated.

Real-time data warehousing. A real-time data warehouse is a historical and analytic component of an enterprise-level data stream. This data stream supports continuous, asynchronous, multipoint delivery of data. In other words, data move straight from the originating source to all uses that do not require some form of staging. This movement takes place soon after the original data are written. Any time delays are due solely to transport latency and (optionally) minuscule processing times to dispatch or transform the instance of data being delivered. Despite its name, the impact of this change is due less to the increase in speed of availability (which is significant) than to a significant reduction in overall processing complexity. A brute force process will be replaced with elegant, yet powerful, simplicity. Real-time data warehousing will solve some of the most vexing data warehouse problems such as change data capture. It will allow a return to co-engineered, end-to-end system architectures (Haisten, 1999). Such a system supports quick reconfiguration and active data warehousing.

2.10   Summary

In this chapter, various fundamental issues related to data warehousing have been discussed. The focus has been on how to make enterprise intelligence and agent-based AI techniques meet. In particular, Web-enabling techniques for data warehousing have been examined, as well as intelligent data analysis in the warehouse environment. With these preparations, fundamentals of data warehousing can be examined in the next chapter in more detail.

References

Agosta, L., Advances in Web computing, *DM Rev. Online*, 2(6), June, 1998. Available at http://www.dmreview.com/.

Baron, J. P., M. J. Shaw, and A. D. Bailey, Jr., Web-based e-catalog systems in B2B procurement, *Comm. ACM*, 43(5), 93–100, 2000.

Berners-Lee, T., *Information management: a proposal*, March 1989 (revised May 1990). http://www.w3.org/History/1989/proposal.html.

Bertino, E., B. Catania, G. P. Zarri, and K. Tristaino, *Intelligent Database Systems*, Addison Wesley, London, 2001.

Bradshaw, J. M., Ed., *Software Agents*, MIT Press, Cambridge, MA, 1997.

Cooley, R., Srivastava, J., and B. Mobasher, Web mining: information and pattern discovery on the world wide web, *Proc. of the 9th IEEE Intl. Conf. on Tools with Artificial Intell.* (ICTAI '97), 1997.

Dyché, J., *e-Data: Turning Data into Information with Data Warehousing*, Addison Wesley, Boston, 2000.

Fayyad, U. M., G. Piatetsky-Shapiro, P. Smyth, and R. Uturusamy (Eds.), *Advances in Knowledge Discovery and Data Mining*, AAAI/MIT Press, Cambridge, MA, 1996.

Fensel, D. and M. A. Musen, The semantic Web: a brain for humankind, *IEEE Intell. Syst.*, 16(2), 24–25, 2001.

Gannon, T. and D. Bragger, Data warehousing with intelligent agents, *Intell. Enterp.*, 1(1), 28–37, 1998.

Goldman, L. F., Customer relationship management: one-to-one marketing — achieving marketing's Holy Grail with clickstream analysis, *DM Rev. Online*, 4(3), March, 2000. Available at http://www.dmmereview.com/.

Haisten, M., Real-time data warehouse, *DM Rev. Online*, 4(3), October, 1999.

Hendler, J., Agents and the semantic Web, *IEEE Intell. Syst.*, March/April 2001, 30–37, 2001.

Hwang, M. and R. Woerner, Next generation data warehousing, *DM Direct Online*, July, 1998.

Inmon, W., A Retrospective look at data warehousing, *DM Rev. Online*, 5(2), February, 2001.

Kimball, R., Clicking with your customer, *Intell. Enterprise*, 2(1), 1–4, 1999.

Kimball, R. and R. Merz, *The Data Webhouse Toolkit: Building the Web-Enabled Data Warehouse*, John Wiley & Sons, New York, 2000.

Kosala, R. and H. Blackeel, Web mining research: a survey, *ACM SIGKDD Explorations*, 2(1), 1–15, 2000.

Loshin, D., Advance knowledge, *Intell. Enterp.*, 3(16), 24–28, 2000.

Maedche, A. and S. Staab, Ontology learning for semantic Web, *IEEE Intell. Syst.*, 16(2), 72–76, 2001.

Malaika, S., Resistance is futile: the Web will assimilate your database, *IEEE Data Eng. Bull.*, 4–13, June, 1998.

Mena, J., *Mining Your Web Site*, Digital Press, Woburn, MA, 1999.

No, A., Frequently asked questions about data warehousing, *DM Rev. Online*, June, 2000.

O'Leary, D. E. and R. Studer, Knowledge management: an interdisciplinary approach, *IEEE Intell. Syst.*, 16(1), 24–25, Jan/Feb, 2001.

Parsaye, K., DataMines for datawarehouses — data mining above, beside and within the warehouse to avoid the paradox of warehouse patterns (an Information Discovery, Inc. White Paper), 1999.

Ramasrisknam, R., *Database Management Systems,* 2nd ed., WCB McGraw-Hill, Boston, 2000.

Ritter, D., Java in the database, *Intell. Enterp.*, 2(1), 76–80, 1999.

Silberschatz, A. et al., *Database System Concepts* (4th ed.), McGraw-Hill, New York, 2001.

Singh, H., *Interactive Data Warehousing,* Prentice Hall, Upper Saddle River, NJ, 1999.

Tanler, R., *The Intranet Data Warehouse: Tools and Techniques for Building an Intranet-Enabled Data Warehouse*, John Wiley & Sons, New York, 1997.

Vassiliadis, P., Gulliver in the land of data warehousing: practical experiences and observations of a researcher, *Proc. DMDW,* 2000 (*online*), 12.1–12.16, 2000.

Weiss, M. A., *Data Structures & Algorithm Analysis in C++*, Addison-Wesley, Reading, MA, 1998.

chapter three

From DBMS to data warehousing

3.1 Overview

This chapter is devoted to the basics of data warehousing. Since building data warehouses is closely related to the construction of database management systems (DBMSs), the chapter begins with a brief review of data management systems, covering issues from data modeling to query processing and transaction processing, as well as advanced database architecture. As for data warehousing itself, its architecture and related issues, such as data marts and metadata, are discussed. We also pay attention to related issues, such as online analytical processing (OLAP). A sketch of viewing data warehousing as materialized views and indexing are also provided.

3.2 An overview of database management systems

3.2.1 Data modeling

A data model is a collection of conceptual tools for describing data, data relationships, data semantics, and consistency constraints. Various models exist at different levels. A conceptual model is the highest level of model. A popular model at this level is the entity-relationship (ER) model. Logic models result when conceptual models are used for development of data models at the logic level. The relational data model is a popular model at logical level abstraction. Other logical level abstractions also exist, including those usually referred to as legacy systems, such as the network data model and hierarchy data model. The physical model occurs at the lowest level, when physical implementations are developed to realize the logic models (not to be discussed in this book).

Conceptual modeling will be discussed in Chapter 5. As an example of the logical model, a relational database consists of structured data stored in a set of relations. Structured data means each relation has a schema that consists of a set of attributes. For example, a company database may have a relation to hold employee information such as employee ID, name, salary, etc. (which form a schema), a relation to hold department information, etc. The contents of a database are referred to as database instance. Intuitively, a relation is just a table; more formally, a relation is defined as a subset of a Cartesian product of a list of domains.

3.2.2   Relational data model

In a relational data model, data are stored in relations (namely, tables). A tuple in a relation is actually a row in a table. In order to access the data stored, relational algebra (RA) operators are used to write queries. The following are some important RA operators:

Select. Find tuples satisfying condition C from relation (r), is expressed as $\sigma_C(r)$.

Project. Find a specific attribute or set of attributes with name A from relation r, is expressed as $\pi_A(r)$.

Union. The results include all tuples in r or s: $r \cup s$ (remove duplicates). A requirement for the union operation is that both relations involved should be union compatible, meaning that the two relations should have the same arity and the corresponding attributes should be in the same domain.

Set Difference. The result includes tuples in r but not in s: $r - s$. Just like the union operation, it requires union compatibility. Note that set difference operation is not commutative: $r - s \neq s - r$

Cartesian Product. $r \times s$ combines information from two relations. If relation r has a schema with three attributes and relation s has a schema with two attributes, the resulting relation will have a schema with five attributes, and each tuple in the resulting relation is constructed by combining a tuple in one table and a tuple in the other table.

Join. Two relations can be combined to form a new relation based on their common values on one or more shared attributes. The duplicated columns in the table are removed. This Cartesian product is followed by a select operation. Join of relations r and s is denoted by $r \bowtie s$. A simple example is given in Table 3.1.

The join operation discussed in Table 3.1 is natural join. A natural join operation can be generalized to outer join. The left outer join takes all tuples in the left relation that did not match with any tuple in the right relation, pads the tuples with null values for all other attributes from the right relation,

Table 3.1 An Example of Natural Join

(a) Relation r(R)			(b) Relation s(S)		(c) Relation r $\bowtie$ s			
A	B	C	C	D	A	B	C	D
4	9	8	7	12	4	9	8	10
5	16	7	4	18	5	16	7	12
2	12	7	8	10	2	12	7	12

Table 3.2 SQL vs. RA

SQL Clause	Corresponding RA operator
Select $A_1, A_2, \ldots A_n$	$\pi_{A1, A2, \ldots, An}$ (NOT σ!)
From $r_1, r_2, \ldots, r_m$	$r_1 \times r_2 \times \ldots \times r_m$
Where(optional) P	σ_P

and adds them to the result of the natural join. The right outer join is symmetric with the left outer join. The full outer join does both of these operations.

Operations discussed here, as well as other RA operators, can be used in combination to form complex queries. Many queries can be written using select (S), project (P), and join (J) operations, hence the term SPJ queries.

Relational algebra is a formal language that has been used for establishing theoretical foundations of the relational model. Queries can also be written in commercial languages, such as structured query language (SQL). SQL clauses can be compared with RA operators, as shown in Table 3.2.

The entire SQL statement "select $A_1, A_2, \ldots A_n$ from $r_1, r_2, \ldots, r_m$ where(optional) P" is equivalent to the following RA expression

$$\pi_{A1, A2, \ldots, An} \left(\sigma_P \left(r_1 \times r_2 \times \ldots \times r_m \right) \right)$$

Nested SQL queries are allowed. For example, any r_i $(i = 1, \ldots, m)$ in the above SQL query could be an SQL query as well. SQL also provides aggregate functions, including avg (average), count (count), min (minimum), max (maximum), and sum (total). In addition, "group by" and "having" clauses can be used in an SQL query. For example, if the headquarters of a retail chain is only interested in stores whose annual average profit is more than 1 million U.S. dollars, then the following query can be submitted:

Select store-number, avg (profit)
From sales
Group by store-name
Having avg (profit) > 1000000

However, these functions are not powerful enough to handle decision support queries in OLAP. That is why additional efforts are needed.

3.2.3   Integrity constraints

An integrity constraint (IC) is a condition specified on a database schema that restricts data that can be stored in an instance of the database. A DBMS enforces ICs in that it permits only legal instances (i.e., those satisfying all ICs) to be stored in the database. In general, ICs provide a means of ensuring that changes made to the database by authorized users do not result in a loss of data consistency. There are several forms of ICs described below.

- Functional dependencies are a very important form of IC and a very important factor affecting relational database design. Among other things, functional dependencies can be used to determine the primary key of a relation. A key (or superkey) in a relation is a set of attributes which uniquely determine the values of all attributes. As a simple intuitive example, in a student relation with schema (name, ID, major, and GPA), the name or ID of a student should determine all the attributes (assuming names and IDs are all unique). Therefore, student name is a key, and ID is another key. Note also that a key combined with any other attributes is still a key. For example, name combined with major is a key. Therefore, it makes sense to define the concept of candidate key, which refers to a set of attributes that uniquely determine the value of other attributes; if any attribute is removed from the candidate key, it will no longer be a key. Apparently, candidate key may not be unique; for example, student name and ID are two candidate keys. Therefore, there is a need to define the concept of primary key, which is the designated candidate key actually used by the database designer. In this example, either student name or ID can be designated as the primary key. Concepts related to keys and functional dependencies play important roles in relational database design, and will be discussed in the next section.
- Referential integrity refers to a particular kind of integrity constraint to ensure data consistency. It is concerned with situations in which change in a relation may affect other relations and usually involves foreign keys. For example, consider a relation for course registration in a university database. If a previously planned course is to be dropped, all the tuples in the registration relation referring to that course should be dropped as well. It is therefore important to preserve the referential-integrity constraint. This issue will be revisited in Section 4.6.6.
- An assertion is a predicate expressing a condition that the database must always satisfy; it may involve several relations.
- Triggers (also called active rules) are statements executed automatically by the system as a side effect of a modification to the database. An active rule consists of condition and action. An active database

is equipped with active rules and can be considered as a special form of a knowledge-based system.

3.2.4   *Normalization and normal forms*

A relational database usually consists of several tables. If a query involves information contained in different tables, join operations are needed. However, join operations could be expensive. So one may wonder why all attributes are not put together to form a big relation. This seems to be quite appealing to naïve people, but a closer look indicates this approach is unrealistic. Take, for example, a simple case of a customer purchase database. If 100 customers purchase the same item, and if the information about the purchased item (such as supplier's information or the product information) is stored along with the sales information, then the same information will repeat 99 times. What is worse, if supplier or product information is changed, then all 99 redundant pieces should be updated as well. Relational database design theory has been developed to avoid these anomalies. An important component of relational database design theory is normalization, which requires that each relation be in certain normal form. For example, third normal form (3NF) is popular in many real-world database applications. It requires that, for any nontrivial functional dependency in a relation, either the left-hand side contains a key (as discussed in Section 3.2.3), or the right-hand side is part of a key. Recent developments in data warehousing have raised many issues related to denormalization (see Section 3.7.1).

3.2.5   *Basics of query processing*

Having discussed data modeling, we now take a brief look at the physical implementation of database management systems (DBMS). Query processing and transaction processing to be discussed in the next section are two key issues in DBMS implementation.

A query (in SQL or other languages) expresses a user's information needs in a DBMS. Query processing refers to the range of activities involved in extracting data from a database. It is concerned with choosing a strategy for processing a query that minimizes the amount of time necessary to compute the answer. Basic steps in traditional on-line transaction processing (OLTP) consist of the following:

1. Parsing and translation translates SQL queries into a system's internal representation (using extended relational algebra).
2. Query optimization refers to the process of selecting the most effective query-evaluation plan for a query. A query evaluation plan is a sequence of primitive operations used to evaluate a query.
3. In a query evaluation, the query is evaluated with the selected plan, and the result of the query is output.

An important concept in query processing is cost model, which makes use of statistical information in the DBMS catalog to determine the optimal cost of alternative operations, so that the optimizer can select the efficient plan with the least estimated cost. The cost of query evaluation can be measured in terms of a number of different resources, including disk accesses, CPU time to execute a query, and the cost of communication in distributed/parallel database systems.

3.2.6   Basics of transaction processing

A transaction is a unit of program execution that accesses and possibly updates various data items in a DBMS. A database transaction should hold the following *ACID* properties: 1. atomicity (*A*): all or no operations of the transaction are executed; 2. consistency (*C*): database should be consistent before and after transaction; 3. isolation (*I*): each transaction is unaware of other transactions executing concurrently in the system; and 4. durability (*D*): changes made by completed transactions should be made persistently, even if there are system failures.

A transaction could be in different status (usually referred to as transaction states), such as active, partially committed (after the final statement has been executed), committed (after successful completion), or aborted. Important issues to be considered in transaction processing include concurrency control and recovery. When several transactions execute concurrently in the same database, the isolation property may no longer be preserved. Concurrency control provides a variety of mechanisms to control the interaction among the concurrent transactions. Recovery refers to the part of the database system responsible for restoration of the database to a consistent database state (or instance) that existed prior to the occurrence of the failure.

It is important to understand how query processing is related to transaction processing. The query manager converts a query into a sequence of requests for stored data (usually involving query optimization). DBMS allows the user to group one or more queries (including possible modification) into a transaction. A transaction usually results from the execution of a user program written in high-level language (such as SQL queries). It is convenient to regard a transaction as a series of read and write operations of database objects (here the term "object" is used in its broad sense) and delimited by statements of the form *begin transaction* and *end transaction*. A system component called transaction manager ensures that all these transactions are executed properly so that ACID properties can be supported.

An important issue in transaction processing is concurrency control, which is concerned with "correct" execution of concurrent transactions. When multiple transactions are executed concurrently (rather than in a serial manner, which means that all statements in one transaction are executed before another transaction is started), an arrangement must be made so that statements in the involved transactions will be executed. This arrangement is called a schedule. Any schedule produced by concurrent processing of a set of transactions should have an effect equivalent to a schedule produced when these transactions are run serially in some order. A system that guarantees this property is said to ensure serializability.

Anomalies may occur when multiple transactions are executed in an interleaved fashion. The reason for concurrency control is to avoid anomalies. An example of anomalies is the lost update problem: when two transactions access the same database item, the value of some database items updated by one of these two transactions is lost. (If two transactions want to access the same data item, and at least one of the transactions wants to update the data item, then these two transactions are called conflict transactions.) Another example of anomalies is the temporary update (dirty read) problem: the transaction that updated one data item failed, but the updated item is accessed by another transaction before it is changed back to its original value.

There are different kinds of protocols used for concurrency control based on the notion of serializability. A popular approach is lock-based protocols, in which each transaction requests a lock on a data item, to be granted by the concurrency control manager.

A popular approach for locking is two-phase locking (2PL). The basic 2PL has a growing phase, during which a transaction may obtain locks, but may not release any lock, and a shrinking phase, during which a transaction may release locks, but may not obtain any new locks. It can be proved that, if every transaction in a schedule follows the 2PL protocol, the schedule is guaranteed to be serializable, obviating the need to test for serializability of schedules. Note that, in the locking protocol, the order between conflicting transactions is determined at the execution time. In contrast, in another mechanism called timestamp protocol, timestamps can be assigned so that selection of an ordering among transactions can be made in advance.

Another important issue in transaction processing is recovery. The recovery mechanism is responsible for the restoration of the database to a consistent state that existed prior to occurrence of the failure. Log-based recovery mechanisms are very popular. There are two basic approaches for log-based recovery. Deferred database modification ensures transaction atomicity by recording all database modifications in the log, but deferring the execution of all write operations of a transaction until the transaction partially commits. If the system crashes before the transaction completes its execution, or if the transaction aborts, then the information on the log is simply ignored (as though the transaction were never executed). Therefore, only redo is needed. In contrast, immediate database modification allows database modifications to be output to the database while the transaction is still in the active state. In the event of a crash or a transaction failure, the system must use the old-value field of the log records to restore the modified data items to their value prior to the start of the transaction. The restoration is accomplished through the undo operation. Unlike deferred database modification, failures at any moment during execution should be handled. Both old and new values are used for recovery.

Data warehousing has posed challenging new issues on query processing and transaction processing. Chapter 7 briefly examines some new problems and approaches to dealing with them.

3.3   Advances in DBMS

Relational databases have achieved tremendous success, and today's data warehousing techniques are largely built on top of relational techniques. Nevertheless, the relational approach has its limitations, such as lack of recursion and reasoning, and lack of an ability to deal with complex objects. In other words, traditional DBMSs are hardly considered "intelligent." Recent development of data warehousing has expanded its arena to more advanced database management systems. Next is a brief examination of advanced DBMSs. This examination justifies the need for data warehousing from a technical perspective.

3.3.1   Basics of deductive databases

A database is a model of a set of integrity constraints, and a query is a formula to be evaluated with respect to this model. From the viewpoint of logic, a DBMS can be seen as a query answering system that views facts (tuples) as axioms of a theorem and queries as the conclusion of a theorem. The inference mechanism provided with logic can be used to deduce the query on the basis of the set of facts and rules. In addition, logic can be used as a uniform language for expressing facts, rules, programs, queries, views, and integrity constraints.

Deductive databases are databases with inference power. As the simplest model of deductive databases, Datalog is a version (or variation, not really a subset) of Prolog (an AI language) suitable for database systems. A Datalog program consists of two parts; a conventional relational database referred to as an extensional database (or EDB), and an intensional database (or IDB) that contains rules operating on the EDB. They are defined by logical rules and are actually views. For example, a table named "parent" with schema (child name, parent name) forms an EDB. The following illustrates possible contents in the EDB, with each tuple represented by a predicate:

> parent (John, Tom),
> parent (Tom, Mary),
> parent (Mary, Bob),
> parent (Ron, John), and
> parent (Ann, John).

Note that the above predicates are equivalent to a flat table as shown in Table 3.3.

The following is an example of an IDB:

Table 3.3 A Parent Table

Child name	Parent name
John	Tom
Tom	Mary
Mary	Bob
Ron	John
Ann	John

ancestor (X, Y) :– parent (X, Y); and
ancestor (X, Y) :– parent (X, Z), ancestor (Z, Y).

There are two rules in the IDB. The first one says if X is Y's parent, then X is Y's ancestor. The second rule says that if X is Z's parent while Z is Y's ancestor, then X is Y's ancestor (that is, the ancestor's ancestor is an ancestor). This is an example of using recursion, because the predicate ancestor appears in both the left-hand side (head) and right-hand side (body) of the same rule. The use of recursion has significantly enhanced the inference power of the database.

3.3.2 Object-relational and object-oriented databases

Another useful direction of extension is object-relational data models that extend the relational data model by providing a richer type system, including object orientation, and add constructs such as SQL to relational query languages, to deal with the added databases. Interestingly enough, the basic idea of object-relational databases can be traced back to nested relations (which are nonflat tables). A more radical approach is object-oriented databases (OODB). These advanced systems are briefly addressed in Chapter 7. Interested readers are referred to Elmasri and Navathe (2000) for more detail.

3.3.3 Distributed and parallel databases

Traditional databases (including relational databases) can be enhanced by introducing more advanced architecture. For example, parallel database systems consist of multiple processors and multiple disks connected by a fast interconnection network. Parallel database architectures include architectures with different tradeoffs on scalability vs. communication speed such as shared memory, shared disk, shared nothing, and hierarchical. In contrast to parallel systems, in which the processors are tightly coupled and constitute a singe database system, a distributed database system consists of loosely coupled (mutually independent) sites that share no physical components. In a distributed database system, the database is stored on several computers that communicate with one another through various communication media, such as high-speed networks or telephone lines. They do not share main memory or disks.

In addition, the database systems that run on each site may have a substantial degree of mutual independence. In recent years, the need has arisen for accessing and updating data from a variety of preexisting databases, which differ in their hardware and software environments and in the schemas under which data are stored. A multidatabase system is a software layer that enables such a heterogeneous collection of databases to be treated like a homogeneous distributed database.

A simple and popular distributed DBMS architecture is called client server. A client server system has one or more client processes (responsible for user-interface issues) and one or more server processes (which manage data and execute transactions). A client process can send a query to any server process. However, the client-server architecture does not allow a single query to span multiple servers. As a consequence, a client process could be quite complex, and its capabilities would begin to overlap with the server. To deal with these problems, collaborating server systems have been developed.

In general, in a distributed database system, the database is stored on several computers located at different sites (or nodes). The computers in a distributed system communicate with one another through various communication media (networks or phone lines). They may vary in size and function and do not share main memory or disks.

In distributed relational databases, relations are usually fragmented. There are two different schemes for fragmenting a relation: horizontal fragmentation splits a relation by assigning each tuple of relation r to one or more fragments; vertical fragmentation splits the relation by decomposing the scheme R of relation r so that the original relation can be reconstructed by joining the fragments back. (It is often convenient to add a special attribute called tuple-ID for this purpose.)

For centralized systems, the primary criterion for measuring the cost of a particular strategy is the number of disk accesses; in a distributed system, it is necessary to take into account several other matters, including cost of data transmission over the network and potential gain in performance from having several sites process parts of the query in parallel.

Distributed environment also brings more challenges for issues related to transaction processing. For example, in order to ensure atomicity, all the sites in which a transaction T is executed must agree on the final outcome of the execution. T must either commit at all sites or abort at all sites. Therefore, the transaction coordinator of T must execute a commit protocol. The simplest and most widely used is the two-phase commit protocol (2PC). Roughly speaking, the first phase is to send prepared messages, while the second is based on the received messages to determine whether to commit or abort.

3.3.4   Motivations of data warehousing: a technical examination

The complexity involved in traditional distributed database systems has stimulated organizations to find alternative ways to achieve decision support. Data warehousing is an emerging approach for effective decision support. According to the popular definition given by the "godfather" of data warehousing technique, William Inmon, a data warehouse is a "subject-oriented, integrated, time-varying, nonvolatile collection of data that is used primarily in organizational decision making" (Inmon, 1996). Although considered by some business people to be a low-key answer for "failed" distributed database systems, data warehousing does take advantage of various techniques related to distributed and parallel computing.

Data warehousing provides an effective approach to dealing with complex decision support queries over data from multiple sites. The key to this approach is to create a copy (or derivation) of all data at one location and to use the copy, rather than going to the individual sources. Note that the original data may be on different software platforms or belong to different organizations.

There are several reasons for the massive growth of volumes of data in the data warehouse environment. Data warehouses may collect historical data and involve the collection of data to satisfy unknown requirements. They include data at the summary level, but may also include data at the very detailed atomic or granule level. Data warehouses contain external data as well (e.g., demographic, psychographic, etc.). Significant amounts of external data are collected to support a variety of data mining activities for prediction or knowledge discovery. For example, data mining tools would use this external data to predict who is likely to be a good customer or how certain companies are likely to perform in the marketplace.

Therefore, data warehouses contain consolidated data from many sources (different business units), spanning long time periods, and augmented with summary information. Warehouses are much larger than other kinds of databases and sizes are much larger; typical workloads involve ad hoc, fairly complex queries, and fast response times are important. Data warehousing encompasses frameworks, architectures, algorithms, tools, and techniques for bringing together selected data from multiple databases or other information sources into a single repository suitable for direct querying or analysis. Data warehousing is especially important in industry today because of a need to gather all information into a single place for in-depth analysis and the desire to decouple such analysis from OLTP systems. Since decision support often is the goal of data warehousing, clearly, warehouses may be tuned for decision support and, perhaps, vice versa.

In its simplest form, data warehousing can be considered as an example of asynchronous replication, in which copies are updated relatively infrequently. However, a more advanced implementation of data warehousing would store summary data or other kinds of information derived from the source data. In other words, a data warehouse stores materialized views (plus some local relations, if needed). Materialized views are briefly discussed below and will be further addressed in Section 3.7.

It is common in a data warehousing environment for source changes to be deferred and applied to the warehouse views in large batches for efficiency. Source changes received during the day are applied to the views in a nightly batch window. (The warehouse is not available to users during this period.) Most current commercial warehousing systems focus on storing the data for efficient access and providing extensive querying facilities. Maintenance of warehousing data (in a large degree, maintenance of materialized views) is thus an important problem (Rundersteiner et al., 2000).

The need for data warehousing techniques is justified largely due to decision support queries, which are ad hoc user queries in various business applications. In these applications, current and historical data are comprehensively analyzed and explored, identifying useful trends and creating summaries of the data, in order to support high-level decision making in a data warehousing environment. A class of stylized queries typically involves group-by and aggregation operators. Applications dominated by such queries are referred to as on-line analytical processing (OLAP), which refers to applications dominated by stylized queries that typically involve group-by and aggregation operators for analysis purposes (Chaudhuri and Dayal, 1997). Such queries are extremely important to organizations in order to analyze important trends so that better decisions can be made in the future. In addition, most vendors of OLAP engines have focused on Internet enabling their offerings. The true promise of the Internet is in making OLAP a mainstream technology, that is, moving OLAP from the domain of analysts to that of consumers. E-commerce has emerged as one of the largest applications of the Internet in decision support. Issues related to OLAP will be revisited after basic features of data warehousing are examined.

As noted in Gupta et al. (1996), the term data warehousing is used for database applications with one or more of the following characteristics: 1. data are integrated from several, possibly heterogeneous sources into a large data store; 2. a large data store functions with access to detailed data for operational and/or decision support applications; and 3. a data warehouse summarizes data along several dimensions and stores the summarized data for aggregate query processing by OLAP and decision support applications. The detailed data may or may not be stored in the warehouse.

In the virtual view model, the integrated database consists purely of the virtual view definitions, a querying interface, and a querying engine. No data are stored in the integrated database. Users submit queries over the virtual views, and the query engine translates them into queries over the remote data sources. The query engine of the integrated database receives the results sent back from the data sources, and combines the results to an answer. This approach resembles distributed databases.

In the materialized view model, the data from remote data sources are brought into the integrated database. The integrated views are computed using data sets, materialized, and stored in the integrated database. User queries are answered by the query engine by looking up data in the materialized views. The latter model is known as a data warehouse.

Note that the term virtual data warehouse is occasionally used in literature. In one sense, in a virtual data warehouse, users are given direct access

Table 3.4 Databases vs. Data Warehouses

	Conventional Database	Data Warehouse
Data	Raw data	Summarized, consolidated
Transaction/queries	Mainly small transactions	Queries are long and complex
Size of data	Megabytes to gigabytes	Gigabytes to terabytes
Temporal aspect	Usually current snapshot (not temporal)	Historical, temporal data
Updates or read-only	Mostly updates	Mostly reads
For whom	End users to retrieve data	Decision makers to analyze data

to source databases. Data are not moved from source databases because there is no target database serving as the data warehouse. The good thing about this concept is that, without an implemented data warehouse, it provides a single, unified front end to multiple hosts, thus hiding the complexity of host systems. However, queries may disrupt optional systems (there are no historical data available). A somewhat different perspective of the virtual data warehouse can be found in Han and Kamber (2000) that refers to a set of views over operational databases; only some of the possible summary views may be materialized. A virtual warehouse is relatively easy to build but requires excess capacity on operational database servers.

Regardless of the meanings actually used by different people, a data warehouse can be viewed as a specialized database. In addition, in many applications, a data warehouse is constructed and managed using relational techniques. However, there are also important differences between data warehouses and specialized databases. Table 3.4 (revised from Wiener, 1997) summarizes some important differences.

Data warehousing has many advantages. First, there is the high query performance; data warehousing also enhances accessibility because data are accessible anytime, even if sources are not available. The data warehouse provides not only logically integrated data obtained from various sources, but also extra information, such as summary data and historical information. In addition, local processing at sources is not affected (Wiener, 1997).

However, the other side of the data warehousing approach should also be understood. Although storage is cheap, many other things involved are not. In particular, maintaining or updating a warehouse is not cheap because propagating updates from source data to the aggregates in the warehouse is a time-consuming process that usually must be done off-line. Many issues should be studied, including how to detect changes and how to develop algorithms for warehouse maintenance that are able to balance update cost against query response time. Another important issue is that of resuming an interrupted data warehouse load (Wiener, 1998). This issue resembles recovery in conventional databases, but with a different emphasis. The goal here is to resume load, after failure, from where it left off (that is, complete what has not been done, similar to redo). Resumption is a challenging issue because efficiency is an important concern, and as little work as possible should be repeated. It is also necessary to guarantee correctness, which refers to achieving the same warehouse state as if no failure had occurred. The basic idea of resumption is to use warehouse contents to avoid repeating work. Incremental algorithms are needed. In addition, incremental resumption can incorporate the use of logs, in which carefully selected items are used to create logs for reduced reprocessing.

3.4 Architecture and design of data warehouses

3.4.1 Operational systems and warehouse data

Chapter 2 presented major components of data warehousing. It is now necessary to revisit the architecture of data warehousing from a more technical perspective. One should first pay attention to the relationship between the parallel universes of operational systems and the warehouse data. Operational data stores (ODSs), also called operational systems, feature standard, repetitive transactions that use a small amount of data as in traditional database systems, while warehouse systems feature ad hoc queries and reports that access a much larger amount of data. High availability and real-time updates are critical to the success of the operational system, but not to the data warehouse. Operational systems are typically developed first by working with users to determine and define business processes. Then application code is written and databases are designed. These systems are defined by how the business operates. The primary goal of an organization's operational systems is efficient performance. The design of both applications and databases is driven by online transaction processing (OLTP) performance. These systems need the capacity to handle thousands of transactions and return information in acceptable user-response timeframes, often measured in fractions of a second. By contrast, data warehouses start with predefined data and vague or unknown usage requirements. Operational systems have different structures, needs, requirements, and objectives from data warehouses. These variations in data, access, and usage prevent organizations from simply using existing operational systems as data warehouse resources. For example, operational data is short-lived and changes rapidly, while warehouse data have a long life and are static. There is a need for transformation of operational data to warehouse data. The architecture of a data warehouse differs considerably from the design and structure of an operational system. Designing a data warehouse can be more difficult than building an operational system because the requirements of the warehouse are often ambiguous. In designing a data warehouse, an organization must understand current information needs as well as likely future needs. This requires a flexible design that ensures the data warehouse can adapt to a changing environment.

Both operational and warehouse systems play an important role in an organization's success and thus need to coexist as valuable assets. This can

Data Marts

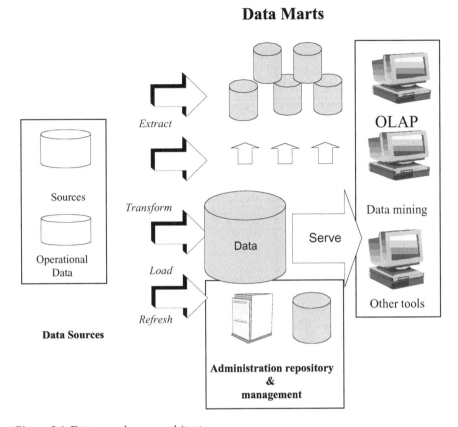

Figure 3.1 Data warehouse architecture.

be done by carefully designing and constructing the data warehouse so that it takes advantage of the power of operational data while also meeting the unique needs of the organization's knowledge workers.

3.4.2   Data warehouse components

The data warehouse is an integrated environment, containing integrated data, detailed and summarized data, historical data, and metadata. The business perspective summarized in Section 2.4 can be described in a form widely accepted by the computer science community (Chaudhuri and Dayal, 1997). A typical data warehousing architecture consists of the following components (as depicted in Figure 3.1):

- A relational database for data storage — as the data warehouse proper, it stores the corporate data. Here data volumes are very high as multiterabyte data warehouses are beginning to appear more frequently;

- Data marts are departmental subsets of the warehouse data focusing on selected subjects. The data mart is where departmental data is stored, and often various external data items are added. The data volumes are usually 15 to 30% of warehouse sizes, and the envelope is being pushed toward the terabyte limit. These databases are also usually based on star-schemas or are in a normalized form. They mostly deal with the data space, but at times some multidimensional analysis is performed;
- Back end (system components providing functionality such as extract, transform, load, and refresh data) and front end (such as OLAP and data mining) tools and utilities;
- Metadata — the system catalogs associated with a warehouse are very large, and are often stored and managed in a separate database called a metadata repository; and
- Other components, depending on design methods and specific needs of the organization.

Data warehousing architecture supported by commercial products may not adopt the exact general architecture described above. For example, consider the Oracle Warehouse, in which differences exist in the component types and perspectives. The Oracle Warehouse emphasizes the role of hardware, database server, and other off-the-shelf tools available in the market that can be integrated to form the infrastructure. In addition to a data model which describes the warehouse data contents (to be discussed in Chapter 5), there are a warehouse server (a powerful machine supporting process and task parallelism at the CPU, disk input/output (I/O), and memory level capabilities of these servers), a data warehouse application server (containing custom codes responsible for periodic refresh, aggregation, and summarization), a middleware layer (containing infrastructure support software such as scheduling, recovery, and monitoring utilities), metadata repositories, backend data scrubbing and transport utilities, data replication engines (providing database-level support for replicating changes of the source data to a remote database), and front-end client analysis tools (Yazdani and Wong, 1997).

3.4.3   Data warehouse design

There are four different views regarding the design of a data warehouse. The top-down view allows the selection of relevant information necessary for the data warehouse. The data source view exposes the information being captured, stored, and managed by operational systems; it includes fact tables and dimension tables. The business query view is the perspective of data in the data warehouse from the viewpoint of the end user. The process of data warehouse design can take several approaches. The top-down approach starts with the overall design and planning, and is useful in cases when business problems are clear and well understood. The bottom-up approach starts with experiments and prototypes, and is useful in the early stages of business modeling and technology development. In addition, a combination of these approaches can be used (Han and Kamber, 2000).

In general, the data warehouse design process consists of the following steps (Inmon, 1996; Kimball et al., 1998):

1. Choose a business process to model, such as sales, shipments, etc.
2. Choose the grain of the business process. The grain is the granularity (namely, fundamental, atomic) level of the data used in the fact table. The data stored there are the primary data on which OLAP operations can be performed.
3. Choose the dimensions that will apply to records in the fact table(s). For example, time is a typical dimension. Dimensions are important because various OLAP operations can be performed on them.
4. Choose the measures that will populate each fact table record. Measures are numeric additive quantities such as sales amount or profit.

The architecture depicted in Figure 3.1 is basically two-tier, namely, warehouse and its front ends. A variation of data warehouse architecture consists of three tiers: the bottom tier is a warehouse database server, typically a relational database system; the middle tier is an OLAP server; and the top tier is a client, containing query and reporting tools.

3.5   Data Marts

3.5.1   Why data marts

As an important component of data warehousing architecture, a data mart is a departmental subset on selected subjects. Therefore, a data mart is an application-focused data warehouse, built rapidly to support a single line-of-business application. Data marts still have all of the other characteristics of data warehouses, which are subject-oriented data that are nonvolatile, time-variant, and integrated. However, rather than representing a picture of the enterprise data, a data mart contains a subset of data specifically of interest to one department or division of an enterprise. Recall that Kimball et al. (1998) insisted that a data warehouse is nothing else but a union of data marts. Although one may not always agree that every data item in the warehouse should be in at least one of the data marts, the importance of data marts should not be overlooked.

The data that reside in the data warehouse are at a very granular level and the data in the data mart are at a refined level. The different data marts contain different combinations and selections of the same detailed data found at the data warehouse. In some cases data warehouse detailed data are added differently across the different data marts, while in other cases a specific data mart may structure detailed data differently from other data marts. In each case the data warehouse provides the granular foundation for all of the data found in all of the data marts. Because of the singular data warehouse foundation that all data marts have, all of them have a common heritage and are able to be reconciled at the most basic level (Singh, 1999).

There are several factors that lead to the popularity of the data mart. As data warehouses quickly grow large, the motivation for data marts increases. More and more departmental decision-support processing is carried out inside the data warehouse; as a result, resource consumption becomes a real problem. Data become harder to customize. As long as the data in the data warehouse are small, users can afford to customize and summarize data every time a decision support analysis is done. But with an increase in magnitude, the user does not have the time or resources to do this each time. The cost of processing in the data warehouse increases as volume of data increases. Software available for the access and analysis of large amounts of data is not nearly as elegant as software that processes smaller amounts of data. As a result of these factors, data marts have become a natural extension of the data warehouse.

There are organizational, technological, and economic reasons why the data mart is so beguiling and is a natural outcome of the data warehouse. Data marts are attractive for various reasons (Kimball et al., 1998; Singh, 1999):

- Customization: when a department has its own data mart, it can customize data as they flow into the data mart from the data warehouse. The department can sort, select, and structure its own departmental data without consideration of any other department.
- Relevance: the amount of historical data needed is a function of the department, not the corporation. In most cases, the department can select a much smaller amount of historical data than that found in the data warehouse.
- Self-determination: the department can do whatever decision-support processing it wants whenever it wants, with no impact for resource utilization on other departments. The department can also select software for the data mart tailored to fit its needs.
- Efficiency: the unit cost of processing and storage on the size of the machine appropriate to the data mart is significantly less than the unit cost of processing and storage for the facilities that house the data warehouse.

3.5.2   Types of data marts

There are several kinds of data mart strategies; two important types (Kimball et al., 1998; Singh, 1999) are worth noting. Dependent data marts evolved from architectural principles and are smaller subsets of the enterprise warehouse specifically designed to respond to departmental or line-of-business issues. In this strategy, data are loaded from operational systems into the enterprise warehouse and then subdivided into the smaller data marts. These marts rely on the central warehouse for their data and metadata rather than obtaining them from the operational systems. While these data marts can solve some performance issues and even some political issues, financial problems and strategic issues are, if anything, exacerbated because the enterprise warehouse must be built before the data marts can be implemented. Independent data marts have been viewed as a viable alternative to the top-down approach of an enterprise warehouse. An organization can start small and move quickly, often realizing limited results in 3 to 6 months. Proponents of this approach argue that, after starting with a small data mart, other marts can proliferate in departments or lines of business that have a need. In addition, by satisfying various divisional needs, an organization can build its way to a full data warehouse by starting at the bottom and working up.

3.5.3 Multiple data marts

In today's environment, data marts have evolved to meet the unique needs of business lines more cost effectively. These marts can be built quickly and contain only data relevant to a specific business unit. For example, data marts may be divided based on departmental lines or by product type. These marts challenge the systems group in terms of managing ongoing changes along with ensuring data consistency across different marts. The architecture must provide for simplifying and reducing costs in this multiple data mart management process. A data mart can overlap another data mart. Kimball et al. (1998) advised considering 10 to 30 data marts for a large organization. For an organization, careful studies and plans are needed for developing multiple data marts. A matrix method for identifying all possible data marts and dimensions has been introduced.

Subsets of the data are usually extracted by subject area and stored in data marts specifically designed to provided departmental users with fast access to large amounts of topical data. These data marts often provide several levels of aggregation and employ physical dimensional design techniques for OLAP.

If a corporation begins its information architecture with an enterprise data warehouse, it will quickly realize the need for subsets of the data levels of summary. A recommended approach is through top-down development, which can spawn marts and select subject area and summary from the enterprise data warehouse. The other approach is one in which a data mart is built first to meet specific user group requirements, but according to a data plan and with roll-up as a goal. The need will arise for the marts to participate in a hierarchy in which detailed information from several subject-area data marts is summarized and consolidated into an enterprise data warehouse.

3.5.4 Networked data marts

Increasingly, multiple data mart systems cooperate in a larger network creating a virtual data warehouse. This results in networked data marts. A large enterprise may have many subject-area marts as well as marts in different divisions and geographic locations. Users or workgroups may have local data marts to address local needs. Advanced applications, such as the Web, extend data mart networks across enterprise boundaries.

In the network data mart world, users must be able to look at and work with multiple warehouses from a single client workstation requiring location transparency across the network. Similarly, data mart administrators must be able to manage and administer a network of data marts from a single location.

Implementation and management of data mart networks requires tools to define, extract, move, and update batches of information as self-consistent units on demand, as well as new software to support subset, catalog, schedule, and publish/subscribe functions in a distributed environment.

3.6   Metadata

Metadata are all of the information in the data warehouse environment that are not the actual data. From a practical perspective, metadata are machine-understandable information about a network resource: what it is, what it is about, and where it is (Davydov, 1999). In addition, in order to deal with heterogeneity of data, the concept of mediated metadata was introduced as a means of distinguishing the description of network resource schemes from the description of export schemes — the portions of such schemes directly relevant for translation and mediation. The main idea is to introduce an explicit description of how to match appropriate e-commerce partners and translate among their heterogeneous data formats, query languages, and metadata schemes.

There are currently several major communities working on metadata standards directly tied to the issue of e-business communications, including the ISO Standard Committee, World Wide Web Consortium (W3C), Internet Engineering Task Force, Meta Data Coalition, Object Management Group (OMG), Voluntary Inter-industry Commerce Standards Council, and Electronic Industries Association. Examples of metadata syntax and formats include XML, XMI (the XML metadata interchange format), and SOIF. Examples of metadata technological frameworks include OIM (which is a set of modeling specifications based on UML that facilitate sharing and reusing metadata) and MDIS (which is a set of definitions that represents the minimum common denominator of metadata elements and integration components).

The coming of data warehouses and data mining has significantly extended the role of metadata in the classical DBMS environment. Metadata describe the data in the database; they include information on access methods, index strategies, and security and integrity constraints, as well as policies and procedures (which are optional).

Metadata have become a major issue with some of the recent developments in data management such as digital libraries. Metadata in distributed and heterogeneous databases guide the schema transformation and integration process in handling heterogeneity and are used to transform legacy database systems to new systems. Metadata can be used for multimedia data management (metadata could be multimedia data such as video and audio). Metadata for the Web include information about various data sources, locations and resources on the Web, usage patterns, policies, and procedures.

Metadata for warehousing include metadata for integrating heterogeneous data sources. They can guide the transformation process from layer to layer in building the warehouse and can be used to administer and maintain the warehouse. Metadata are used in extracting answers to various queries posed.

Regardless of their actual form, metadata can be viewed as a kind of data reduction.

Figure 3.2 illustrates metadata management in a data warehouse. The metadata repository stores and maintains information about the structure and content of the data warehouse components. In addition, all dependencies between the different layers of the data warehouse environment, including operational layer, data warehouse layer, and business layer, are represented in this repository. Figure 3.2 also shows the role of three different types of metadata (Miller et al., 1999; Singh, 1999):

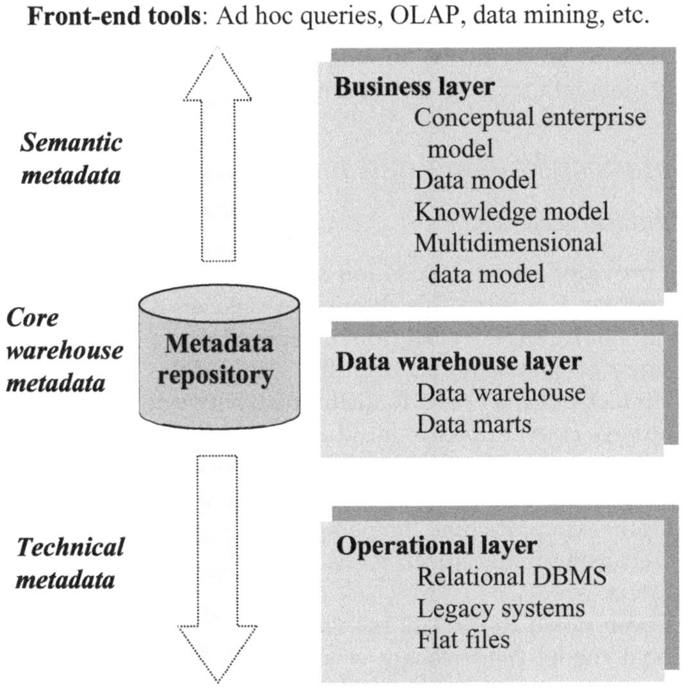

Front-end tools: Ad hoc queries, OLAP, data mining, etc.

Figure 3.2 Metadata management in a data warehouse.

- Semantic (or business) metadata intend to provide a business-oriented description of the data warehouse content. A repository addressing semantic metadata should cover the types of metadata of the conceptual enterprise model, multidimensional data model, etc., and their interdependencies.
- Technical metadata cover information about the architecture and schema with respect to the operational systems, data warehouse, and OLAP databases, as well as the dependencies and mappings among the operational sources, data warehouse, and the OLAP databases on the physical and implementation levels.
- Core warehouse metadata are subject-oriented and based on abstractions of the real world. They define the way in which the transformed data are to be interpreted, as well as any additional views created.

When data mining is performed in a data warehouse, metadata for specific types of data mining require specific techniques. For example, for multimedia data, metadata may be extracted from the multimedia databases and then used to mine the data. Metadata related to security and privacy can be regarded as part of the metadata, and can thus be used to guide the process of data mining so that privacy issues are not compromised through mining. Another type of metadata is concerned with Web mining. Since Web information is semistructured, direct mining may be challenging. It may be necessary to extract metadata from the data, then either mine them or use this metadata to guide in the mining process. XML could play a role in describing metadata for Web documents.

3.7   Data warehousing and materialized views

3.7.1   Materialized views

Chapter 2 provided a brief discussion on data warehouses based on a business perspective. However, this discussion requires some further technical clarification. For example, recall from Chapter 2 that a data warehouse consists of a copy of data acquired from the source data. What does this copy look like? In fact, one may need to distinguish between a "true" copy (duplicate), a derived copy, approximate duplicate, or something else. Later in Section 3.3.4, several perspectives were presented on what a data warehouse is. For this reason, it is necessary to examine the concept of data warehouse in more depth — in particular, the perspective that a data warehouse can be characterized using materialized views and indexing. These two issues are examined next.

It has been noted that relational views are the most important asset of the relational model (Silberschatz et al., 2001). Recall the following basic concepts in relational databases: a relation (base table) is a stored table; an external view (also called a virtual view or "just a view") is a virtual table (derived relation defined in terms of base relations); and a materialized view a view stored in the database, rather than computed from the base relations in response to queries.

For example, suppose a database schema of d(ABC) with functional dependencies {A → B, B → C}. Also assume that r(AB) and s(BC) are the two relations. If frequent queries exist to retrieve A and C together, then it would be ideal to materialize the view AC or ABC. This way, it is possible to avoid expensive join operations.

Materialized views have been studied in the database community for many years. Data warehousing marks a rejuvenation of materialized views, but with some new requirements. The general idea is to materialize certain expensive computations that are frequently inquired, especially those involving aggregate functions, such as count, sum, average, max, etc., and usually to store such materialized views in a multidimensional database (called a data cube) for decision support, knowledge discovery, and many other applications.

The benefit of using materialized views is significant. Since index structures can be built on materialized views, consequently, database access to the materialized view can be much faster than recomputing the views. A materialized view is just like a cache, which is a copy of the data that can be accessed quickly. Integrity constraint checking and query optimization can also benefit from materialized views.

The traditional relational database design emphasizes normalization. However, one may also argue that data warehouse design cannot be simply reduced to relational database design. In fact, frequently materialized views are the result of performing joint operation, and are no longer in appropriate normal forms (as discussed in database management systems; see discussion in Section 3.2.4). Although normalized data guarantee integrity constraints and avoiding anomalies, in the business community, it is not uncommon for people to feel that normalized designs are hard to comprehend. Denormalized designs tend to be more self-explanatory, even though denormalized tables have longer records. Typical multiattribute search-and-scan performance is better on denormalized data because fewer tables are involved than in normalized designs. Denormalization data provide an intuitive productive environment for users who need to be trained or retrained. On the other hand, denormalization is the greatest cultural hurdle for most incremental data mart design teams because they are used to dealing with OLTP. As a result of denormalization, data are redundant. For example, two relations, along with the joined result, coexist. In particular, consider the previous database schema ABC with functional dependencies {A → B, B → C}. AB and BC are the two relations. Apparently both AB and BC are in third normal form. However, if frequent queries exist to retrieve A, B, and C together, then it would be ideal to materialize the view ABC. That the result is not in third normal form can be easily verified.

Another note should be made here on the impact of entity-relationship (ER) modeling to data warehouse design. This will be further discussed in Chapter 5. Briefly, there are two schools of thought in enterprise data warehouse design. The ER normalized school (Inmon, 1996) still starts from fundamentally normalized tables and then spawns off subset data marts that are denormalized. In contrast, Ralph Kimball and his school (Kimball et al., 1998) endorse a consistent, denormalized star schema environment across all enterprise data warehouses.

3.7.2   Indexing techniques

Due to the close relationship between materialized views and indexing, it is worthwhile to take a look at the issue of indexing. Traditional indexing techniques (Silberschatz et al., 2001) can be used, but there are also additional issues unique to a data warehousing environment.

The most read environment of OLAP systems makes the CPU overhead of maintaining indices negligible; the requirement of interactive response times for queries over very large datasets makes the availability of suitable indices very important. With a bitmap index, the idea is to record values for sparse columns as a sequence of bits, one for each possible value. For example, the biological gender of a customer (male or female) can be represented using a bitmap index. This method supports efficient index operations such as union and intersection; it is more efficient than hash index and tree index. The join index method is used to speed up specific join queries. A join index maintains the relationships between a foreign key and its matching primary keys. The specialized nature of star schemas makes join indices especially attractive for decision support.

Indexing is important to materialized views for two reasons: indices for a materialized view reduce the cost of computation to execute an operation (analogous to the use of an index on the key of a relation to decrease the time needed to locate a specified tuple) and indexing reduces the cost of maintenance of the materialized views. Maintenance of materialized views can be a very time consuming process. (Advances achieved in view maintenance are discussed in Chapter 7.)

The following example illustrates the idea of join index. Consider the two relations "sale" and "product" as shown in Table 3.5 (a) and (b).

If join is performed on sale.prod-id = prod-id, and the result is precomputed, the join index can be obtained, as shown in Table 3.6. Note that the result shown in Table 3.7 has the same effect of Table 3.6, which represents a materialized view.

3.7.3   Indexing using metadata

Another interesting aspect of indexing in the warehousing environment is its relationship with metadata. Recently, indexing using metadata has received much attention. Recall that metadata is the information that records the characterization and relationship of the source data. It helps to provide succinct information about the source data that may not be recorded in the source itself due to its nature or an oversight. As noted in Desai (1995), the

Table 3.5 (a) The Sale Table

Rid	Prod-id	Store-id	Date	Amount
R1	P1	C1	1	12
R2	P2	C1	1	11
R3	P1	C3	1	50
R4	P2	C2	1	8
R5	P1	C1	2	44
R6	P1	C2	2	4

Table 3.5 (b) The Product Table

ID	Name	Price
P1	Bolt	10
P2	Nut	5

Table 3.6 Example of Join Index

Product.id	Sale.prod-id
P1	R1, R3, R5, R6
P2	R2, R4

Table 3.7 A Materialized View

Rid	Prod-id	Name	Price	Store-id	Date	Amount
R1	P1	Bolt	10	C1	1	12
R2	P2	Nut	5	C1	1	11
R3	P1	Bolt	10	C3	1	50
R4	P2	Nut	5	C2	1	8
R5	P1	Bolt	10	C1	2	44
R6	P1	Bolt	10	C2	2	4

problem with current automatically generated index databases is their inadequate semantic information. It is evident that professional cataloging of the ever-growing information resources would be prohibitively expensive. This is particularly true in a data warehousing environment. Thus, the design of adequate metadata to describe and establish the semantic contents of resources and to establish their semantic dependencies on other resources is of utmost importance. Metadata can provide an instrument to describe the semantic content of a resource. In many cases, the resources themselves may not be able to provide the semantic dependencies or it could be computationally too expensive to do so. Therefore, when the resource itself is not as easily accessible as the index, using metadata as an index could become extremely valuable in data warehousing. Metadata could also be used to express semantic dependencies that are inherent in a collection of objects. This means that the structure of the objects could be expressed using metadata as their surrogates and the actual sources could be separated from their metadata. This simplifies the storage of the resources and allows for the recognition of redundancies. In addition, using metadata and extracting salient features of a resource can also support retrieval by content. Automatic processing of the contents of a source by extractors has been done on an ad-hoc basis but has been found to be unreliable.

Using metadata as indexing could also further advance the current status of query processing. In fact, an initial query processing could be done on the metadata and thus avoid access to most of the resources and the possibility of their computationally bound interpretation. This becomes more advantageous when there are costs (time, money, network bandwidth, and overloading) involved in accessing resources. The cost of accessing metadata would be much smaller than the cost of accessing the resource.

3.8 Data warehouse performance

3.8.1 Measuring data warehouse performance

The massive amount of data (in terabytes) in data warehouses makes high performance a crucial factor for the success of data warehousing techniques. Successful implementation of a data warehouse on the World Wide Web requires a high-performance, scalable combination of hardware that can integrate easily with existing systems. Data warehousing involves extracting data from various sources and transforming, integrating, and summarizing them into relational management systems residing over a span of World Wide Web servers. Typically part of the client/server architecture, such data warehouse servers may be connected to application servers, which improve the performance of query and analysis tools running on desktop systems. Possibly the most important factor to consider in arriving at a high-performance data warehouse environment is that of end-user expectations. These expectations represent unambiguous objectives that provide direction for performance tuning and capacity planning activities within the data warehouse environment (Inmon et al., 1999).

The basis for measuring query performance in the data warehouse environment is the time from submission of a query to the moment the results are returned. A data warehouse query has two important measurements: 1. the length of time from the moment of submission to the time when the first row/record is returned to the end user, and 2. the length of time from submission until the row is returned. Therefore, data warehouse performance goes beyond query optimization in traditional DBMSs.

The data warehouse environment attracts volumes of data never before experienced in the information processing milieu. In previous environments, volumes of data were measured in the thousands (kilobytes) and millions (megabytes) of bytes of data. In the data warehouse environment volumes of data are measured in gigabytes and terabytes of data. Thus, there are many orders of magnitude of difference between these measurements. Some aspects of improving performance have already been discussed earlier, such as indexing and denormalization. There are also other important aspects, such as user hardware architecture that is parallelized.

Optimizing data structures in the data warehouse environment is an important, but difficult, issue because many different sets of requirements must be satisfied at once. Great care must be taken in the physical organization of the data in the warehouse.

3.8.2   Performance and warehousing activities

Performance issues are closely tied to data warehousing activities at various stages (Inmon et al., 1999).

> Base level architecture hardware and software. Issues that need to be considered include whether the hardware platform supports the volume of data, the types of users, types of workload, and the number of requests that will be run against it, whether the software platform organizes and manages the data in an efficient and optimal manner, etc.
>
> Design and implementation of the data warehouse platform based on usage and data. There are various issues related to different aspects, such as:
>
> - Database design. For example, one needs to know whether the different elements of data have been profiled so that the occurrences of data that will exist for each entity are roughly approximated.
> - Usage and use profiles. For example, one needs to know whether the database design takes into account the predicted and/or known usage of the data.
>
> Creation of the programs and configuration of tools that will make use of the data. For example, one needs to know whether the queries or other programs that will access the data warehouse have been profiled, information about the programmers, etc.
>
> Post warehousing development. After programs are written and the data warehouse is being populated, the ongoing system utilization needs to be monitored and system guidelines service management contracts need to be established.

If an organization follows these guidelines and carefully considers performance at each appropriate point in time, the organization will arrive at a point where performance is truly optimal.

A final remark must be made here about data mart performance. Although performance related to a data mart shares many considerations with a data warehouse as a whole, limiting a data mart's scope ensures that the resulting data mart will fit within the scalability limits of an OLAP database server. It also permits the analysis at hand to be conducted without distractions presented by extraneous data. Using an OLAP database server, in turn, allows the use of OLAP indexing and presummarization techniques to deliver rapid response times and intuitive access.

3.9   Data warehousing and OLAP

3.9.1   Basics of OLAP

We have repeatedly mentioned the close relationship between data warehousing and OLAP. We examine this issue below in more detail.

OLAP, as a multidimensional analysis, is a method of viewing aggregate data called measurements (e.g., sales, expenses, etc.) along a set of dimensions such as product, brand, stored, month, city and state, etc. An OLAP typically consists of the following conceptual tokens: 1) *Dimension*. Each dimension is described by a set of attributes. A related concept is domain hierarchy; for example, country, state, and city form a domain hierarchy. 2) *Measure*. Each of the numeric measures depends on a set of dimensions, which provide the context for the measure. The dimensions together are assumed to determine the measure uniquely. Therefore, the multidimensional data view a measure as a value in the multidimensional space of dimensions.

There are two basic approaches to implementing an OLAP. ROLAP (Relational OLAP) is an OLAP system that stores all information (including fact tables) as relations. Note that the aggregations are stored with the relational system itself. MOLAP (Multidimensional OLAP) is an OLAP system that uses arrays to store multidimensional datasets.

In general, ROLAP is more flexible than MOLAP, but has more computational overhead for managing many tables. One advantage of using ROLAP is that sparse data sets may be stored more compactly in tables than in arrays. Since ROLAP is an extension of the matured relational database technique, SQL can be used. In addition, ROLAP is very scalable. However, one major advantage is its slow response time. In contrast, MOLAP abandons the relational structure and uses a sparse matrix file representation to store the aggregations efficiently. This gains efficiency, but lacks flexibility, restricts the number of dimensions (7 to 10), and is limited to small databases. (Note on dimension: a relation can be viewed as a 2D table or *n*-D table [each attribute represents a dimension].) One advantage of using MOLAP is that dense arrays are stored more compactly in the array format than in tables. In addition, array lookups are simple arithmetic operations which result in an instant response. A disadvantage of MOLAP is long load times. Besides, MOLAP design becomes very massive very quickly with the addition of multiple dimensions. To get the best of both worlds, one can combine MOLAP with ROLAP. Other approaches also exist.

3.9.2   Relationship between data warehousing and OLAP

Having described the basic architecture of data warehouses, the relationship between data warehousing and OLAP may be further edescribed as follows. Decision-support functions in a data warehouse involve hundreds of complex aggregate queries over large volumes of data. To meet the performance demands so that fast answers can be provided, virtually all OLAP products resort to some degree of these aggregates. According to a popular opinion from the OLAP Council, a data warehouse is usually based on relational technology, while OLAP uses a multidimensional view of aggregate data to provide quick access to strategic information for further analysis. A data warehouse stores tactical information that answers "who" and "what" questions about past events. OLAP systems go beyond those questions; they are able to answer "what if" and "why" questions. A typical OLAP calculation is more complex than simply summarizing data.

Most data warehouses use star schemas to represent the multidimensional data model. In a star schema, there is a single fact table (which is at the center of a star schema and contains most of the data stored in the data warehouse) and a set of dimension tables which can be used in combination with the fact table (There is a single dimension table for each dimension.). An example of a star schema is shown in Figure 3.3.

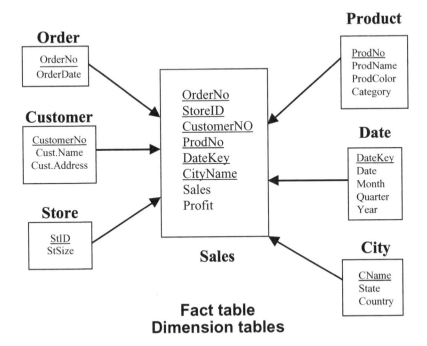

Figure 3.3 A star schema.

The star schema model of data warehouses makes join indexing attractive for cross table search because the connection between a fact table and its corresponding dimension tables is the foreign key of the fact table and the primary key of the dimension table. Join indexing maintains relationships between attribute values of a dimension and the corresponding rows in the fact table. Join indices may span multiple dimensions to form composite join indices.

A very useful concept for OLAP is data cube, which presents a materialized view involving multidimensional data and will be discussed in Chapter 5.

3.10 Summary

This chapter has first reviewed basics of DBMSs. Discussion has focused on relational databases, but more advanced DBMS and modeling issues have also been briefly addressed. Due to space limitations, only a very brief review on query processing and transaction processing has been provided. A good understanding of these materials is needed for understanding new algorithms developed for data warehousing (such as those described in Chapter 7).

As for the data warehousing proper, issues examined included metadata, data marts (DMs), and materialized views (MVs). It is interesting to note relationships between these concepts and the data warehouse itself: while metadata contain condensed information of the data stored in the data warehouse (DW), each data mart contains a subset of the warehouse data, and each materialized view represents a restructuring of the original data. Another interesting aspect is that, while the business perspective tends to exploit the formula of

$$DW = \cup_i DM_i$$

where DM_is are all data marts corresponding to DW, the database research community has put emphasis on

$$DW = \cup_j MV_j$$

where MV_is are all materialized views.

However, as noted by Elmasri and Nevathe (2000), views may provide only a subset of the functions and capabilities of data warehouses. Views and data warehouses are similar in that they both have read-only extracts from databases and subject-orientation. However, data warehouses are different from views in a number of ways, in that unlike views, data warehouses exist as persistent storage instead of being materialized on demand; views are usually relational, but data warehouses are usually multidimensional; data warehouses can be indexed to optimize performance, while views cannot be indexed independent from of the underlying databases; data warehouses characteristically provide specific support of functionality, but views cannot; and data warehouses provide large amounts of integrated and often temporal data, while views are usually an extract of a database. Nevertheless, in our opinion, materialized views offer a unique opportunity for extending traditional database methodologies to dealing with new data warehousing challenges, and this is an important aspect to be emphasized in this book.

References

Chaudhuri, S. and U. Dayal, An overview of data warehousing and OLAP technology, *SIGMOD Rec.*, 26(1), 65–74, 1997.

Davydov, M. M., E-business grail (metadata management), *Intell. Enterprises*, 2(1), 33–39, 1999.

Elmasri, R. and S. B. Navathe, *Fundamentals of Database Systems*, Addison-Wesley, Reading, MA, 2000.

Gupta, A. and I. S. Mumick, What is the data warehousing problem? (Are materialized views the answer?), *Proc. VLDB*, 1996, 602.

Han, J. and M. Kamber, *Data Mining: Concepts and Techniques*, Morgan Kaufmann, San Francisco, 2000.

Kimball, R., L. Reeves, M. Ross, and W. Thornthwaite, *The Data Warehouse Lifecycle Toolkit*, John Wiley & Sons, New York, 1998.

Inmon, W. H., *Building the Data Warehouse*, John Wiley & Sons, New York, 1996.

Inmon, W. H., K. Rudin, C. Buss, W. H. Anmon, and R. Sousa, *Data Warehouse Performance*, John Wiley & Sons, New York, 1999.

Müller, R., T. Stöhr, and E. Rahm, An integrative and uniform model for metadata management in data warehousing environments, *Proc. DMDW 1999 (Online)*, 12.1–12.16, 1999.

Rundersteiner, E. A., A. Koeller, and X. Zhang, Maintaining data warehouses over changing information sources, *Commun. ACM*, 43(6), 57–62, 2000.

Silberschatz, A., H. Korth, and S. Sudarshan, *Database System Concepts* (3rd ed.), McGraw-Hill, New York, 2001.

Singh, H., *Interactive Data Warehousing*, Prentice Hall, Upper Saddle River, NJ, 1999.

Wiener, J., Data warehousing: what is it? and related Stanford DB research, available at http://www-db.stanford.edu/warehousing/warehouse.html, 1997.

Wiener, J., Research talk: resuming an interrupted data warehouse load, available at http://www-db.stanford.edu/warehousing/warehouse.html, 1998.

Yazdani, S. and S. S. Wong, *Data Warehousing with Oracle*, Prentice Hall PTR, Upper Saddle River, NJ, 1997.

Part II

chapter four

Data preparation and preprocessing

4.1 Overview

This chapter and the next two chapters examine the major stages in the overall data warehousing lifecycle. This chapter addresses various issues for data preprocessing such as data cleansing, data integration, data reduction, and related issues. Also included are two case studies that illustrate how to prepare data for later analysis.

But first, we should emphasize the importance of requirements analysis based on a well-defined goal. It has been noted that data warehousing development projects often fail because of faulty requirements analysis. Therefore, a sound requirements methodology should be applied before the actual data preparation activities start (Riggle, 2001).

4.2 Schema and data integration

An important issue in the data preparation stage of data warehousing is how to handle uncertainty in integrated use of data. The primary consideration here is dealing with data from miscellaneous sources. Therefore, it is necessary to start from fundamental issues such as schema integration and data cleansing, followed by issues more related to database semantics.

Issues affecting warehouse creation, as identified by Srivastava and Chen (1999), include warehouse architecture selection (database conversion and synchronization), enterprise schema creation (enterprise data model, schema integration, and constraints), and warehouse population (semantic issues, scalability, and incremental updates). The following are some aspects related to uncertainty in effecting warehouse creation:

Constraints. In addition to structural and semantic mismatches of schema entities, there is the additional problem of constraint mismatches, which are often not evident from the definitions of entity types. For example, one database may have a constraint such as EMP.age ← 70 while another may have the constraint on age as EMP.age ← 62. In integrating such databases, in general, there seems to be no right approach to resolving such constraint incompatibilities.

Scalability. Since warehouses store information about the database as it progresses over time, they tend to grow much more rapidly than on-line databases. It is quite common to start with an initial warehouse of size 10 to 100 gigabytes, and subsequently have a periodic (weekly or monthly) update rate of 1 to 10 gigabytes. The data integration tasks typically range in complexity from $O(n \ log \ n)$ to $O(n^2)$ for n data items. Given tens to hundreds of GBs of data, this can be very time consuming, and hence improved algorithms for integrated use of data are needed.

Many steps discussed in data preparation of data mining (Pyle, 1999) are also valid for preparation of warehouse data. The following are major stages in organizations for conducting integrated data warehousing and intelligent data analysis:

1. Define the problem, including accurately describing the problem, determining the appropriateness of using data mining, deciding the form of input and output, deciding cost effectiveness, etc.
2. Collect/select data, including deciding what data to collect and how to collect them.
3. Prepare data, such as transforming data to a certain format, data cleansing, or integrating data from different sources (usually there is a need to deal with the uncertainty of data).
4. Data preprocessing is mainly concerned with enhancement of data quality.
5. Select an appropriate data analysis or mining method, which consists of two substeps:
   a. Selecting a model or an algorithm: for example, to decide whether to use a parametric or nonparametric algorithm, whether to use regression, use a particular algorithm in an artificial neural network, or use a particular clustering algorithm (such as k-means algorithm); and
   b. Selecting model/algorithm training parameters, such as the number of nodes at each level when an artificial neural network is used.
6. Train/test the data or apply the algorithm; use an evaluation set of data in the trained architecture.
7. Finally, integrate and evaluate the generated model.

Data integration requires resolving modeling, semantic, and query capability differences, as well as inconsistencies between data sources. As the result of this process, an integrated view, or a set of views, is defined over the different data sources. The view describes how the data are going to be combined together (Gupta and Mumick, 1998). As discussed in Chapter 3, when these views are stored, they become materialized views.

The result of data integration can be captured by a special form of materialized views called data cubes. Data cubes are a convenient way of thinking about multiple aggregate views derived from a fact table using different subsets of group-by attributes. Data cubes are popular in OLAP because they provide an easy and intuitive way for analysts to navigate various levels of summary information in the database. A summary table is a materialized aggregate view. In a data cube, attributes are categorized into dimension attributes on which grouping may be performed, and measures which are the results of aggregate functions. A data cube with k dimension attributes is a shorthand for 2^k aggregate queries. In addition, the aggregate queries represented by a data cube can be organized into a lattice. Data cubes will be discussed in Chapter 6.

4.3   Data pumping

Data pumping is both an application of materialized views and a way of building a data warehouse over the Web. A data pumping (also called push or broadcast) service pumps data into several users' machines distributed over a network, giving each user the ability to view only that portion of data of interest to the user. The user also has the ability to see data in the preferred format and layout. Data pumping services are becoming very common over the Internet. Materialized views provide a framework within which one can study performance problems faced by data pumping services. User profiles can be treated as materialized views. Each user of a data pumping service defines one or more views over the data to be pumped to the users. The user then requires the views to be materialized locally to the user, who happens to be remote from the data server containing the data to be pumped. One can thus envision numerous materialized views defined remotely from a data source. Each materialized view could be in a separate remote machine. In addition, as the data in the source change, it is necessary to maintain the materialized view in the user machines. A good solution to the problem of maintaining a large number of materialized views over a common set of data sources would result in a scalable data pumping service.

In order to maintain thousands of materialized views in a distributed framework, a naïve solution could be to broadcast all changes in the data sets to each client that stores materialized views and to let each client maintain its views locally. This solution requires that the views at each client be self-maintainable, namely, using local data only, without accessing the base data. and that each client be willing to receive and process changes to all data sets, even those irrelevant to the interests of the node. Although the self-mainte-nance assumption is reasonable, the second requirement presents significant overhead upon client resources, especially when the clients are PCs and the data sets are huge. A solution is needed wherein each client receives only changes relevant to the views at the client. One attempt would be to cluster views into equivalent classes in which the views in each class have the same set of relevant updates. Since all the views may not be strictly equivalent with respect to relevant updates, it may be necessary to study in which cases they should be grouped approximately (Gupta and Mumick, 1998).

4.4 Middleware

Middleware is a loosely defined term referring to products that help customers deal with disparate, heterogeneous environments more effectively. In the DBMS arena, middleware products provide a consistent interface to different local and remote data sources. Typically, data sources are supported through one or more specific drivers that (among other things) pass requests to a given data source and enable the results to be returned to the application.

From a customer's viewpoint, typical elements of data access middleware offerings include: 1. an application programming interface (API) consisting of a series of available function calls in C and a series of data access statements in dynamic SQL; 2. a component called middleware engine for routing requests to various drivers and performing other functions (structures of middleware engine differ, depending on whether a global catalog or directory exists.); and 3. drivers to translate requests issued through the middleware API to a format intelligible to the various back-end data sources. Gateways may be considered an early attempt at middleware; they provide specific point-to-point connectivity rather than broad-based connectivity.

In Chapters 2 and 3 the logical architecture of data warehousing was discussed. Now, including the roles of the middleware, one can redraw the architecture in Figure 4.1. Each data mart contains a portion of the data stored in the data warehouse. Also note that source data are assisted by wrappers that facilitate conversion of data for integration.

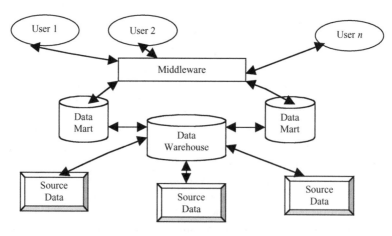

Figure 4.1 Logical architecture of a data warehouse.

Table 4.1 Result of a Query

Gender	Count
M	2002
F	1859
O	11
U	27
0	154
1	38

4.5   Data quality

An important aspect in data integration is data quality. SQL queries can be used for testing data quality. For example, in a database table T1 containing juvenile criminal data, the following query was used:

```
Select distinct (*)
From T1
Group by gender;
```

The result could be what is shown in Table 4.1. Although the expected value for attribute gender is 2, there are actually 6 values returned. In addition to "normal" values of M and F, there are values such as O, U, 0, and 1. In fact, using 0 and 1 may be another way of denoting male and female (or female and male). But 0 may also have been used to denote a missing value. In addition, the letter O may have been used to denote "other" (in this sense, it could be the same as U, which stands for unknown), but it may also have been a typo for the number 0.

In order to illustrate another scenario for data quality, take a look at Table 4.2. A manual examination indicates that only the first tuple is good. All the other tuples have problems, particularly in the "age of accident" column: the second tuple has wrongly entered the date of accident as age of accident, the third tuple has entered date of birth as accident, which is entered in the age column as well, and the problem for the last tuple seems to be missing the name value, so that all data in that row have shifted one column. Can we still use such data after shifting? If the affected attribute is always the name column, and if the name column will eventually be

Table 4.2 Problems of Data Quality

Name	Gender	Date of Birth	Date of Accident	Age of Accident
Anderson, R	M	5/09/1984	06/07/2001	17
Clark, M	F	11/06/1985	05/28/2001	05/28/2001
Fagin, K	0	12/15/1981	12/15/1981	12/15/1981
F	11/18/83	11/18/83		

eliminated in the attribute selection, then these kinds of tuples can still be used in further analysis.

Imposing a better data type could reduce the problem (such as shifting to the left, as shown in the previous example). For example, if the attributes of name and gender are of two different data types, then this would not occur. But a more interesting problem would be how to detect such a data field shift by an intelligent data cleansing program.

In general, data warehouse quality is a very important issue, and data quality is only a part of it. Due to the importance of this issue, data warehouse quality metrics have been introduced (Calero et al., 2001) and a quality management system has been developed (Hinrichs and Aden, 2001).

4.6   Data cleansing

Data cleansing (also called data cleaning) is a very important step to improve the quality of data. The general requirement for data cleansing is removal or correction of questionable data so that data can be used for data mining or other purposes of data analysis. There are plenty of commercial tools for data cleansing; most of them, however, are application-specific. The term data cleansing is sometimes used loosely; for example, some commercial products claim to be data cleansing products, but their own function is simply to divide a long character string into tokens (such as a name field, age field, etc.). From a theoretical perspective, the task of data cleaning can be formed as the problem of identifying approximate duplicates. The duplicate detection problem is also referred to in many academic papers as the semantic integration problem, instance identification problem, or merge/purge problem (Hernandez and Stolfo, 1998), and the data cleansing problem has been described as the matching of approximate duplicate data base records (Monge and Elkan, 1997; Monge, 2000).

4.6.1   General aspects of data cleansing

Data cleansing which is aimed to improve data quality by detecting and removing errors and inconsistencies from data, is considered to be one of the biggest problems in data warehousing.

As noted by Rahm and Do (2000), data cleansing problems can be categorized as having two dimensions: single vs. multi-source problems and schema vs. instance levels. Consequently, data cleansing problems can be discussed in these four possible combinations: single source at schema and instance levels, and multi-source at schema and instance levels. The data quality of a source largely depends on the degree to which it is governed by schema and integrity constraints controlling permissible data values. Single-source problems at the schema level usually are the result of violating integrity constraints. For example, data values of an attribute could go beyond the domain range, two employees have the same social security number, or referencing a non-existing value, etc. Examples for single-source problems at the instance level could be missing values, "approximately" duplicated records (two records are almost same, with one or more spelling differences), as well as others. The problems present in single sources are aggravated when multiple sources need to be integrated. Data cleansing methods for single source data could be conducted before the data integration, while data cleansing methods for multi-source data could be applied after the integration.

Regardless of single source or multi-source, data cleansing involves several tasks or phases, including data analysis using data profiling (which focuses on the instance analysis of individual attributes) or data mining (which tries to discover specific data patterns in large data sets), definition of transformation workflow and mapping rules, conflict resolution at schema and instance levels, and backflow of cleaned data (so that the dirty data in the original sources can be replaced the cleaned data). (Rahm and Do, 2000).

There are plenty of commercial tools for data cleansing; most of them, however, are application-specific. The term data cleansing is sometimes used in a loosely fashion; for example, some commercial products are claimed as data cleansing products, but their own function is simply dividing a long character string into tokens (such as a name field, age field, etc.). Various commercial tools may either concentrate on a specific problem domain (such as cleaning name and address data), or a specific cleaning task (such as data analysis or duplicate elimination). These tools must be assisted by other tools to address the broad spectrum of cleansing problems. In the data warehousing environment, data cleansing is intertwined with the data extraction, transformation and loading (usually referred to as the ETL) process). ETL tools provide comprehensive transformation and workflow capabilities to cover a large part of data transformation and cleansing process, although they may have limited interoperability.

From a theoretical perspective, the task of data cleansing can be formed as the problem of identifying *approximate duplicates* (Monge and Elkan, 1997; Monge 2000). The duplicate detection problem is also referred to as the *semantic integration problem*, *instance identification problem*, or *merge/purge problem* (Hernandex and Stolfo, 1998). Various algorithms and approaches have been proposed. For example, Galhardas et al. (2001) discussed an approach of designing a data flow graph to generate clean data. In this approach, a data lineage facility is provided that enables the user to interactively inspect intermediate data and exceptions.

4.6.2   Data cleansing methods

Below, we summarize several useful methods to illustrate the diversity of data mining techniques.

4.6.2.1   Domain relevance

Most duplicate detection methods can be classified as domain-dependent and domain-independent. Domain-dependent duplicate detection methods require some knowledge of the data source to be implemented. For instance, the person implementing the duplicate detection method may need to know what data fields would be the most distinguishing or uniquely identifying data fields because most of the domain-dependent methods require the data source to be sorted based on these fields. In contrast, domain-independent methods do not require any familiarity with the data fields within the data source. Domain-independent methods use text strings within the records to search for matches. The text strings might consist of data from several of the text fields within the data source.

4.6.2.2 Sorted neighborhood duplicate detection method

One of the most common duplicate detection methods is the *sorted neighborhood method*. The effectiveness of this approach depends on the quality of keys chosen to do the sorting. The data cleanser should choose sort keys that bring the attributes that have the most distinguishing value among the records to the top of the sorting key. The steps involved in the sorted neighborhood method can be summarized as following:

- *Create Keys:* Compute a key for each record in the list by determining the most distinguishing field of data.
- *Sort Data:* Sort the records in the data list using the key which was previously determined.
- *Merge:* Using a fixed size window, advance the window through the list of records only searching for matching records within the window. Assuming the size of the window is w, then the first record in the window will be compared to the next w-1 records for matches. Then the window will be advanced one record and the record that was just compared will no longer be considered since it is now outside of the window.

4.6.2.3 Multi-pass sorted neighborhood duplicate detection method

A variation to the sorted neighborhood method is the multi-pass sorted neighborhood method. The multi-pass sorted neighborhood method involves using multiple passes of the initial sorted neighborhood method. During each pass, the three steps, create keys, sort data, and merge, are performed selecting a different key field for each pass. Once the duplicate records are identified during a pass, all but one of the duplicates is eliminated from the data source. The output modified data source from any previous pass is used for any subsequent pass. It has been shown by that the multi-pass sorted neighborhood method provides better results. In general, several passes involving a small window size and cheap execution time and resource cost is better than performing one pass over the data with a large window size and expensive execution time and resource cost. Throughout the remainder of this section, the original sorted neighborhood duplicate detection method will be referred to as the 'one-pass sorted neighborhood duplicate detection method' to clearly distinguish this method from the multi-pass sorted neighborhood method.

4.6.2.4 Transitive closure

The idea of computing the transitive closure of duplicate relationships can be presented by utilizing a graph representing the relationships among the records and the union-find data structure to identify if any two records are already within the same path. If it can be determined that two records are already within the same path, then the record matching comparison can be avoided.

Assume the starting state involves a graph G with n vertices where each vertex represents one record in the database. Initially, all n vertices are unconnected to any other vertex. An undirected edge will be added between two vertices if it can be determined from the duplicate detection algorithm that the two records match. Before the duplicate detection algorithm does a record match comparison for any two records, the graph will be examined to see if the records belong to the same connected component. If the records do belong to the same connected component, it is known that the records do match and do not need to be compared. If the records do not belong to the same connected component, a record match comparison will need to be performed. Then, if the records are determined to match, an edge between the two records will be added to the graph. The connected components within the graph represent the transitive closure of the previously detected "is a duplicate of" relationships.

Next, consider three nodes R1, R2, and R3 and their corresponding nodes N1, N2, and N3. If it is determined that R1 and R2 are duplicates, an edge is added to graph G between nodes N1 and N2. Once the edge has been added, N1 and N2 are in the same connected component. Then, if it is determined that R2 and R3 match, an edge is added to graph G between nodes N2 and N3. It can then be discovered through transitivity (R1 = R2 and R2 = R3, so R1 must = R3), that R1 and R3 are also duplicates. Therefore, an edge must exist between N1 and N3 as well.

4.6.2.5 Union-find algorithms

Union-find algorithms are used to track the sets of connected components. The algorithm has basic two operations (Weiss, 1998):

- *Union (x,y)* combines the sets that contain node x and node y, say sets S_x and S_y, into a new set that is their union $S_x \cup S_y$, A representative for the union is chosen, and the new set replaces S_x and S_y in the collection of disjoint sets.
- *Find (x)* returns the representative of the unique set containing x. If Find (x) is invoked twice without modifying the set between the requests, the answer is the same.

The algorithm begins with n single sets containing only a single element. Then, for every edge (R1,R2) that exists in the set of edges within graph G, if Find (R1) is not equal to Find (R2) then the Union (R1,R2) will be computed. Two nodes R1 and R2 are in the same connected component only if their sets are the same, meaning Find (R1) = Find (R2). When this algorithm is applied to data cleansing, records differ in minor aspects will be accessed by the find operation, and grouped into one class using the union operation.

4.6.2.6   K-way sorting method

Examining the sorted neighborhood method shows it is not very effective in detecting duplicate records in cases where the data source does not contain a primary key field of reference. For instance, consider a typical customer mailing list example containing first name, last name, street address, city, state, and zip code data elements. The sorted neighborhood method would be much more effective if the customer mailing list had a data field which was similar to a primary key and provided a distinguishing characteristic. Then, by sorting on the primary key data element the duplicate records could be easily identified. However, the assumption of using a primary key may not always be realistic; for example, including a field of social security number in cleaning a customer mailing list, although makes things easy to handle, is unrealistic, because it is hard to imagine that people should provide their social security numbers when ordering magazines!

The *k-way sort duplicate detection method* is designed to effectively detect duplicates in data sources that do not have any uniquely distinguishing data fields. K-way sorting represents a new domain-independent duplicate detection method but the data sources it was designed for do have a common feature.

The concept behind the k-way sort method follows.

1. Let k be the number of columns to be used for sorting.
2. Select the k most meaningful combinations of sort keys based on the k selected columns.
3. Assign a record identifier to each record.
4. Sort records based on the selected sort key combinations.
5. For each sorted set of data, compare adjacent rows within a given window size. If more than half of the k columns used for sorting match, then the records should be considered pairwise matches for that sort. Repeat with all subsequent windows of records, until all records have been examined.
6. Draw k graphs, one for each sort, with undirected connectors between the record identifiers that were identified to be pairwise matches.
7. Examine the k graphs collectively. For all pairwise matches, if the matches occur between the same record identifiers exceeds certain pre-defined threshold (such as 0.5, which means matches occur on more than half of the k graphs), then it should be mapped onto the summation graph. The summation graph should represent all

pairwise matches that existed on certain number of the *k* sort graphs (determined by the threshold).

8. The summation graph should then be handled by computing the transitive closure utilizing the Find/Union processes.

A closer examination of the k-way sort concept reveals that some areas of complexity may be able to be simplified. For example, the initial methodology suggested selecting k most meaningful combinations of sort keys and then sorting the data k times using these sort keys. The benefit of the sorting is that similar records would sort near or adjacent to each other. Then, only directly adjacent records are compared to determine whether or not the records are duplicates. Another concept presented was using a given window size to limit the number or record comparisons to be mapped on to each undirected graph.

The sorting of the data is done so that similar records will be near to each other after the sort. Nearness of duplicate records is needed if small comparison windows are used so that the duplicate records will be compared and one can be eliminated. If the data was not sorted, a record may be near the beginning of the array of records and a duplicate record may be near the end of the array of records. If the window size were chosen as n/2 where n is the total number of data source records, the duplicate records would never be compared or detected by the duplicate detection method. Although these concepts limit the number of record comparisons necessary, the concepts require a great deal of memory tracking and recording of information in addition to k sorts of the data.

By eliminating the k sorts of the data and the window size from the algorithm and comparing all records against all other records in search of duplicates, the k-way sort complexity can be minimized. These changes require more record-to-record comparisons, but the need for the summation table and summation graph is eliminated and the amount of memory tracking and information recording is reduced. More detail of the K-way sorting methods can be found in Feekin and Chen (2000), where some experimental results are also reported.

4.7   Dealing with data inconsistency in multidatabase systems

A data warehouse contains integrated data. An interesting question is what will happen if the data are not already integrated. This leads us to take a look at the issues of data inconsistency and resolution function in multidatabase systems (Yu and Meng, 1998), where independent management of a component database system is the main reason data inconsistency occurs. Usually, the schema integrator at the front end cannot modify the involved values in component databases to resolve the inconsistency because the integrator may not be authorized to do so or the integrator cannot be certain which values are incorrect. As a result, data inconsistency is often handled at the front end. To retain the ability to identify instances from different databases representing the same real-world object, it is necessary to assume that data inconsistency does not occur on the ID attribute.

Sometimes an apparent inconsistency does not necessarily mean that one of the involved values must be incorrect. For example, suppose a salary value of 25k is recorded for Mary in the first database, while a value of 30k is recorded in the second database. This apparent inconsistency may have different explanations. It is possible that the apparent inconsistency is a real inconsistency in the sense that the two values should be the same but they are not. However, it is also possible that it is not a real inconsistency. For instance, it is possible that Mary has two different salaries in the two databases because she has two different part-time jobs. In this case, both salary values for Mary are correct and they should both be used to define the salary value for Mary in the integrated schema.

In general, when two values (either different or identical) exist for the same attribute of a real-world object in two databases, the following three cases exist: 1. There is no data inconsistency, and only one of the two values is needed; 2. There is a data inconsistency, but both values are needed to define the value of the object for the same attribute in the integrated schema; or 3. There is no data inconsistency, but both values are needed (as in the case illustrated earlier). Different methods may be used to define the value of the object under an attribute in the integrated schema from the two corresponding values in the component databases. In general, for cases 2) and 3) above, the global value in the integrated schema can be defined by a definition function. Since cases 2) and 3) can be handled uniformly through the use of definition functions, for the convenience of presentation, when an attribute is involved in either case 2) or 3), a data inconsistency is said to be on the attribute and the corresponding definition function is called a resolution function.

4.8   Data reduction

One particular concern in data preparation is data reduction (which was discussed in Section 2.10). As frequently noted (Weiss and Indurkhya, 1998), the data may be too big for some prediction programs. The expected time for inducing a solution may be too long. Therefore, reduction of big data, or shrinking the size of the database by eliminating both rows and columns, may be helpful for predictive data mining. In fact, better answers are sometimes found by using a reduced subset of the available data. Prediction programs can potentially fit their solutions to any size data. The bigger the data are, the more exceptions must be fit. Even with completely random data, many programs will first attempt to fit all the training data. By fitting so many exceptions, some prediction programs are more likely to err on the optimistic side, finding a concept that is not there.

The main theme for simplifying the data is dimension reduction. One can delete a column (namely, a feature), delete a row (which represents a case), or reduce the number of values in a column (smooth a feature). The emphasis here is to use simple techniques to implement and preserve the character of the original data, although advanced techniques, such as the method of principal components, can be used to replace the features with composite features.

Dimension reduction is the goal of the new process that mediates between data preparation and prediction methods. Methods that transform data into a new set of attributes (referred to as features in pattern recognition literature) can also be considered data preparation methods. Dimension reduction can be done by feature selection. The objective of feature selection is to find a subset of features with predictive performance comparable to the full set of features. This perspective on dimension reduction is independent of the prediction methods.

Data reduction techniques, along with prediction methods themselves, form the two types of tools that can contribute to the task of predictive data mining. Because data reduction is much faster than data modeling, the data are filtered to narrow the search space of the prediction methods. However, the reduction methods make assumptions that potentially could degrade results. These assumptions can be viewed as sources that cause a kind of uncertainty in data preprocessing. In order to deal with such uncertainty, empirical comparisons of the different data reduction techniques have been made. These techniques are then matched to prediction methods to see which combinations work best. This kind of comparison of different approaches to data reduction and mining should aid in gaining experience in picking the right tools for the job (Weiss and Indurkhya, 1998).

Data reduction is usually used as a data preparation step, but it can be used for data analysis in its own right. Chapter 8 contains a case study of intelligent data analysis using a reduction approach. The rest of this chapter describes sample projects for data preparation.

4.9   Case study: data preparation for stock food chain analysis

4.9.1   Overview

The concept of stock food chain consists of the relationship between big companies and the companies that sell them parts/services. Once this relationship is established, their stock prices can then be compared to determine how closely a smaller company's stock depends on the large company or the large company's stock on the smaller one. This may provide a good indication on when to buy or sell a stock. The following case study (Plum, 2001) describes how to establish a data warehouse prototype which can be used for further analysis.

Figure 4.2 represents a subset of the stock food chain for Microsoft. Companies at level 3 sell to companies at level 2, which in turn sell to companies at level 1, which sell to Microsoft. This illustrates the purpose

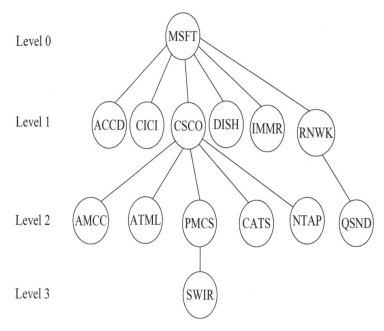

Figure 4.2 Microsoft stock food chain.

of the stock food chain. As can be seen, if Microsoft's stock falls, it can easily cause a chain reaction in other companies' stocks. Microsoft would not be able to purchase as many goods from companies at level 1, so their sales would be greatly reduced, causing their stock price to fall also, and the same logic may be applied to levels 2 and 3. For example, consider what happened when Cisco's stock price plummetted: Cisco Systems' share price fell sharply after the network equipment maker announced second quarter earnings that failed to fulfill Wall Street expectations and predicted that revenue would not likely grow during the next 6 months. Stocks below Cisco in the food chain, or in a related field to those stocks, plummeted, while Microsoft — above Cisco in the food chain (Microsoft buys from Cisco) — was essentially unchanged.

The objective of this case study is to establish a small data warehouse prototype consisting of stocks and their weekly prices that contains accurate, quality data. The data warehouse will also contain a relationship that describes the stock food chain. This relationship is essential to quality of the data warehouse and therefore will be one of the main emphases of this project. This will be accomplished by collecting stock data, establishing the relationships between the stocks that define the stock food chain, and performing the data preprocessing required when creating a data warehouse.

This study required a great deal of research in order to collect the required amount of data on each individual stock, as well as determining the complicated relationship between these stocks that establishes the stock food chain. Before stock data could be collected, it was first necessary to decide which stocks to collect and what data from those stocks would be valuable for the necessary analysis. Because of interest in technology stock, the top 100 NASDAQ stocks were selected, as well as other stocks considered to be in the computer hardware or software category. Overall, data for almost 300 stocks were collected.

The data included the date, price, stock category, stock symbol, company name, market that the stock traded on, and volume for that date. The majority of these data were exported from a program called TeleChart 2000, which analyzes historical stock data. Some of the stock data were also taken from the Internet. Sites such as Yahoo! and Microsoft's Money Central provide historical data, but it required a great deal of effort in order to get that information from the Web page into the stock data warehouse.

The relationship between stocks that defines the stock food chain turned out to be somewhat complicated to establish. The information that defines the food chain is the relationship that says company A buys from company B, which buys from company C. However, the information is not provided in this manner in the profiles of these companies on the Internet. Instead, they provide the information in this manner: company C sells to company B, which sells to company A. This may seem like only a subtle difference, but it made it much harder to target a company at the top of the food chain. For example, one could not go to the profile on IBM (a company at the top of the food chain) and find all of the companies that IBM buys from. Instead one must start at a company at the bottom of the food chain, such as Read-Rite Corporation, and find out that it sells to Maxtor Corporation, then look at the profile of Maxtor Corporation and find out that it sells to IBM.

Internet sites such as http://moneycentral.msn.com/ and http://finance.yahoo.com were used to collect relationship data from company profiles. Here are a few examples of the profiles: Exabyte's customers are primarily computer makers (IBM accounts for 15% of sales and Sun Microsystems for 11%) and resellers (Ingram Micro accounts for 14% of sales). Compaq and IBM account for 23 and 15% of sales, respectively. The profiles of each of the nearly 300 stocks were read and the information on to whom they sell was recorded in the food_chain relationship in the data warehouse.

The first task was to use Microsoft Access to design and create a data warehouse that would allow for stock data to be stored in a manner allowing useful information on the stock food chain to be extracted. The second major task was data preprocessing — possibly the most important part of the data mining process. If the data warehouse does not contain quality data, then there will be no quality results. Several data preprocessing methods were applied to the stock data in order to ensure their quality.

4.9.2   Preparing the data

Conceptual modeling techniques such as the entity-relationship (ER) model can be used for data modeling. The two entities were stock and price. The stock entity contained the following attributes: stock symbol, company name, business category, and stock exchange where traded. The price entity contained the stock symbol, week (1 to 52), year, price, and volume traded. The two relationships were food_chain and stock_price. The food_chain relationship related the stock entity to itself in order to establish the stock food chain relationship. The stock_price relationship related each stock in the stock entity to its weekly price in the price entity.

The data warehouse was created with the aforementioned specifications using Microsoft Access. Three tables were created: stock (the stock entity), price (the price entity), and food_chain (the food_chain relationship). The stock_price relationship was represented by adding the stock symbol to the price table.

4.9.2.1   Data integration

Much of the original data was exported from a stock analysis program in a format that did not fit directly into the stock food chain data warehouse. The stock information was simply exported from the program into a tab-delimited file with each record representing a line in the file. The stock data also comprised the daily price of the stock and not the weekly price that the data warehouse required. In order to integrate the data, a series of SQL statements were applied to the data.

The first step in data integration was to import the information into the stock entity. This information was brought into a temporary table; then the data were added to the stock entity by grouping on the stock symbol (the primary key of the stock entity) to produce a single row for each stock.

The second step was to integrate the price data. As mentioned previously, the stock price data represent the daily price of the stocks, so the data must first be transformed before they can be integrated into the price entity (to be discussed in a later section). After data transformation was performed, the data were inserted into the price entity. The stock_price relationship was now established because both the stock and price entities contained the stock symbol. The food_chain relationship was more complicated to establish; it involved a great deal of research followed by data entry.

4.9.2.2   Data cleaning

Data cleaning was applied in order to ensure that all the records contained valid dates and stock prices. SQL was used to search for out of range or NULL dates and stock prices. Because the price entity represents weekly prices, the valid values are 1 through 52. However, after the stock data were transformed and imported, some weeks contained the value of 53. This is technically a legal value because leap years contain 52 weeks and 1 day or 53 weeks. However, because week 53 does not represent an entire week, its value was averaged into the data of week 52 for that year.

Any stock prices that were NULL were then either filled in with the actual average for that week by researching the stock on the Internet or, if this information was unavailable, the average price of the stock from the week before and the week after was used to fill in the missing value.

4.9.2.3 Data transformation

The stock price data were transformed in order to condense the daily stock prices into weekly stock prices. This was done by placing all of the daily price data into a temporary table and separating the date into two new attributes: week and year. Then SQL was used to group by stock symbol, week, and year while averaging the stock price and volume. This produced a new set of data containing the average stock price and volume for each week, year, and stock symbol. Transforming the data in this manner helped greatly reduce the amount of data. The price data went from 1,050,000 records to 115,000 records while maintaining its quality for the purpose of the stock food chain.

4.9.2.4 Data reduction

The dimension of the data was reduced by removing attributes that were not applicable to the stock food chain project. Such attributes as the company P/E ratio and the minimum and maximum price for each day were removed from the data before they were placed in the data warehouse.

4.9.2.5 SQL query examples

SQL was used in the creation of the stock food chain data. The following are some examples.

```
INSERT INTO stocks (Symbol, Company, Category, Exchange)
SELECT
   [CompHardStocks].[symbol] AS symbol, [CompHardStocks].[com-
      pany] AS company,
   [CompHardStocks].[catagory] AS catagory,
   [CompHardStocks].[exchange] AS exchange
FROM
   CompHardStocks
GROUP BY
   [CompHardStocks].[symbol],
   [CompHardStocks].[company],
   [CompHardStocks].[catagory],
   [CompHardStocks].[exchange]
ORDER BY [CompHardStocks].[symbol];

SELECT
[prices_hard].[symbol] AS symbol INTO hard_stock_symbols
FROM prices_hard
GROUP BY
   [prices_hard].[symbol]
```

HAVING ((([prices_hard].[symbol]) Not In (select symbol from
weekly_price group by symbol)));

SELECT
    food_chain.parent AS [level 0],
    food_chain.child AS [level 1],
    food_chain_1.child AS [level 2],
    food_chain_2.child AS [level 3]

FROM (food_chain AS food_chain_1
RIGHT JOIN
    food_chain ON food_chain_1.parent = food_chain.child)
LEFT JOIN
    food_chain AS food_chain_2 ON
    food_chain_1.child = food_chain_2.parent
GROUP BY
    food_chain.parent, food_chain.child, food_chain_1.child,
        food_chain_2.child
HAVING
    (((food_chain.parent) Not In (select child from food_chain group by
        child)))
ORDER BY
    food_chain.parent, food_chain.child, food_chain_1.child,
        food_chain_2.child;

INSERT INTO weekly_price (symbol, [Year], Week, AvgOfPrice,
    AvgOfVolume)
SELECT
    prices_hard.symbol AS symbol,
    DatePart("yyyy",[date]) AS [Year],
    DatePart("ww",[date]) AS Week,
    Avg(prices_hard.price) AS AvgOfprice,
    Avg(prices_hard.volume) AS AvgOfvolume
FROM hard_stock_symbols, prices_hard
GROUP BY
    prices_hard.symbol, DatePart("yyyy,"[date]), DatePart("ww,"[date])
ORDER BY
    prices_hard.symbol, DatePart("yyyy,"[date]), DatePart("ww",
        [date]);

SELECT
    [weeks].symbol AS symbol,
    [weeks].Year AS year,
    [weeks].Week AS week,
    Avg([weeks].price) AS AvgOfPrice,
    Avg([weeks].volume) AS AvgOfVolume

```
FROM weeks, stocks
WHERE
    (((([weeks].[symbol]) Not In (select stocks.symbol from stocks)))
GROUP BY [weeks].symbol, [weeks].Year, [weeks].Week
ORDER BY [weeks].symbol, [weeks].Year, [weeks].Week;

SELECT
    food_chain.parent, food_chain.child, stocks.Company,
    Avg(weekly_price.AvgOfPrice) AS AvgOfAvgOfPrice,
    Max(weekly_price.AvgOfPrice) AS MaxOfAvgOfPrice,
    Min(weekly_price.AvgOfPrice) AS MinOfAvgOfPrice,
    Avg(weekly_price_1.AvgOfPrice) AS [parent avg],
    Max(weekly_price_1.AvgOfPrice) AS [parent max],
    Min(weekly_price_1.AvgOfPrice) AS [parent min]
FROM
    weekly_price AS weekly_price_1
INNER JOIN
    ((food_chain INNER JOIN stocks ON food_chain.child = stocks.
        Symbol) INNER JOIN weekly_price ON stocks.Symbol =
        weekly_price.symbol) ON weekly_price_1.symbol =
        food_chain.parent
GROUP BY
    food_chain.parent, food_chain.child, stocks.Company
ORDER BY food_chain.parent, food_chain.child;
```

4.9.3   Building the hierarchies

How to collect data and process the data to the required form have been discussed. But how to organize the different stocks into a hierarchical structure? Of the stocks collected, it was necessary to read their profiles from several sites and record the company to whom they sold, then manually enter this information into the food_chain relationship. The entry was simplified somewhat by connecting the stock table to the food_chain relationship based on the child field. This allowed simple entering of the parent information (whom they sold to) for each stock — information collected from the Web. When the parent field was entered, the child field for that stock would then be automatically entered into the food_chain relationship and, therefore, hierarchical structure would be established.

4.9.4   Resulting data

The result of this case contains well-organized data containing almost 300 company stocks and over 115,000 weekly prices. The stock price data range from 1984 to 2001. There are also over 150 valid stock food chain relationships established in the data warehouse.

Table 4.3 is an example of the stock food chain relationship for Hewlett-Packard Company (HWP) and Microsoft Corp. (MSFT).

Table 4.3 Stock Food Chain Relationships

Level 0	Level 1	Level 2	Level 3
HWP	AESP		
HWP	BVSN		
HWP	CPWR		
HWP	CREAF		
HWP	CSCO	AMCC	
HWP	CSCO	ATML	
HWP	CSCO	BRCM	
HWP	CSCO	CATS	
HWP	CSCO	NTAP	
HWP	CSCO	PMCS	SWIR
HWP	CSCO	PSEM	
HWP	CSCO	VNWK	
HWP	CSCO	VTSS	
HWP	CSCO	XLNX	
HWP	DSS		
HWP	FDRY		
HWP	HDD		
HWP	INPH		
HWP	INTC	AMAT	
HWP	INTC	CREAF	
HWP	INTC	ESCC	
HWP	INTC	IONN	
HWP	INTC	NWRE	
HWP	IOM		
HWP	KTCC		
HWP	MOLX		
HWP	SMSC		
HWP	SNDK		
HWP	SSPI		
HWP	STK	CRDS	
HWP	VRTS		
HWP	WDC	KMAG	
HWP	WDC	RDRT	
HWP	ZOOX		
MSFT	ACCD		
MSFT	CICI		
MSFT	CSCO	AMCC	
MSFT	CSCO	ATML	
MSFT	CSCO	BRCM	
MSFT	CSCO	CATS	
MSFT	CSCO	NTAP	
MSFT	CSCO	PMCS	SWIR
MSFT	CSCO	PSEM	
MSFT	CSCO	VNWK	
MSFT	CSCO	VTSS	
MSFT	CSCO	XLNX	
MSFT	DISH		

Table 4.3 Stock Food Chain Relationships *(Continued)*

Level 0	Level 1	Level 2	Level 3
MSFT	IMMR		
MSFT	KTCC		
MSFT	RNWK	QSND	
MSFT	SIGM		
MSFT	VRSN		
MSFT	VRTS		

Table 4.4 Stock Entry Data

Symbol	Company	Category	Exchange
CSCO	Cisco Systems Inc.	COMPUTER HARDWARE — Networking & Communication Dev.	NASDAQ
EMLX	Emulex Corp.	COMPUTER HARDWARE — Computer Peripherals	NASDAQ
HWP	Hewlett-Packard Co.	COMPUTER HARDWARE — Diversified Computer Systems	NYSE
IBM	International Business Mach	COMPUTER HARDWARE — Diversified Computer Systems	NYSE
INTC	Intel Corp.	ELECTRONICS — Semiconductor – Broad Line	NASDAQ
MSFT	Microsoft Corp.	COMPUTER SOFTWARE & SERVICES — Application Software	NASDAQ
PMCS	Pmc-Sierra Inc.	ELECTRONICS — Semiconductor – Integrated Cir.	NASDAQ

Table 4.5 Sample Results for Cisco

Symbol	Year	Week	Price	Volume
CSCO	1992	1	$0.47	706,261.50
CSCO	1992	26	$0.63	613,905.80
CSCO	1992	52	$1.03	680,511.50
CSCO	1995	1	$1.90	451,699.25
CSCO	1995	26	$2.80	518,007.80
CSCO	1995	52	$4.23	648,337.00
CSCO	1999	26	$30.45	543,501.20
CSCO	1999	52	$51.78	323,006.00

Table 4.4 contains a sample of the stock entity data for several companies.
Table 4.5 contains a sample of the weekly stock price and volume data for
Cisco (CSCO) in years 1992, 1995, and 1999 and the 2nd, 26th, and 52nd weeks.

4.10   Web log file preparation

Earlier it was mentioned that documents available from the Web have made
Webhouse possible. In this section a case study of Web log file preparation

and preprocessing is described. This study has been carried out in two environments: one is Sybase running in HP UNIX (Scenario 1), the other combines the use of UNIX with ORACLE running in Window NT (Scenario 2). The main language is Korn shell scripting and SQL. The following briefly describes the first scenario.

> Input: the log file with input size of 1067 rows of data.
> This is a text file ftp to UNIX from desktop.
>
> #Software: Microsoft Internet Information Server 4.0
> #Version: 1.0
> #Date: 2000-10-18 11:52:22
> #Fields: time c-ip cs-method cs-uri-stem sc-status
> 11:52:22 144.163.64.30 GET /Forms/ 401
> 11:52:31 144.163.64.30 GET /Forms/Default.asp 200
> 11:52:40 144.163.64.30 GET /Forms/Default.asp 200
> 11:53:16 144.163.64.30 GET /Forms/run.asp 200
> 14:08:37 144.163.64.24 GET / 401
> 14:08:58 144.163.64.24 GET /Default.html 200
> 14:08:58 144.163.64.24 GET /welcome.html 200
> 14:08:58 144.163.64.24 GET /header.asp 200
> 14:08:58 144.163.64.24 GET /images/helpbutton-new.jpg 200
> 14:08:58 144.163.64.24 GET /images/qwest.jpg 200
>
> . . . . . .

In this input file there is a comment line following each field. The first field is the time (hour/minute/second), the second field is the IP address of log-on user's workstation, the third field is the command issued by the user, the fourth field is the path the user entered into, and the fifth field is return value of the command, fail or succeed.

> Main Procedure:
> Preliminary processing
> Read the input file
> Get rid of blank line
> Get rid of comment line
> Get the date
> Put the processed file into a temporary file
> Set up connection to database
> Create the table in database
> If table exists
>   Remove the table
> Else
>   Create

Get the total number of lines of the cleaned data file
Insertion (tuple t)
If the number of parameters is not equal to m
Skip //data incomplete
      Decrement count
else
      Set date format
      Insert into table with value of all fields of the
      tuple
Populate Table
Initialize n to 1
While n is less than or equal to the total number of
lines in the data file
  Get a line from temporary file
  Parsing the line and put each field into an array
  Add row id
Prepending date to time
  Connect to database
  Insertion (all fields)
  Verify table exists
      Set row count equals to k (a predefined value)
      Show all the attributes
  Find knowledge pattern
Enter the database
      Find the number of logged on users during
      each hour in the day
      Using the hour and am/pm as identifier,
      search through the table
      Get the total number of rows
      Convert the global variable into integer
      Set array to hold the results spilled
      from data server
      Process the results and format into a given
      format
  Find the total number of distinguish users during
  the day
      Issue query to get the distinguished users
  Process the data spilled from data server and
  display as user
  interpretable format.

Part of the output created in the database is shown in Table 4.6.
It also shows in the text format of the number of users logged onto the
site each hour in the day,

The number of logged on users at 1PM clock is: 0

Table 4.6 Sample Output

row_id	log_on	user_addr	command path	ret_val
1	Oct 18 2000 11:52AM	144.163.64.30	GET /Forms/	401
2	Oct 18 2000 11:52AM	144.163.64.30	GET/Forms/Default.asp	200
3	Oct 18 2000 11:52AM	144.163.64.30	GET /Forms/Default.asp	200

The number of logged on users at 2PM clock is: 1
The number of logged on users at 3PM clock is: 2

4.11   Summary

The process of data preparation needed for data warehouse construction has been reviewed in this chapter. In order to make data warehouses effectively achieve their goals, a careful requirement analysis should be first carried out, and the data should be integrated and preprocessed in appropriate forms.

References

Feekin, A. and Z. Chen, Duplicate detection using k-way sorting method, *Proc. ACM SAC Conf.*, 323–327, 2000.

Gupta, A. and I. S. Mumick, Applications of materialized views, in *Materialized Views: Techniques, Implementations, and Applications*, MIT Press, 1998, 13–18.

Hernandez, M. A. and J. Stolfo, Real world data is dirty: data cleansing and the merger/purge problem, *Data Mining and Knowledge Discovery*, 2(1), 9–37, 1998.

Hinrichs, H. and T. Aden, An ISO 9001: 2000 Complaint Quality Management System for Data Integration in Data Warehouse Systems, *Proc. DMDW '2001 (online)*, Ch. 1(1.1–1.12).

Monge, A. E., Matching algorithms within a duplicate detection system, *IEEE Data Eng. Bull.*, 23(4), 14–20, 2000.

Monge, A. E. and C. Elkan, An efficient domain-dependent algorithm for detecting approximately duplicate database records, *Workshop on Research Issues on Data Mining and Knowledge Discovery (DMKD '97)*, 1–16, 1997.

Plum, D., Preparation for stock food chain analysis, term project paper, Department of Computer Science, University of Nebraska at Omaha, 2001.

Pyle, D., *Data Preparation for Data Mining*, Morgan Kaufmann, San Francisco, CA, 1999.

Srivastava, J. and P. Y. Chen, Warehouse creation — a potential roadblock to data warehousing, *IEEE Trans. Knowledge Data Eng.*, 11(1), 118–126, 1999.

Weiss, M. A., *Data Structures & Algorithms Analysis in C++*, Addison-Wesley, Menlo Park, CA, 1998.

Weiss, S. W. and N. Indurkhya, *Predictive Data Mining*, Morgan Kaufmann, San Francisco, CA, 1997.

Yu, C. and W. Meng, *Principles of Database Query Processing for Advanced Applications*, Morgan Kaufmann, San Francisco, 1998.

chapter five

Building data warehouses

5.1 Overview

This chapter examines the process of building data warehouses in more detail. As noted by Moody and Kortink (2000), data warehousing is based on a supply chain metaphor. The data product is obtained from data suppliers (operational systems or external sources) and is temporarily stored in a central data warehouse. The data are then delivered via data marts to data consumers (end users). Data warehousing consists of various processes to be executed at design time, build time, and run time (Gatziu et al., 2000).

Chapter 4 already discussed some basic methods for data preparation. These methods can be used for building data warehouses, but also for individual file preparation. This chapter summarizes existing and proposed approaches of building data warehouses mainly from an application-oriented perspective, with an emphasis on higher-level aspects, such as conceptual modeling. Both entity-relationship (ER) and dimensional modeling approaches are discussed.

5.2 Conceptual data modeling

5.2.1 Entity-relationship (ER) modeling

Conceptual modeling of a data warehouse employs high-level formalisms. The ER approach provides an effective way for conceptual modeling of data. The underlying idea is simple: data can be described in terms of "things" and their connections. Consequently, there are two kinds of basic constructs in an ER model: entity sets consist of entities and relationship sets connect the entity sets. Both entity sets and relationship sets can be described by attributes. ER modeling typically makes use of ER diagrams (ERDs) which are graphical expressions of the overall logical structure of a database. In an ERD, each entity set is represented by a rectangle, each relationship set is represented by a diamond and is connected to associated entity sets by lines, and each attribute is represented by an oval.

Although the ER approach seems to be simple, there are a lot of design issues to be considered. For example, one should decide which things should be treated as entity sets. Other issues should be considered, including which attributes should go to an entity set and which should go to a relationship set takes, etc.

There are major constructs involved in ER modeling. An entity set (i.e., a strong entity set) is a set of entities of the same type that share the same properties (or attributes). An entity is a thing or object in the real world that is distinguishable from all other things and represented by a set of attributes. Entity sets do not need to be disjoint.

A relationship set is a set of relationships of the same type. A relationship is an association among several entities. The degree of a relationship set is determined by the number of entity sets associated. Typically there are binary relationship sets, but there can also be n-ary relationship sets. A relationship set may have its own attributes (just like an entity set). An important aspect of a relationship set is the mapping constraint (namely, cardinalities):

- One to one (1:1) $\longleftrightarrow$. For example, a student can only take one course and each course can only have one student. (Of course, this restriction is not realistic.)
- One to many (1:N) $\longleftarrow$. For example, a student can take many courses, while each course can have only one student. (Again, not realistic in the current example.)
- Many to one (N:1) $\longrightarrow$. For example, many students can take one course, and each course can have many students.
- Many to many (M:N) $\longrightarrow$. For example, each student can take one or more courses and each course may have more than one student. This is a reasonable assumption in this example.

The function that an entity plays in a relationship is called that entity's role. For example, a graduate student can play the role of a student as well as that of an instructor.

Both entity sets and relationship sets are described by attributes. There are different kinds of attributes, such as simple vs. composite, single-valued vs. multivalued, null, and derived (such as age being derived by date of birth and today's date). The collection of attributes is referred to as the schema (discussed earlier in this book).

Relational databases have concepts related to keys, such as candidate key or primary key. These concepts can be extended to entity-relationship models. There are several different types of keys for entity sets. A superkey is a set of attributes which uniquely identifies an entity in the entity set. A candidate key is the minimal super key (attributes used as candidate key are usually underlined). The primary key is the designated candidate key. In addition, the notion foreign key denotes a set of attributes that form the primary key of another relation. Primary keys for relationship sets are formed from primary keys of associated entity sets.

After the ER diagrams are constructed, the next step is to map them into relations. ERDs can be converted to a form closely related to predicate logic, which is a relation. For an entity set E, E is represented by a table with distinct columns; each column corresponds to one of the attributes of E. Each row corresponds to an entity of the entity set. Relationship set R can be represented by a table with distinct columns; each column corresponds to one of the attributes in primary keys of associated entity sets or R's own descriptive attributes.

When the ER approach is used, primary keys and foreign keys in the converted tables can be determined from the primary keys in the corresponding constructs (entity sets or relationship sets) in the ERD:

- Entity relation: the primary key of the entity set in ERD becomes the primary key of the entity relation.
- Relationship relation: the union of the primary keys of the related entity sets becomes a superkey of the relation. (Note here that union means to put together all the attributes in both primary keys.)

5.2.2 Dimension modeling

OLAP or multidimensional analysis is a method of viewing aggregate data called measurements (e.g., sales, expenses, etc.) along a set of dimensions such as product, brand, stored, month, city and state, etc. An OLAP typically consists of the following conceptual elements: *dimension:* each dimension is described by a set of attributes. A related concept is domain hierarchy. For example, "country," "state," and "city" form a domain hierarchy; *measure:* each of the numeric measures depends on a set of dimensions, which provide the context for the measure. The dimensions together are assumed to uniquely determine the measure. Therefore, the multidimensional data view a measure as a value in the multidimensional space of dimensions.

Gallas (1999) described differences between different schools in building data warehouses, where ERDs take a controversial role. According to Kimball (2000), while ER modeling is a useful technique for beginning the process of understanding and enforcing business rules, it falls far short of providing any kind of completeness or guarantee. Reasons include:

- ER modeling is incomplete. There is no test of an ER model to determine if the designer has specified all possible one-to-one, many-to-one, or many-to-many relationships.
- ER modeling is not unique. A given set of data relationships can be represented by many ER diagrams.
- Most real data relationships are many-to-many. This is a kind of catch-all declaration that does not provide any discipline or value.
- Most large ER models are ideal, not real.

Regardless of whether ER models will be used or not, in general, the data warehouse design process consists of the following steps (Inmon, 1996; Kimball et al., 1998): 1. choose a business process to model, such as sales, shipments, etc.; 2. choose the grain of the business process. The grain is the granularity (namely, fundamental, atomic) level of the data used in the fact table. The data stored there are the primary data based on which OLAP operations can be performed; 3. choose the dimensions that will apply to records in the fact table(s). For example, time is a typical dimension; and 4. choose the measures that will populate each fact table record. Measures are numeric additive quantities such as sales amount or profit.

As noted in Chapter 3, according to the business perspective, data warehousing can be considered as a union of data marts. Therefore, building data marts plays a central role in warehouse construction. Once all the possible data marts and dimensions have been identified, the design of individual fact tables within these data marts can be made very specific.

A matrix approach has been recommended in building data marts. The rows of the data warehouse bus architecture matrix are the data marts and the columns are the dimensions. With the rows and columns of the matrix defined, one systematically marks all the intersections where a dimension exists for a data mart. For example, if dimension Dim 1 exists for data mart 1, one puts a check mark in the entry located at the intersection of data mart 1 and dim 1. Table 5.1 illustrates this approach, where two data marts with four possible dimensions are shown.

Table 5.1 Matrix Approach for Building Data Marts

	Dim 1	Dim 2	Dim 3	Dim 4
Data Mart 1	✓	✓		
Data Mart 2	✓		✓	✓

A data mart can overlap another data mart. It is advisable to list 10 to 30 data marts for a large organization.

Kimball et al. (1998) used the four-step method to design each fact table: choose the data mart, declare the grain, choose the dimensions, and choose the facts. Kimball (1999) further discussed dimension modeling issues related to clickstream data mart.

5.3   Data warehouse design using ER approach

5.3.1   An example

Although Kimball argues that modeling in a data warehousing environment is radically different from modeling in an operation (transaction processing) environment, in the database research community, researchers still feel that ER modeling is equally applicable in a data warehousing context as in an operational context and provides a useful basis for designing both data warehouses and data marts. The issue of data warehouse design using the ER approach is examined in a simple example next.

Consider building a data warehouse for a grocery chain. Suppose that the marketing department wants to analyze all of the sales promotions made during the 2000 calendar year. It is necessary to start with the ERD of the existing operational database. First a multidimensional data model (snow-flake schema) for the data warehouse is built and then a multidimensional data structure (a cube) to enable fast response times when the marketing analysts query the data warehouse.

The following steps are involved in developing a data warehouse and data cube for the above mentioned test scenario: 1. identification of appropriate relations and their attributes from ERD; 2. identification of the fact table and its measures; 3. identification of dimension tables; 4. design of the snow-flake schema; 5. building the data warehouse; and 6. building the data cube.

First is the identification of appropriate relations and their attributes from ERD. The target is to calculate all of the sales promotions made during the 2000 calendar year. For this, one would first analyze the existing ERD of the database. After the entity sets and relationship sets are mapped to relational tables, the resulting ERD is shown in Figure 5.1.

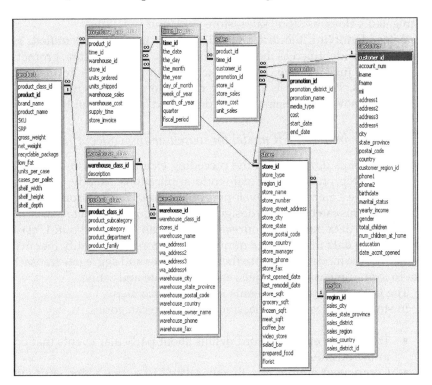

Figure 5.1 An ERD for a retail chain.

From this ERD, the following potential relations necessary to achieve the task were found:

1. Product relation gives the description about each product supplied by this company. The description includes ID of the product and the ID of the class to which it belongs, name of product, and its brand name and weight, etc.
2. Product_class relation gives the information about the class to which a particular product belongs.
3. Sales relation contains sales information for each product in a store and other related information.
4. Promotion relation contains information about the method adopted to promote the product.
5. Store relation contains information regarding a particular store and its related details.
6. Time_by_day relation contains information related to the periods.

The next step is identification of the fact table and its measures. Among all the relations, the sale relation contains the numerical measures. It contains names of the facts or measures as well as keys to each of the related tables. So sale relation is selected as the fact table. This fact table has measures, the aggregated values, as store_sales, store_cost, and unit_sales.

After identifying the fact table, dimension tables are identified. Here four tables are identified as the dimension tables. These are store, promotion, product, and time_by_day. The product table in the ERD is normalized to product_class. But there is only one dimension that covers both tables. Finally, the snowflake schema can be developed, as shown in Figure 5.2.

5.3.2   Steps in using ER model for warehousing conceptual modeling

The simple steps illustrated in the preceding example need to be extended into a multistep procedure in real-world applications. Moody and Kortnik (2000) describe a method for developing dimensional models from traditional ER models. This can be used to design data warehouses and data marts based on enterprise data models. A four-step process can be carried out: 1. classify entities in the data model into a number of categories; 2. identify hierarchies that exist in the model; 3. collapse these hierarchies and aggregate transaction data to form dimensional models; and 4. evaluate and refine.

The following are more details related to each step.

In step 1, entities can be classified into three categories:

- Transaction entities record details about particular events that occur in the business.
- Component entities are directly related to a transaction entity via a one-to-many relation. They define the details or components of each business transaction.

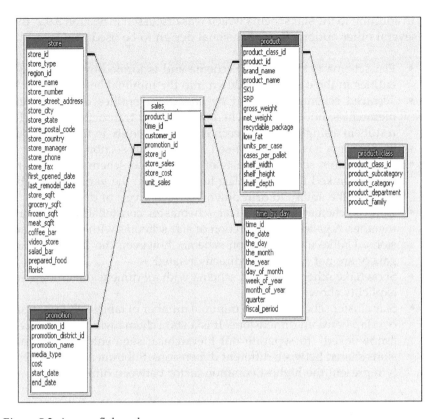

Figure 5.2 A snowflake schema.

- Classification entities are entities related to component entities by a chain of one-to-many relationships; they are functionally dependent on a componet entity (directly or transitively). Classification entities represent hierarchies embedded in the data model, which may be collapsed into component entities to form dimension tables in a star schema.

In some cases, entities may fit into multiple categories. Ambiguities are resolved by using precedence hierarchy, where transaction entities are given highest precedence while component entities are given lowest precedence.

In step 2, note that a hierarchy in an ER model is any sequence of entities joined together by one-to-many relationships, all aligned in the same direction. A hierarchy is called maximal if it cannot be extended upward or downwards by including another entity. An entity is called minimal if it is at the bottom of a maximal hierarchy and maximal if it is at the top.

In step 3, two operators exist for producing dimensional models: collapse hierarchy in which higher level entities can be collapsed into lower level entities within hierarchies; and aggregation, which can be applied to a transaction entity to create a new entity containing summarized data.

In addition to the star schema which was discussed in Section 3.9.2, there are several other options for dimensional design to be used in this step:

- Flat schema is the simplest schema and is formed by collapsing all entities in the data model down into the minimal entities.
- Terraced schema is formed by collapsing entities down maximal hierarchies, but stopping when they reach a transaction entity. This results in a single table for each transaction entity in the data model.
- Star schema has been discussed in a previous section.
- Constellation schema consists of a set of star schemas with hierarchically linked fact tables. The links between the various fact tables provide the ability to drill down between levels of detail.
- Galaxy schema is a set of star schemas or constellations combined together. A galaxy is a collection of star schemas with shared dimensions. Unlike a constellation schema, however, the fact tables in a galaxy are not necessarily directly related.
- Snowflake schema is a star schema with all dimensional hierarchies explicitly shown.
- Star cluster schema has the minimal number of tables while avoiding overlap between dimensions. It is a star schema which is selectively "snowflaked" to separate out hierarchical segments or subdimensions shared between different dimensions. Subdimensions effectively represent the highest common factor between dimensions.

Finally, in step 4, evaluation and refinement include the following possible activities: combine fact tables, combine dimension tables, and handle many-to-many relationships. Most of the complexities that arise in converting a traditional ER model to a dimensional model result from many-to-many relationships or intersection entities. Many-to-many relationships cause problems in dimensional modeling because they represent a "break" in the hierarchical chain, and cannot be collapsed. Discussion on this issue can be found in Song et al. (2001). In addition, Abello et al. (2001) has advocated the idea of treating relationships between different aggregation levels as part-whole relationships to deal with semantic problems.

5.3.3   Research work on conceptual modeling

Much work on ER-based conceptual modeling for data warehousing has been carried out from the database community. For example, an extension to ER diagrams which allows modeling aggregation over different dimensions was proposed by Franconi and Sattler (1999), as indicated in their data warehouse conceptual data model (CDWDM). In addition, the models can be mapped to description logic expressions which enables reasoning on the conceptual level of warehouse design such as the detection of inconsistencies. Modeling data warehouses is a complex task focusing, very often, on internal structures and implementation issues. In Tryfona et al. (1999), based on a real mortgage business warehouse environment, a set of user modeling requirements is presented and the concepts involved are discussed. Understanding the semantics of these concepts, allows the building of a conceptual model — namely, the starER model — for efficient handling. The starER model combines the star structure, which is dominant in data warehouses, with the semantically rich constructs of the ER model; special types of relationships have been further added to support hierarchies. An evaluation of the starER model is presented as well as a comparison of the proposed model with other existing models, pointing out differences and similarities. Examples from a mortgage data warehouse environment in which starER is tested reveal the ease of understanding the model, as well as the efficiency in representing complex information at the semantic level.

Baekgaard (1999) used the event-entity-relationship model (EVER) to illustrate the use of entity-based modeling languages for conceptual schema design in data warehouse environments. EVER is a general purpose information modeling language that supports the specification of both general schema structures and multidimensional schemes that are customized to serve specific information needs. EVER is based on an event concept that is very well suited for multidimensional modeling because measurement data often represent events in multidimensional databases.

Boehnlein and Ende (1999) showed that the conceptual data models of underlying operational information systems can support construction of multidimensional structures. The special features of the structured entity relationship model (SERM) are not only useful for the development of big operational systems but can also help with the derivation of data warehouse structures. The SERM is an extension of the conventional entity relationship model (ERM) and the conceptual basis of the data modeling technique used by the SAP Corporation. To illustrate the usefulness of this approach, the derivation of the warehouse structures from the conceptual data model of a flight reservation system is explained.

5.4 Aspects of building data warehouses

Building data warehouses is a complex task. Many aspects other than conceptual modeling are involved. This section presents research work concerning various aspects at different stages of building data warehouses.

5.4.1 Physical design

During physical data warehouse design, the conceptual model is mapped to a specific implementation, such as MOLAP or ROLAP. This process requires decisions about physical optimization techniques, such as indexing schemes, physical clustering, precomputation strategies, and denormalization. Related issues will be further discussed in Chapters 6 and 7.

At the design level, a data warehouse is defined as a hierarchy of view expressions. One key problem of the design is selection of a set of views to materialize in order to meet performance requirements (minimizing both the query evaluation cost and the maintenance cost of the materialized views). Existing approaches either propose algorithms to explore the search space by enumerating and evaluating all the possible solutions, or introduce heuristics that restrict the search space. Bouzeghoub and Kedad (2000) proposed a framework to support the physical design of a data warehouse based on a logical model called the view synthesis graph. In this framework, a level of overlapping is defined to characterize the graph. This level allows to order the search space. The framework integrates some quality factors that can be used either to drive the exploration of the search space, or to reduce the search space, or both. Physical aspects of data warehouse management have also been discussed by Karayannidis and Sellis (2001), Pieringer et al. (2001), and Ciaccia et al. (2001).

5.4.2 Using functional dependencies

A methodology for automated selection of the most relevant independent attributes in a data warehouse, as presented by Last and Maimon (2000), is based on the information-theoretic approach to knowledge discovery in databases. Attributes are selected by a stepwise forward procedure aimed at minimizing the uncertainty in the value of key performance indicators (PKIs). The method selects features (attributes) by constructing information-theoretic connectionist networks, which represent interactions between the classifying features and each dependent attribute (which is a key performance indicator). The approach starts with an extended relational data model, on which the feature selection procedure can be conducted. Functional dependencies are then extracted from the network through association. Note that functional dependencies indicate a kind of determination while an association between X and Y refers to the probability distribution of Y when the values of X are given.

Functional dependencies should also play an important role in conceptual warehouse design (Husemann et al., 2000). Business-oriented practice in data warehousing and its applications demonstrated a radical departure from the principles of normalized schema design. In addition, the database research community has not been paying much attention to developing complete design methods for data warehouses in general or for conceptual design in particular, or to establishing guidelines for good schema design or integrity constraints within the context of multidimensional models. There is a discrepancy between traditional database design as applied to operational databases and the design principles applied to data warehouses.

In order to deal with this problem, Husemann et al. (2000) showed that a conceptual warehouse schema that is in a normal form called generalized multidimensional normal form can be systematically derived from the multidimensional data models.

5.4.3 Loading the warehouse

The loading processes running on a data warehouse rely on complex specifications of parallel and interacting streams of operations on the data extracted from the data sources. To make this process more effective, a declarative representation of the dependency between sources and warehouse has been proposed, which allows the generation of mediators for extraction and loading, rather than for the overall loading process. This conceptual representation of data sources and their interrelationship is termed correspondences. Whenever a new view is introduced in the warehouse, its specification is rewritten using the correspondences. The result is a mediator program which refers to the data sources and applies conversion, matching, and reconciliation routines on and among them.

One important aspect in the loading processes is refreshment. Although it is often considered a view maintenance problem or part of the loading process, it has been argued that the refreshment process is more complex than the view maintenance problem, and different from the loading process (Bouzeghoub et al., 1999). The loading phase is the initial computation of the data warehouse contents, and consists of four steps: preparation (including data extraction, cleaning, etc.), integration, aggregation, and customization. Refreshment differs from the loading process in several aspects, such as it may have a complete asynchronization between the activities mentioned in the four steps involved in loading or a high level parallelism within the preparation activity itself, etc. The propagation of changes during the refreshment process is carried out through a set of independent activities, including maintenance of materialized views. This process is similar to the materialized view maintenance problem except that, in data warehouses, the changes to propagate into the aggregated views are not exactly those occurring in the data sources, but the result of pretreatments performed by other refreshment activities, such as data cleaning and multisource data reconciliation.

5.4.4 Metadata management

As already discussed in Section 3.6, metadata are important to data warehousing because they maintain information about the data warehouse needed in installation and evolution, with an emphasis on the logical and physical aspects of the actual data stored. Orr (1996) introduced data warehouse architecture with eight layers, including a metadata layer. These layers represent the overall structure of data, communication, processing, and presentation that exists for end user computing within the enterprise. Kimball et al. (1998) proposed data warehouses with a "bus structure" based on conformed dimension and standard fact definitions. This is a practical, flexible architecture for data warehouse systems.

It would be interesting to ask questions about the relationship between metadata and actual data, such as: what kinds of metadata are needed and will more information handled by metadata benefit warehouse design and implementation? In order to get some insight about this issue, one should take a look at a concrete study (Quix, 1999) in which a process model used metadata to capture the dynamics of a data warehouse. The evolution of a data warehouse is represented as a special process and the evolution operators are linked to the corresponding architecture components and quality factors they affect. The idea used here is to provide complementary metadata which track the history of changes and provide a set of consistency rules to enforce when a quality factor has to be reevaluated. As an interesting example to illustrate the usefulness of the proposed process model, consider the following scenario. An analyst has detected that the views (V) he is using are changed often, and would like to be notified about future changes. A view in the metadata repository monitoring changes of V can be established for this purpose. Overall, the management of the metadata in the repository system called ConceptBase allows query and analysis of the stored metadata for errors and deficiencies. In addition, active rules can be used to keep warehouse users up to date on the status of the warehouse.

Recent work in data warehousing has paid increasing attention to object-relational data warehouses. It has been observed that, for developing the DW and OLAP systems, the dominant relational database reaches its limitations (Gopalkrishnan et al., 1999). In an object-relational data warehousing (ORDW) environment, the semantics of data and queries can be explicitly captured, represented, and utilized based on is-a and class composition hierarchies, resulting in more efficient OLAP query processing. A particular aspect of such an environment is metadata, which can play an important role and provide the foundation for all actions in all stages. Metadata can be considered the glue sticking together all individual parts of these systems. Data warehouse architecture and interoperability with an investigation of the role of metadata has been discussed by Binh et al. (2001).

5.4.5   Operation phase

At the run time, a data warehouse is operational to handle user queries. An important issue at this phase is run-time system optimization, including caching and scheduling optimization. Golfarelli and Rizzi (2000) consider query represented by nested GPSJ (generalized projection, selection, and join) expressions, in which a sequence of aggregate operators may be applied to measures and selection predicates may be formulated, at different granularities, on both dimensions and measures.

5.4.6   Using data warehouse tools

Various vendors have provided various kinds of tools for data warehousing. But can a data warehouse be effectively designed using a particular tool, such as Microsoft SQL server? A star schema can be designed together with data flow graphs specifying how data sources are fed into the warehouse, a process referred to as data pumping. The data transfer is either implemented by SQL queries or by user-defined programs. As a case study provided by Sorensen and Alnor (1999) showed, available tools could be sufficient and easy to use for designing the data warehouse and source integration.

5.4.7   User behavior modeling for warehouse design

The design of interactive multidimensional data analysis tools (mostly OLAP systems) can be considered part of the data warehouse design itself. Therefore, there is a need for modeling user query behavior. The benefits of the OLAP design, which is driven mainly by the user's analysis requirements, should not be overlooked (Sapia, 1999). In fact, integrating user behavior into system design is an important aspect of achieving intelligent data warehousing. The schema of the data model is static, but it is closely related to the dynamic aspect of the system concerning the query behavior of the user. Therefore, the design of the conceptual data warehouse schema should be driven by a model of the user query behavior. This integration will also eliminate users' difficulties in understanding the static schema necessary to answer their queries. Besides conceptual modeling, knowledge about anticipated user behavior is also a key input for subsequent physical data warehouse design so that reasonable workloads for certain design tasks, such as view selection problems (see Chapter 7), can be automatically generated. In addition, user and task profiles that contain information about typical query sequences can be used for run-time system optimization. Since the user is engaged in an interactive dialogue with the system, it is possible for the system to predict next steps of the user. This information can be used in an intelligent data warehousing environment for system optimization. Of particular interest is using prediction to speculatively execute possible next queries. If the user does ask a predicted query, the system answering time will be greatly reduced (Sapia, 1999).

The actual modeling technique for user behavior, as explained by Sapia (1999), is based on the observation that, although the contents of user queries against the multidimensional data will change, the structure of these queries is likely to remain the same. Therefore, a query prototype can be defined from this structure. Of great interest is modeling typical interaction patterns in query behavior. These patterns describe similarities between different sessions that are similar with respect to the intention or task the user had in mind when executing the session. In particular, two sessions have a common pattern if they contain similar queries. Therefore, one can first define the notion of similarity of queries, as well as the distance between two queries. The structure of individual sessions can then be modeled. The next issue is to define further user or task profiles, which can be captured by a graphical representation. An architecture for the prediction of user behavior has been proposed based on these notions. It is hoped that this architecture could be implemented on the top of a commercial OLAP system.

As can be seen in previous sections, use of auxiliary data must be investigated in the view selection problem. Auxiliary data can also be stored for efficient lineage trancing as well. Cui and Widom (2000) studied the problem of selecting auxiliary views to materialize in order to minimize the total view maintenance and lineage tracing cost, which are the two parts of performance in the lineage tracing problem. In order to get this done, first the search space for the optimization problem needs to be defined and the cost model developed. Algorithms can then be developed, which take the primary view definition and a set of statistics as the input, and produce a set of auxiliary views as output.

5.4.8   Coherent management of warehouses for security

As noted by Rosenthal and Sciore (2000), a key challenge for data warehouse security is how to manage the entire system coherently. Permissions on the warehouse must satisfy the restrictions of the data owners and be updated quickly as local concerns (such as sources and views) evolve. The notion of access permission on a table consists of two separately administered issues: information permission (which is concerned with who is allowed to access what information) and physical permission (which is concerned with who is allowed to access which physical tables). The former is the result of an enterprise-wide decision, while the latter is local, and physical permissions do not have to be consistent. For example, the decision that "employee salary information is releasable to payroll clerks and cost analysts" is an information permission, while the decision that "cost analysts are allowed to run queries on the warehouse" is a physical permission. Each kind of permission can be treated independently.

5.4.9   Prototyping data warehouses

Summarizing the overall process of data warehouse design, we can recognize that the process of developing and evolving complex data warehouse systems is intrinsically exploratory in nature. Data warehouse projects are notoriously difficult to manage and many of them end in failure. One explanation for the high failure rate is the lack of understanding of the requirements and missing proof-of-concepts for a decision support for the knowledge workers of an organization. Driven from these considerations, Huynh and Schiefer (2001) described a prototyping approach for data warehouse environments, with the hope that prototyping can support an incremental and iterative requirement development. Different types of prototypes and their applicability for data warehouse systems have been discussed, and a tool supporting a rapid development of prototypes by automatically generating the mass sample data for a data warehouse system was introduced.

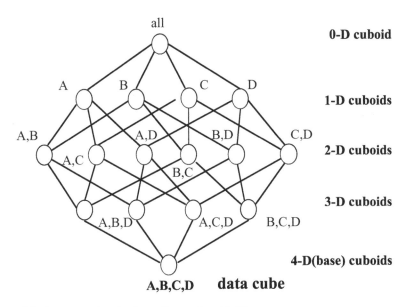

Figure 5.3 An example of a four-dimensional lattice.

5.5   Data cubes

Previous sections of this chapter have addressed a wide range of issues in data warehouse design. In addition to these general studies, conceptual modeling for multidimensional database design and OLAP has also been extensive studied (Tiso et al., 2001; Niemi et al., 2001). In order to have a better understanding of the design concerns for multidimensional modeling, below we take a closer look on data cubes.

Data cubes present materialized views involving multidimensional data. A data cube consists of a lattice of cuboids, each corresponding to a different degree of summary of the given multidimensional data. (Recall that a lattice is a partially ordered set in which every subset consisting of two elements has a least upper bound and a greatest lower bound.) Partial materialization refers to the selective computation of a subset of the cuboids in the lattice. Full materialization refers to the computation of all of the cuboids in the lattice. If the cubes are implemented using MOLAP, then multiway array aggregation can be used. A four-dimensional data cube is depicted in Figure 5.3.

We now use data cubes to examine OLAP operations. The two most well-known operations for OLAP queries are 1. roll-up which takes the current data object and does a further group-by on one of the dimensions. For example, given total sale by day, one can ask for total sale by month; and 2. drill-down which, as the converse of roll-up, tries to get more detailed presentation. For example, given total sale by model, one can ask for total sale by model by year. Other operations include: pivot (whose result is called a cross-tabulation), slice (which is an equality selection, reducing the dimensionality of data), and dice (which is the range selection).

In the following, the motivation behind the operation of pivot is illustrated. This example also illustrates the basic idea of the roll-up operator. Consider a relational database on auto sales. The database is assumed to be in 3NF. More specifically, consider a relation in this database with schema (model, year, color, dealer, and sales date). Now it is necessary to have data aggregated by model, then by year, and, finally, by color. Suppose the result is as shown in Table 5.2.

Table 5.2 Sales Roll Up

Model	Year	Color	Sales by model by year by color	Sales by model by year	Sales by model
Toyota	1998	black	130		
		light	120		
				250	
Toyota	1999	black	130		
		light	110		
				240	
					490

For a better summary, one can use the cross tabulation (namely, pivot) as shown in Table 5.3. The operation involved here is called the pivot. Note how the cross tabulation table can be obtained in a systematic way: when pivot is performed, the values that appear in columns of the original presentation (such as "black" and "light" for color, and "1998" and "1999" for year) now become labels of axes in the result presentation.

Table 5.3 Toyota Sales Cross Tabulation

Toyota	1998	1999	Total (ALL)
Black	130	130	260
Light	120	110	230
Total (ALL)	250	240	490

The cross tabulation in this example is a 2D (two dimensional) aggregation. But this is just a special case. For example, if other automobile models (such as Dodge, Ford, etc.) are added, it becomes a 3D aggregation. Generally speaking, the traditional GROUP BY clause in SQL can be used to generate the core of the N-dimensional data cube. The N-1 lower-dimensional aggregates appear as points, lines, plains, cubes, or hyper-cubes in the original data cube.

5.6 Summary

This chapter described conceptual modeling and other important design aspects for data warehouse construction. Both dimension modeling and ER-based approaches were presented. In particular, ER-based approaches were described in some detail, because even the business community has different opinions on ER modeling. In the author's view, ER-based approaches are still appealing to many database researchers and practitioners, not only because ER modeling has been well accepted in long time practices of the database community, but also because ER models can readily lend themselves to dimension modeling. Other aspects in various stages of data warehouse construction were also discussed. Additional information or design and management of data warehouses can be found in Jensfeld and Stendt (2001).

References

Abello, A., J. Samos, and F. Saltor, Understanding analysis dimensions in a multidimensional object-oriented model, *Proc. Int. Workshop Design Manage. Data Warehouse (DMDW 2001).*

Baekgaard, L., Event-entity-relationship modeling in data warehouse environments, *Proc. ACM Second Int'l. Workshop on Data Warehousing and OLAP (DOLAP),* 9–14, 1999.

Berry, M. J. A. and G. Linoff, *Data Mining Techniques: For Marketing, Sales, and Customer Support,* John Wiley & Sons, New York, 1997.

Binh, N. T., A. M. Tjoa, and O. Mangisengi, Meta Cube-X: An XML metadata foundation for interoperability search among Web data warehouses, *Proc. Int. Workshop Design Manage. Data Warehouse (DMDW 2001),* 8.1–8.8.

Boehnlein, M. and A. U. Ende, Deriving initial data warehouse structures from the conceptual data models of the underlying operational information systems, *Proc. ACM Second Intl. Workshop on Data Warehousing and OLAP,* 15–21, 1999.

Bouzeghoub, M., F. Fabret, and M. Matulovic-Broque, Modeling data warehouse refreshment process as a workflow application, *Proc. Int. Workshop Design Manage. Data Warehouse (DMDW 1999),* 6.1–6.12.

Bouzeghoub, M. and Z. Kedad, A quality-based framework for physical data warehouse design, *Proc. Int. Workshop Design Manage. Data Warehouse (DMDW 2000).*

Calero, C., M. Piattini, and C. Pascual, Towards data warehouse quality metrics, *Proc. Int. Workshop Design Manage. Data Warehouse (DMDW 2001).*

Calvanese, D., G. De Giacomo, M. Lenzerini, D. Nardi, and R. Rosati, A principled approach to data integration and reconciliation in data warehousing, *Proc. Int. Workshop Design Manage. Data Warehouse (DMDW 1999).*

Ciaccia, P., M. Golfarelli, and S. Rizzi, On estimating the cardinality of aggregate views, *Proc. Int. Workshop Design Manage. Data Warehouse (DMDW 2001).*

Cui, Y. and J. Widom, Storing auxiliary data for efficient maintenance and lineage tracing of complex views, *Proc. Int. Workshop Design Manage. Data Warehouse (DMDW 2000).*

Franconi, E. and U. Sattler, A data warehouse conceptual data model for multidimensional aggregation, *Proc. DMDW 1999 (online),* 13.1–13.10, 1999.

Galhardas, H., D. Florescu, D. Shasha, E. Simon, and C. Saita, Improving data cleaning quality using a data lineage facility, *Proc. Int. Workshop Design Manage. Data Warehouse (DMDW 2001)*, 3.1–3.13.

Gallas, S., Kimball vs. Inmon, *DM Direct*, September, 1999.

Gatziu, S., M. Jeusfeld, M. Staudt, and Y. Vassilious, Design and management of data warehouses, Report on the DMDW '99 Workshop, *SIGMOD Record*, 28(4), 7–10, 1999.

Golfarelli, M. and S. Rizzi, View materialization for nested GPSJ queries, *Proc. Int. Workshop Design Manage. Data Warehouse (DMDW 2000)*, 10.1–10.8.

Gopalkrishnan, V., Q. Li, and K. Karlapalen, Star/snow-flake schema driven object-relational data warehouse design and query processing strategies, *Proc. 1st Int. Data Warehousing Knowl. Discover. Conf. (DaWak '99)*.

Husemann, B., J. Lechtenborger, and G. Vossen, Conceptual data warehouse design, *Proc. Int. Workshop Design Manage. Data Warehouse (DMDW 2000)*, 6.1.

Huyn, T. N., O. Mangisengi, and A. M. Tjoa, Metadata for object-relational data warehouse, *Proc. Int. Workshop Design Manage. Data Warehouse (DMDW 2000)*.

Inmon, W. H., *Building the Data Warehouse*, John Wiley & Sons, New York, 1996.

Jeusfeld, M. A. and M. Staudt (Eds.), Special issue on design and management of data warehouses, *Int'l. J. Cooperative Info. Syst.*, 10(3), 2001.

Karayannidis, N. and T. Sellis, SISYPHUS: a chunk-based storage manager for OLAP cubes, *Proc. Int. Workshop Design Manage. Data Warehouse (DMDW 2001)*, 10.1–10.12.

Kimbal, R., There are no guarantees, *Intell. Enterp.*, 3(12), 28–30; 45, 2000.

Kimball, R., Clicking with your customer, *Intell. Enterp.*, 2(1), 1999.

Kimball, R., L. Reeves, M. Ross, and W. Thornthwaite, *The Data Warehouse Lifecycle Toolkit*, John Wiley & Sons, New York, 1998.

Last, M. and O. Maimon, Automated dimensionality reduction of data warehouses, *Proc. Int. Workshop Design Manage. Data Warehouse (DMDW 2000)*, 7.1–7.10.

Masand, B. and M. Spiliopoulou, WEBKDD'99: Workshop on Web usage analysis and user profiling, *SIGKDD Explorations*, 1(2), 108–111, 2000.

Moody, D. L. and M. A. R. Kortink, From enterprise models to dimensional models: a methodology for data warehouse and data mart design, *Proc. Int. Workshop Design Manage. Data Warehouse (DMDW 2000)*, 5.1–5.12.

Niemi, T., J. Nummenmaa, and P. Thanisch, Logical multidimensional database design for ragged and unbalanced aggregation, *Proc. Int. Workshop Design Manage. Data Warehouse (DMDW 2001)*, 7.1–7.8.

Orr, K., Data warehousing technology (white paper), The Ken Orr Institute, 1996.

Parsaye, K., Surveying decision support: new realms of analysis? *Database Programming Design*, April, 1996, 26–33.

Pieringer, R., V. Markl, F. Ramsak, and R. Bayer, HINTA: a linearization algorithm for physical clustering of complex OLAP hierarchies, *Proc. Int. Workshop Design Manage. Data Warehouse (DMDW 2001)*, 11.1–11.11.

Quix, C., Repository support for data warehouse evolution, *Proc. Int. Workshop Design Manage. Data Warehouse (DMDW 1999)*, 4.1–4.9.

Rosenthal, A. and E. Sciore, View security as the basis for data warehouse security, *Proc. Int. Workshop Design Manage. Data Warehouse (DMDW 2000)*, 8.1–8.8.

Sapia, C., On modeling and predicting query behavior in OLAP systems, *Proc. DMDW 1999 (online)*, 2.1–2.10, 10, 1999.

Sarawagi, S., R. Agrawal, and N. Megiddo, Discovery-driven exploration of OLAP data cubes. *Proc. Int. Conf. Extending Database Technol.*, 168–182, 1998.

Singh, H., *Interactive Data Warehousing*, Prentice Hall, Upper Saddle River, NJ, 1999.

Song, I. Y., B. Rowan, C. Medsker, and E. Ewen, An analysis of many-to-many relationships between fact and dimension tables in dimensional modeling. *Proc. Int. Workshop Design Manage. Data Warehouse (DMDW 2001)*.

Sorensen, J. O. and K. Alnor, Creating a data warehouse using SQL server, *Proc. Int. Workshop Design Manage. Data Warehouse (DMDW 1999)*.

Srivastava, J., R. Cooley, M. Deshpande, and P.-N. Tan, Web usage mining: discovery and applications of usage patterns from Web data, *SIGKDD Explorations*, 1(2), 12–23, 2000.

Stohr, T., R. Muller, and E. Rahm, An integrative and uniform model for metadata management in data warehousing environments, *Proc. Int. Workshop Design Manage. Data Warehouse (DMDW 1999)*.

Tryfona, N. F., B. Busborg, and J. G. B. Christiansen, Star ER: a conceptual model for data warehouse design, *Proc. ACM Second Intl. Workshop on Data Warehousing and OLAP (DOLAP)*, 3–8, 1999.

Tsois, A., N. Karayiannidis, and T. Sellis, MAC: conceptual data modeling for OLAP, *Proc. Int. Workshop Design Manage. Data Warehouse (DMDW 2001)*.

Vassiliadis, P., Gulliver in the land of data warehousing: practical experiences and observations of a researcher, *Proc. Int. Workshop Design Manage. Data Warehouse (DMDW 2000)*.

chapter six

Basics of materialized views

6.1 Overview

From a computer science perspective, a data warehouse is a collection of materialized views (MVs) derived from base (i.e., source) relations that may not reside at the warehouse. Therefore, a data warehouse is considered as a definer and storage of views. This chapter examines this perspective using simple examples. Note that view management from traditional databases may not be applied in a data warehousing environment, because there may not be enough information available in a data warehouse on changes related to the source data (as in the case of conventional databases).

In order to examine the perspective of data warehousing as materialized views, it is necessary to start with a brief review. There are two approaches toward providing integrated access to multiple, distributed, heterogeneous databases: 1. lazy or on-demand approach to data integration, which often uses virtual view(s) techniques; and 2. the data warehousing approach, where the repository serves as a warehouse storing the data of interest. This approach uses materialized views.

According to the perspective of materialized views, at the most abstract level the contents of the data warehouse are regarded as a set of materialized views defined over the data sources. These materialized views are designed based on the users' requirements (e.g., frequently asked queries). The topic of data warehousing encompasses architectures, algorithms, and tools for bringing together large quantities (up to several terabytes) of selected data from distributed, autonomous, and possibly heterogeneous data sources into a single separate repository, called a data warehouse, suitable for direct querying or complex data analysis and decision support activities. The source data for a data warehouse are often the operational databases used for on-line transaction processing, but may also be nontraditional sources such as flat files, news wires, legacy systems, and structured documents. The warehouse approach presents some advantages over the traditional (which can be considered as on-demand or lazy) approach to the integration of multiple sources because queries can be answered without accessing the original information sources; therefore, it facilitates OLAP operations (which are now decoupled from OLTP). OLAP and DSS applications make heavy use of complex grouping or aggregation queries. These data intensive queries require sequential scans. In order to ensure high query performance, the queries are evaluated in a centralized (at least logically) data warehouse using exclusive materialized views, without accessing the original base relations (Theodoratos and Sellis, 1999).

As already mentioned in Chapter 3, a view is a derived relation defined in terms of base (stored) relations. A view can be materialized by storing the tuples of the view in the database. A materialized view provides fast access to data; the speed difference is critical in applications where the query rate is high and the views complex or over data in remote databases, so that it is not feasible to recompute the view for every query (Gupta and Mumick, 1996).

The "kernel" of a data warehouse is the multidimensional database. Many important data warehousing tuning aspects are related to this kernel, including special methods for optimization concerning cache management and indexing. It has already been shown that the warehouse cache can contain precomputed data specified at design time as materialized views. In addition, a warehouse can also contain precomputed data based on actual data warehouse usage (Gatziu et al., 2000).

The balance of this chapter presents several basic ideas related to materialized views, with an emphasis on data cubes, as well as selection of views to materialize. A case study is also presented.

6.2   Data cubes

6.2.1   Materialization of data cubes

A data cube allows data to be modeled and viewed in multiple dimensions. It is defined by dimensions and facts (already discussed). The interesting property of cubes is that the n-D data can be represented as a series of (n–1)-D cubes. The data cube is a metaphor for multidimensional data storage. The actual physical storage of such data may differ from their logical representation. The important thing to remember is that data cubes are n-dimensional and do not confirm data to 3-D.

Decision support applications involve complex queries on very large databases. Since response times should be small, query optimization is critical. Users typically view the data as multidimensional data cubes. Each cell of the data cube is a view consisting of an aggregation of interest, like total sales. The values of many of these cells are dependent on the values of other cells in the data cube. A common and powerful query optimization technique is to materialize some or all of these cells rather than compute them from raw data each time. Commercial systems differ mainly in their approach to materializing the data cube. In this and the next section, continuing the discussion on data cubes started in Chapter 5 and following the presentations of Chaudhuri and Shim (1994), Harinarayan et al. (1996), Fiege (1996), and Gupta (1997), the issue of which cells (views) to materialize when it is too expensive to materialize all views is further examined. A lattice (as discussed in Chapter 5) is used to express dependencies among views.

While operational databases maintain state information, data warehouses typically maintain historical information. As a result, data warehouses tend to be very large and to grow over time. In addition, decision-support queries are much more complex than OLTP queries and make heavy use of aggregations. The size of the data warehouse and the complexity of queries can cause queries to take very long to complete. This delay is unacceptable in most DSS environments, as it severely limits productivity.

A commonly used technique for performance improvement is to materialize (precompute) frequently asked queries. The data warehouse at a typical department store chain could have over 1000 precomputed tables to improve query performance. Selecting the right set of queries to materialize is a nontrivial task, since by materializing a query people may be able to answer other queries quickly. For example, one may want to materialize a query that is relatively infrequently asked if it helps answer many other queries quickly.

There are two basic implementation approaches that facilitate OLAP. The first approach is to eschew SQL and relational databases and to use proprietary multidimensional database (MDDB) systems and APIs for OLAP. So while the raw data are in relational data warehouses, the data cube is materialized in an MDDB. Users query the data cube, and the MDDB efficiently retrieves the value of a cell given its address. To allocate only space for those cells present in the raw data and not every possible cell of the data cube, a cell-address hashing scheme is used. Note, this approach still materializes all the cells of the data cube present in raw data, which can be very large. Another approach is to use relational database systems and let users directly query the raw data. The issue of query performance is attacked using smart indices and other conventional relational query optimization strategies. However, MDDBs retain a significant performance advantage. Performance in relational database systems, though, can be improved dramatically by materializing parts of the data cube into summary tables.

The relational approach is very scalable and can handle very large data warehouses. MDDBs, on the other hand, have much better query performance, but are not very scalable. By materializing only selected parts of the data cube, one can improve performance in the relational database, and improve scalability in MDDBs. There are products in both the relational world and the MDDB world that materialize only parts of the data cube.

Users of data warehouses work in a graphical environment and data are usually presented to them as a multidimensional data cube whose 2-D, 3-D, or even higher-dimensional subcubes they explore trying to discover interesting information. The values in each cell of this data cube are some measures of interest. As an example, consider the TPC-D decision-support benchmark (Raab, 1995).

Example 1:

The TPC-D benchmark models a business warehouse. Parts are bought from suppliers and then sold to customers at a sale price SP. The database has information about each such transaction over a period of 6 years. There are three dimensions people are interested in: parts, suppliers, and customers. The measure of interest is the total sales: sales. So for each cell (p, s, c) in this 3-D data cube, people store the sales of part p that was bought from supplier s, and sold to customer c. In the general case, a given dimension may have many attributes. Users are also interested in consolidated sales: for example, what are the total sales of a given part p to a given customer c? In this question users want the total sales of a given part p to a given customer c for ALL suppliers. The query is answered by looking up the value in cell (p, ALL, c).

The presentation of the data set as a multidimensional data cube to the user has been discussed above. The following implementation alternatives are possible:

1. Physically materialize the whole data cube. This approach gives the best query response time. However, precomputing and storing every cell is not a feasible alternative for large data cubes, as the space consumed becomes excessive. It should be noted that the space consumed by the data cube is also a good indicator of the time it takes to create the data cube, which is important in many applications. The space consumed also affects indexing and so adds to the overall cost.

2. Materialize nothing. In this case one needs to go to the raw data and compute every cell on request. This approach punts the problem of quick query response to the database system where the raw data are stored. No extra space beyond that for the raw data is required.

3. Materialize only part of the data cube. This approach will be described below. In a data cube, the values of many cells are computable from those of other cells in the data cube. This dependency is similar to a spreadsheet where the value of cells can be expressed as a function of the values of other cells. Such cells are called "dependent" cells. For instance, in Example 1, one can compute the value of cell (p, ALL, c) as the sum of the values of cells of (p, s_1, c), ..., $(p, s_{Nsupplier}, c)$, where $N_{supplier}$ is the number of suppliers. The more cells one materializes, the better query performance is. For large data cubes, however, one may be able to materialize only a small fraction of the cells of the data cube, due to space and other constraints. It is thus important to pick the right cells to materialize.

Any cell that has an ALL value as one of the components of its address is a dependent cell. The value of this cell is computable from those of other cells in the data cube. If a cell has no ALLs in its components, its value cannot be computed from those of other cells, and one must query the raw data to compute its value. The number of cells with ALL as one of their components is usually a large fraction of the total number of cells in the data cube. The problem of which dependent cells to materialize is a very real one. For example, in the TPC-D database (Example 1), 70% of all cells in the data cube are dependent.

The cells of the data cube are organized into different sets based on the positions of ALL in their addresses. Thus, for example, all cells whose addresses match the address (-, ALL, -) are placed in the same set. Here, "-" is a placeholder that matches any value but ALL. Each of these sets corresponds to a cell's different SQL query. The values in the set of (-, ALL, -) are output by the SQL query (R refers to the raw-data relation):

> SELECT Part, Customer, SUM(SP) AS Sales
> FROM R
> GROUP BY Part, Customer

The queries corresponding to the different sets of cells differ only in the GROUP-BY clause. In general, attributes with ALL values in the description of the set of cells do not appear in the GROUP-BY clause of the SQL query above. For example, supplier has an ALL value in the set description (-, ALL, -). Hence it does not appear in the GROUP-BY clause of the SQL query. Since the SQL queries of the various sets of cells differ only in the grouping attributes, one can use the grouping attributes to identify queries uniquely. Deciding which sets of cells to materialize is equivalent to deciding which of the corresponding SQL queries (views) to materialize.

6.2.2   Using the lattice

6.2.2.1   Hierarchies in lattice

Consider two queries, Q_1 and Q_2. $Q_1 \subset Q_2$ can be defined if Q_1 can be answered using only the results of Q_2. It is then said that Q_1 is dependent on Q_2. For example, in TPC-D benchmark, the query (part) can be answered using only the results of the query (part, customer). Thus, there is (part) $\subset$ (part, customer). There are certain queries that are not comparable with each other using the $\subset$ operator. For example: (part) $\not\subset$ (customer) and (customer) $\not\subset$ (part).

The $\subset$ operator imposes a partial ordering on the queries. This is related to the views of a data cube problem forming a lattice. In order to be a lattice, any two elements (views or queries) must have a least upper bound and a greatest lower bound according to the $\subset$ ordering. However, in practice, one only needs the assumptions that $\subset$ is a partial order and that there is a top element, a view upon which every view is dependent.

In most real-life applications, dimensions of a data cube consist of more than one attribute, and the dimensions are organized as hierarchies of these attributes. A simple example is that of organizing the time dimension into the hierarchy: day, month, and year. Hierarchies are very important, as they underlie two very commonly used querying operations: drill-down and

Figure 6.1 Hierarchy of time attributes.

roll-up. Drill-down is the process of viewing data at progressively more detailed levels. For example, a user drills down by first looking at the total sales per year and then total sales per month, and, finally, sales on a given day. Roll-up is just the opposite: it is the process of viewing data in progressively less detail. In roll-up, a user starts with total sales on a given day, then looks at the total sales in that month, and, finally, the total sales in that year.

In the presence of hierarchies, the dependency lattice is more complex than a hypercube lattice. For example, consider a query that groups on the time dimension and no other. If one wants to use the time hierarchy given earlier, the following three queries are possible: (day), (month), (year) — each of which groups at a different granularity of the time dimension. Further, (year) $\subset$ (month) $\subset$ (day). In other words, if one has total sales grouped by month, for example, the results can be used to compute the total sales grouped by year. Hierarchies introduce query dependencies that one must account for when determining what queries to materialize.

Note that hierarchies often are not total orders but partial orders on the attributes that make up a dimension. Consider the time dimension with the hierarchy day, week, month, and year. Since months and years cannot be divided evenly into weeks, if the grouping is not done by week, one cannot determine the grouping by month or year. In other words: (month) $\not\subset$ (week), (week) $\not\subset$ (month), and similarly for week and year. When one includes the "none" view corresponding to no time grouping at all, the lattice for the time dimension shown in the diagram of Figure 6.1 is obtained.

6.2.2.2 Composite lattices for multiple, hierarchical dimensions

There are query dependencies of two types: those caused by the interaction of different dimensions with one another, and those within a dimension caused by attribute hierarchies.

If one is allowed to create views that independently group by any or no member of the hierarchy for each of n dimensions, then each view can be represented by an n-tuple $(a_1, a_2, \ldots, a_n)$, where each a_i is a point in the

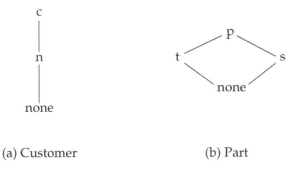

(a) Customer   (b) Part

Figure 6.2 Hierarchies for the customer and part dimensions.

hierarchy for the ith dimension. This lattice is called the direct product of the dimensional lattices. A $\subset$ operator is directly obtained for these views by the rule: $(a_1, a_2, \ldots, a_n) \subset (b_1, b_2, \ldots, b_n)$ if and only if $a_i \subset b_i$ for all i.

Example 2:
    In Example 1, the TPC-D benchmark database was mentioned. In order to illustrate the direct-product lattice in the presence of hierarchies we now take a look at two dimensions: part and customer. Each of these dimensions is organized into hierarchies. The dimensional lattices for the dimension queries are given in Figure 6.2. These dimension lattices have already been modified to include the attribute (none) as the lowest element.
    The customer dimension is organized into the following hierarchy. One can group by individual customers c, or customers can also be grouped more coarsely, based on their nation n. The coarsest level of grouping is none at all — none. For the part dimension, individual parts p may be grouped based on their size s or based on their type t. Note that neither s nor t is $\subset$ the other. The direct-product lattice is shown in Figure 6.3.

6.2.2.3   The cost analysis
To see the effect of the materialized view we now provide an analysis, assuming that the cost of answering a query is equal to the rows scanned by the view from which the query is answered.
    To answer a query Q, choose an ancestor of Q, e.g., Q_A, which has been materialized. One thus needs to process the table corresponding to Q_A to answer Q. The cost of answering Q is a function of the size of the table for Q_A. For illustration purposes, the simplest cost-model is used: the cost of answering Q is the number of rows present in the table for that query Q_A used to construct Q.
    As in the TPC-D benchmark example, not all queries ask for an entire view, such as a request for the sales of all parts. It is at least as likely that the user would like to see sales for a particular part or for a few parts. If there is an appropriate index structure, and the view (part) is materialized, then the answer can be obtained in O(1) time. If there is not an appropriate

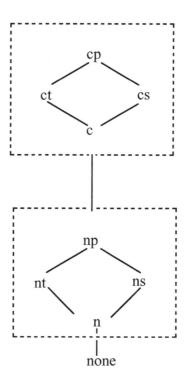

Figure 6.3 Combining two hierarchical dimensions.

index structure, then one must search the entire (part) view; the query for a single part takes almost as long as producing the entire view.

If, for example, one wants to answer a query about a single part from some ancestor view such as (part, supplier), that entire view needs to be examined. It would cost more because the table of (part, supplier) view contains more rows than that of (part) view in most cases. On the other hand, if one wishes to find the sales for each part from the ancestor view (part, supplier), one needs to do an aggregation over this view. Either hashing or sorting (with early aggregation) can be used to do this aggregation. The cost is a function of the amount of memory available and the ratio of the number of rows in the input to that in the output. In the best case, a single pass of the input is sufficient (for example, when the hash table fits in main memory). In practice, it has been observed that most aggregations take either one or two passes of the input data.

While the actual cost of queries that ask for single cells, or small numbers of cells, rather than a complete view is thus complex, it is appropriate to make an assumption of uniformity. Assume that all queries are identical to some element (view) in the given lattice. If the view for answering the specific query has been materialized, the answer can be obtained in constant time. If the direct ancestor view for answering a query has been materialized, one can get the answer efficiently; but if it is necessary to use the indirect ancestor view or raw data to answer a query, it would be costly because a large number of rows must be scanned, and some aggregation must be calculated.

6.3 Using a simple optimization algorithm to select views

The most important objective is to develop techniques for optimizing the space-time tradeoff when implementing a lattice of views. The problem can be approached from many angles, since one may, in one situation, favor time, in another, space, and in a third, be willing to trade time for space as long as one gets good "value" for what is traded away. Here we make use of two assumptions: there is a need to minimize the average time taken to evaluate the set of queries identical to the views; and there is a constraint to materialize a fixed number of views, regardless of the space they use (Kong, 2001).

Even in this simple setting, the problem is NP-complete: there is a straightforward reduction from set-cover. Thus, one is looking for heuristics to produce approximate solutions. The obvious choice is to use a heuristic algorithm, where one selects a set of views that have more children than others. This approach is relatively simple and, in some cases, can be shown to produce optimal selection of views to materialize.

One can then use a simple optimization algorithm for a selecting a set k views to materialize. The set of views materialized should always include the top view, because no other view can be used to answer the query corresponding to that view. Thus, in addition to the top view, one must select (k–1) views to materialize. The algorithm is shown here:

S = {top view};
For I=1 to (k–1) do begin
       Select that view v not in S such that v has the most
       children among the rest candidate views;
       S = S union {v};
End;
Resulting S is the optimal selection.

Example 3:
Consider a set of views (which are elements of a lattice structure) shown in Figure 6.4. There are 37 views, labeled 1 through 37. Suppose one wants to choose four views to materialize.

The topmost view must be chosen because no other view can be used to answer the query corresponding to that view. To execute the optimal algorithm, one can obtain the rest of the three views. Table 6.1 indicates that each of these four views has more children than others. Figure 6.5 shows four selected materialized views in this lattice. The reason why the view with more children has the priority to be chosen is that the more children it

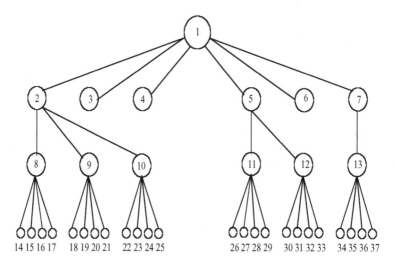

Figure 6.4 Hierarchy in a lattice.

Table 6.1 Number of Children of Each View

View	Number of Children	View	Number of Children
1	36	20	0
2	15	21	0
3	0	22	0
4	0	23	0
5	10	24	0
6	0	25	0
7	5	26	0
8	4	27	0
9	4	28	0
10	4	29	0
11	4	30	0
12	4	31	0
13	4	32	0
14	0	33	0
15	0	34	0
16	0	35	0
17	0	36	0
18	0	37	0
19	0		

has, the more chance that it can be involved in the various queries, and that it is relatively popular and frequent. Therefore, the algorithm can provide the optimal solution in selecting the view to materialize.

This section has explored the problem of deciding which set of cells (views) in the data cube to materialize in order to minimize query response times. Materialization of views is an essential query optimization strategy for decision-support applications. The case shows that the correct selection

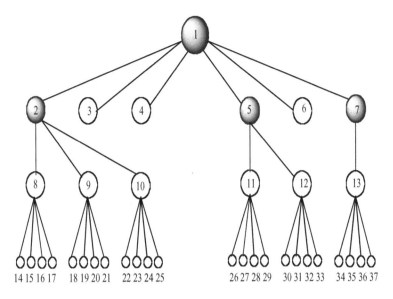

Figure 6.5 Example lattice with selected materialized views.

of views to materialize is critical to the success of this strategy. The TPC-D benchmark database was used as an example database in showing why it is important to materialize some part of the data cube, but not all of the cube. The algorithm works on the lattice and picks the right views to materialize, but may be subject to various constraints.

6.4   Aggregate calculation using preconstructed data structures in data cubes

In order to demonstrate how to use materialized views for calculating aggregation, let us examine a new approach for aggregate calculations using preconstructed data structures called PRE_SUM cube and PRE_MAX tree (Chen, 2000). Examples are used to illustrate the proposed approach.

In the multidimensional model of data warehousing, there are sets of measures and dimensions. Since aggregate is the most frequently used operation in this model, one expects an efficient approach for calculating aggregate in data cube. Below is a new approach for aggregate calculation is introduced using preconstructed data structures in data cube. This begins with preliminaries of aggregation functions, and then some operators are discussed, with emphasis on how to construct necessary data structures for further processing.

6.4.1   Preliminaries of aggregation functions

Basic formulas for calculating some basic aggregate operations in data cube are now introduced. Suppose there is a data cube C and there are n dimensions D_1, D_2, ... D_n. Without loss of generality, suppose there is one measure to be aggregated called M. M is represented by $m[d_1, d_2, ..., d_n]$, $d_1 \in D_1$, $d_2 \in D_2 ... d_n \in D_n$.

1. SUM of the measure value $m \in M$ in data cube C.

$$SUM(C) = \sum_{d_n \in D_n} \cdots \sum_{d_2 \in D_2} \sum_{d_1 \in D_1} m(d_1, d_2, ... d_n)$$

2. COUNT of measure value $m \in M$ in data cube C.

$$COUNT(C) = \sum_{d_n \in D_n} \cdots \sum_{d_2 \in D_2} \sum_{d_1 \in D_1} 1$$

3. AVG of the measure value $m \in M$ in data cube C.

$$AVG(C) = SUM(C)/COUNT(C)$$

4. MAX measure value $m \in M$ in data cube C.

$$MAX(C) = MAX(\{m[d_1, d_2, ... d_n] | d_1 \in D_1, d_2 \in D_2, ... d_n \in D_n\})$$

5. MIN measure value $m \in M$ in data cube C.

$$MIN(C) = MIN(\{m[d_1, d_2, ... d_n] | d_1 \in D_1, d_2 \in D_2, ... d_n \in D_n\})$$

Based on the definitions shown here, apparently AVG can be computed with SUM and COUNT, and MAX operation can be handled in a way similar to MIN. Therefore, this discussion will focus on SUM and MAX. In addition, since COUNT can be considered as a special case of SUM, a brief remark on COUNT operation is also provided.

6.4.2 Aggregation operations defined on data cubes

6.4.2.1 Calculating SUM on data cube using PRE_SUM cube

In order to see the motivation clearly, consider a simple example of a data cube in one dimension. As shown in Table 6.2, the measure of sum in cube C is precomputed, and the result stored as PRE_SUM cube.

Table 6.2 Precomputation for Measurement of a Sum

Dimension ID	1	2	3	4	5	6	7	8	9	10	...
Measure M (value)	5	2	9	7	6	3	1	9	11	17	...
PRE_SUM (for Measure M)	5	7	16	23	29	32	33	42	53	70	...

The PRE_SUM cube can be used in a number of ways. For example, to calculate the sum of measure M "dimension id" from 1 to 4, simply retrieve the value from PRE_SUM cube, and get pre_sum[4] = 23. On the other hand, if one wants to compute the sum of measure M "dimension id" from 2 and 8, simply use pre_sum [8] − pre_sum [2] = 42 − 7 = 35, where pre_sum is the cell in PRE_SUM cube.

More generally, the following formula calculates PRE_SUM cube:

$$pre\_sum[d_1, d_2, \ldots, d_n] = m[d_1, d_2, \ldots, d_n] +$$

$$\sum_{s=1}^{n} \sum_{\substack{i_1, i_2, i_n = 0 \\ i_1 + i_2 + \ldots i_n = s}}^{1} (-1)^{s+1} pre\_sum[d_1 - i_1, d_2 - i_2, \ldots, d_n - i_n]$$

For example, in 3-D cube C, cell pre_sum[d1,d2,...,dn] is calculated by:

$$pre\_sum[d_1, d_2, d_3]$$

$$= m[d_1, d_2, d_3]$$

$$+ pre\_sum[d_1 - 1, d_2, d_3] + pre\_sum[d_1, d_2 - 1, d_3]$$

$$+ pre\_sum[d_1, d_2, d_3 - 1]$$

$$- (pre\_sum[d_1 - 1, d_2 - 1, d_3] + pre\_sum[d_1 - 1, d_2, d_3 - 1]$$

$$+ pre\_sum[d_1, d_2 - 1, d_3 - 1])$$

$$+ pre\_sum[d_1 - 1, d_2 - 1, d_3 - 1]$$

It is not difficult to prove that the time complexity of construct PRE_SUM cube is $O(n^2)$. The formula to calculate SUM using PRE_SUM cube is very similar to that to calculate pre_sum cell. More detail is given in Chen (1999). The time complexity of SUM using PRE_SUM cube is $O(1)$.

6.4.2.2   Calculating COUNT

COUNT can be considered a special case of SUM. In this case, set the measure value for each cell in C to be 1 and construct PRE_SUM cube for such an aggregate function. Note that special considerations should be given in dealing with distinct COUNT.

Table 6.3 Precomputing for *MAX*

Dimension ID	1	2	3	4	5	6	7	8	9	10	11	...
Value	160	90	30	110	90	50	70	120	40	45	190	...

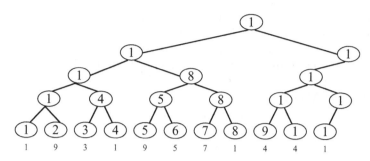

Figure 6.6 A PRE_MAX tree.

6.4.2.3   Calculating MAX by constructing PRE-MAX tree

A simple one-dimensional cube example (Table 6.3) is used to illustrate the basic idea of constructing a PRE-MAX tree to calculate MAX. For the data in Table 6.2, the PRE_MAX tree is shown in Figure 6.6.

The algorithm to compute MAX is

1. Find the common parent of all selected cells, mark (+) the path, and insert common parent to a set N.
2. In the set N, select node d that has the largest value in N.
   If d is marked, go to step 4.
   If d is a leaf node, go to step 4.
   Else delete d from set N. Input its left child as d_0 and right child d_1 to step 3.
3. If d_0 is not in the selected cells, insert d_1 into set N, go to step 2.
   If d_1 is not in the selected cells, insert d_0 into set N, go to step 2.
   Insert d_0 and d_1 into set N, go to step 2.
4. d is largest value. End.

The process to find the largest element between elements 3 to 10 is shown in Figure 6.7, from steps (a) to (h).

This section has briefly summarized a new approach for aggregate operations based on construction of data structures such as PRE_SUM cube and PRE_MAX tree. This approach has incorporated technical considerations discussed by other authors (Ho, 1997; Yvan et al., 1998).

6.5   Case study: view selection for a human service data warehouse

Data warehouses are the queryable source of information in an enterprise. They store information from multiple sources in a manner that optimizes query access to support data analysis. Materialized views are used in data warehouses to improve query performance. The view selection problem is to select which views to materialize in order to minimize query response time, given a maintenance cost constraint that must be met, such as storage

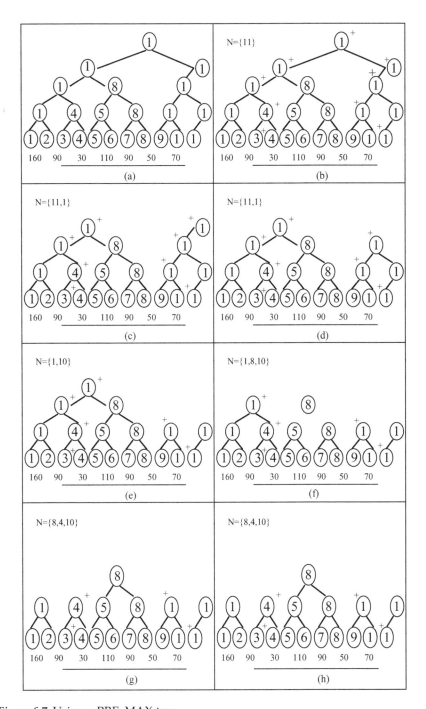

Figure 6.7 Using a PRE_MAX tree.

space limitations or the length of the warehouse refresh window. Below a view selection application is described (Engebretson, 2000) where a genetic algorithm is used to solve the view selection problem for a human services data warehouse. The case study is restricted to finding optimal solutions based on a single OR view graph. Actual query times and view maintenance costs were collected using the data warehouse to support this analysis. The GA implementation found the optimal set of views to materialize for the OR view graph considered.

6.5.1   Overview of the case study

One technique used to improve query performance within a data warehouse is materialized views, which are database tables that contain the results of queries. Using these views to satisfy queries can greatly improve query response time; however, there are maintenance costs associated with materialized views. When the data in the warehouse are updated or refreshed, materialized views must also be refreshed. Incremental updates to materialized views are typically more efficient than regeneration of the entire view. Another maintenance cost associated with materialized views is the storage space each view requires.

Materializing a large number of views will provide a greater query benefit, but will also result in larger maintenance costs. In some cases, these maintenance costs have a fixed ceiling such as a limit on the time the warehouse is unavailable to users while views are maintained, or a disk space limitation. Balancing the query performance provided by materialized views with associated maintenance costs is the view selection problem. This section describes a method of solving the view selection problem for a particular type of problem based on OR view graphs.

A view graph for a data warehouse is a directed graph where each node represents a view and each edge represents a path to a source view or table from which the view can be generated. An OR view graph is a special case in which any view in the graph can be computed from any of its related views. That is, each view in the graph has zero or more ways to be constructed from other source views, but each way involves only one other view. Figure 6.2 is an example of an OR view graph. Development of OR view graphs from a set of queries is described in Gupta (1997) and Roussopoulos (1992).

OR view graphs are particularly applicable to data warehouses because of the popularity of data cubes. Each view in a data cube is derived from the same base view. Selecting which views to materialize in a data cube and which views to compute from the base view is basically the problem addressed in this project.

Heuristic algorithms have been used to solve the view selection problem in the past. However, the solution used in this project is based on genetic algorithms. This is a randomized technique that has been applied successfully to many optimization problems. Lee and Hammer (1999) report that the genetic algorithm finds solutions within 10% of optimal with only a linear increase in run time. This case study follows their description. A genetic algorithm is used to select a near-optimal set of views to materialize on a data warehouse. This technique is based on selection of views from an OR view graph as described earlier. The first step to construct an OR view graph for the data warehouse is to find a set of related views, or queries, to consider.

6.5.2 Background information

A pilot data warehouse architecture for human services, including all source data to be loaded into the data warehouse for the pilot project, resides on an IBM S/390 mainframe. Most of the data is in IDMS (an IBM hierarchical database) records, but some reside in indexed (VSAM) files. The data warehouse resides on the NCR Worldmark 4800 multiprocessor machine running the Teradata RDBMS. The NCR/Teradata architecture is highly optimized for decision support because of its ability to distribute large queries efficiently among multiple processors. At the front end of the data warehouse, users can access data via front-end client tools installed on their PCs or over the Web through the front-end server software running on the NT Server. Metadata are available to users through a combination of their front-end client tools and a metadata Web site.

As is typical of a data warehouse, the data go through an extraction, transformation, and loading process. All data extraction and transformation occurs on the IBM mainframe. First, data are copied from source files and databases into record-based, displayable files. For the IDMS source files, foreign key data are added to each record to establish relationships between tables when the data are loaded into the data warehouse. After the data extraction phase, transformation programs are run to further prepare the data for loading into the warehouse by cleansing them as well as generating additional primary/foreign key information. After data transformation, the data are loaded into the data warehouse using the Teradata FastLoad and MultiLoad tools that also run on the IBM mainframe. These tools load the data directly into data warehouse tables through a FIPS channel interface. This interface directly connects the mainframe to the NCR Worldmark machine.

6.5.3 Data model

The data model for the data warehouse is based on the ER modeling approach and the tables are close to 3NF. The ER model was selected because it is the recommended model for the Teradata database. Because Teradata's high-end query performance is based on its ability to partition the work among multiple processor nodes, NCR recommends this model. Queries against denormalized data do not lend themselves to as high a level of partitioning. The ER model was also selected because it more closely matched the model used by the source systems. Mapping the source data to

Table 6.4 Data Warehouse Views

View	Description
BV1	Child abuse incidents for 1998–1999
V1	Child abuse incidents in county C for 1998–1999
V2	Registered child abuse incidents for 1998–1999
V3	Child abuse incidents for 1999
V4	Child abuse incidents in county C for 1999
V5	Registered child abuse incidents in county C for 1998–1999
V6	Registered child abuse incidents for 1999
V7	Registered child abuse incidents in county C for 1999

the data warehouse was straightforward because it was very similar to the data model used on the mainframe.

6.5.4   Queries selected

The queries considered in this project are listed in Table 6.4. BV1 actually represents a table in the data warehouse. This table contains a record for each child abuse incident that was investigated in a region in the U.S. during 1998–1999 and maps almost directly from a similar IDMS table on the IBM mainframe. Views 1 through 7 have the same schema as the base view. They simply represent different slices of the data in BV1. These views were selected based on analysis performed. Policy analysts are frequently interested in yearly totals, making views that specify a single year useful. Registered child abuse incidents represent specific types of confirmed child abuses. For example, many types of sexual abuse must be registered, making these types of abuse a hot topic for the region studied. Finally, policy analysts for the state are often interested in data for particular counties.

These seven views can be described as a "select * from BV1 where XYZ" with XYZ representing the different qualifiers described in the descriptions in Table 6.1. For example, the "where" clause of V4 would be "County = 'C' and DateOfIncident >= 01/01/1999 and DateOfIncident <= 12/31/1999." Another observation is that these queries in general become more precise as the view number increases. Views 4 through 7 can also be generated using a "select *" on views 1 through 3. The OR view graph in the next section illustrates these relationships.

6.5.5   Development of the OR view graph

Figure 6.8 is the complete OR view graph based on the queries in Table 6.4. The base view on the bottom of the diagram provides the basis for all other views. Each of the next three layers provides a more highly qualified view of the data. For example, while V2 contains all of the registered incidents for 1998–1999, V6 contains only the registered incidents for 1999. Edge 8 illustrates the fact that V6 is a subset of V2 as well as V3. Therefore, V6 can be thought of as "select * from V2 where DateOfIncident >= 01/01/1999 and

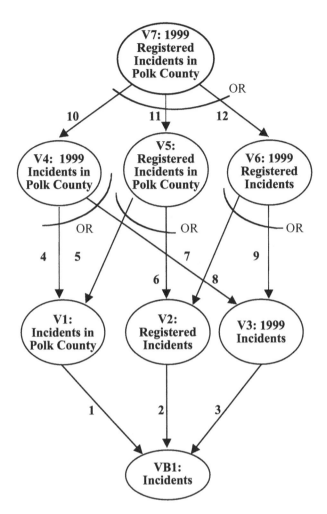

Figure 6.8 Complete OR view graph.

DateOfIncident <= 12/31/1999." Alternatively, V6 can be thought of as "select * from V3 where RegisteredFlag = true." However, V6 is not a subset of V1 since V1 contains only those incidents that occurred in county C. V7 can be generated from V4, V5, or V6 since it combines all of the restrictive qualifiers.

6.5.6   Implementation

The view selection problem is an NP-hard problem. Basically, the solution space for this type of problem grows exponentially as the problem size increases (i.e., more views are considered), so it is very difficult to find an optimal solution. Heuristic algorithms can be used to solve this type of problem in a short period of time. However, the quality of the solution may be far from optimal. Randomized algorithms can be applied to NP-hard problems; they often find a reasonable solution within a few percentage points of the optimal solution in a relatively short time (Lee and Hammer, 1999). A genetic algorithm, a specific type of randomized algorithm, was used to solve the view selection problem in this project and is described in the next few sections.

6.5.6.1　Genetic algorithm description

A genetic algorithm (GA) is a randomized algorithm inspired by the evolutionary processes of natural selection and genetics. Basically, a set of potential solutions to a problem is created, often randomly. This set is referred to as the GA's population. Each entity in the population, or solution, is called a genome. A fitness function is used to evaluate the fitness of each genome and must provide higher scores for more optimal solutions to support the natural selection process.

At a high level, the genetic algorithm works as follows:

1. Evaluate the fitness of each genome in the population.
2. Eliminate some portion of the genomes with the lowest fitness from the population.
3. Use reproduction of the remaining genomes to replenish the population.
4. Randomly mutate genomes in the population.
5. Repeat steps 1 through 4 for a selected number of generations or until convergence occurs.

Convergence occurs in a GA when the genomes in the population all approach the same solution. This indicates that a near-optimal solution has been found, but does not guarantee it is the optimal solution. Convergence may occur quickly or may take many hundreds of algorithm iterations.

6.5.6.2　Solution encoding, reproduction, and mutation

Before a GA can be applied to a problem, the solutions must be encoded as genomes. For this project, binary strings were used. Each digit in the binary string represents one view from the OR view graph with a "1" indicating the view is materialized. For example, the string "1110001" indicates that V1, V2, V3, and V7 are materialized for the OR view graph in Figure 6.2. If this solution were implemented, the queries represented by V4, V5, and V6 would go against the materialized views V1, V2, and V3. A solution of "0000000" would indicate all queries must be satisfied by querying the base table, VB1.

Reproduction for this project is implemented as a crossover of two genomes. This is accomplished by selecting a random crossover point for the genomes and then creating two offspring consisting of part of each of the parent genomes. Consider the following example:

Genome 1: 1111111
Genome 2: 0000001
Crossover point: 4
Resulting genome 1': 1111001
Resulting genome 2': 0000111

Mutation is simply applied to the entire population by randomly flipping each bit in each genome with a certain probability.

6.5.6.3 Description of the fitness function

The fitness function is very important since it indicates to the GA which solutions are more near-optimal. This is vital to the elitist portion of the GA represented by step 2 of the algorithm where the worst genomes are eliminated from the population. The fitness function used for this project came from Lee and Hammer (1999). Lee and Hammer tested several possible fitness functions but obtained the best results with what they called the divide function. The fitness of a genome x on view graph G with the set of materialized views M is

- Fitness(x) = B(G, M)/Penalty(x)   if Penalty(x) > 1
- Fitness(x) = B(G, M)   if Penalty(x) <= 1

B(G, M) is the query benefit of materializing the set of views M for view graph G. The Penalty(x) represents the cost of materializing the views specified by genome x. It is ignored when it is less than 1 because that indicates the maintenance cost is being met, so the penalty is not a factor. The maintenance cost is related to the storage space used by the materialized views or the time it takes to materialize those views. These values are calculated based on parameters associated with the views and edges in the OR view graph. Table 6.5 describes those parameters.

Table 6.5 View Graph Parameters

Parameter	Description
	Node (View)
RC	Read cost of the view; also represents size of the view.
QF	Query frequency: represents the number of queries on the view during a given period of time.
UF	Update frequency: represents the number of updates on the view during a given time interval. Based on incremental updates.
	Edge
QC	Query cost: represents the cost to calculate a view from one of its source views.
MC	Maintenance cost: represents the cost for updating a view using one of its source views.

6.5.6.4   Query benefit function

The query benefit function is defined as follows: B(G, M) = T(G, b) – T(G, M). T(G, M) is the total query cost for view graph G in the presence of a set of materialized views M. The first component of the query benefit function, T(G, b), is the total query cost for view graph G in the presence of only the base views. This represents the worst case if no views are materialized. Therefore, the query benefit realized is the worst case minus the query cost based on the set of views materialized. The total query cost equation is

$$T(G, M) = \sum_{v \in V(G)} QF_v * Q(v, M)$$

Notice that this is a summation over all views in the view graph G. This equation takes the frequency at which a query is executed into account to minimize the impact of views that would be infrequently accessed and maximize the impact of those used frequently.

Q(v, M) is the cost of answering query v in the presence of a set of materialized views M. This is the minimum query length of a path from view v to the first materialized view in the view graph. This is implemented as a depth first traversal of the view graph starting at view v.

6.5.6.5   Penalty function

The exponential penalty function was selected from Lee and Hammer (1999) since it provided the best results in that work. Therefore, the penalty function is defined as: Penalty(x) = $(1 + \text{rho} (U(M) - S))^2$ where rho is defined as a constant calculated from the given OR view graph G, U(M) is the total maintenance cost of the set of materialized views M, and S is the maintenance cost constraint. Notice that this penalty function will always be greater than or equal to 1 so it will always be applied in the fitness function.

The total maintenance cost equation is similar to the total query cost and is defined as follows:

$$U(M) = \sum_{v \in V(M)} UF_v * UC(v, M)$$

This summation differs from the total query cost in that it only considers those views that are in the materialized set M. It also considers the update frequency so that frequently updated views are more costly. UC(v, M) is the cost of maintaining a materialized view v in the presence of a set M of materialized views. This is the minimum maintenance length of a path from v to a materialized source view, and again is implemented as a depth first traversal of the view graph.

The constant ρ is defined as follows:

$$\rho = \underset{v_i \in V(G)}{Max} (B(G, \{v_i\}) \, / \, U(\{v_i\}))$$

As illustrated by the equation, ρ is based on the query benefit and maintenance cost of materializing a single view.

6.5.6.6   Total query cost and maintenance cost calculation example

Consider the small view graph presented in Figure 6.9. This is a subset of the larger view graph presented earlier. Some sample calculations will be considered based on this view graph.

Assume $M = \{V2, V4\}$ (i.e., $x = 01010$). To calculate the total query cost for V5 one must perform a depth first traversal of the view graph to a materialized view. There are two alternative paths based on edge numbers: $\{5, 3, 1\}$ or $\{6\}$. Since the second path has only one edge, assume it will provide the minimum query cost. Therefore, $Q(V5, M) = QC_6 + RC_{V4}$. Similarly, the total maintenance cost based on that path is $UC(V5, M) = MC_6$. Now consider the case of V4, which is materialized. In this case, $Q(V4, M) = RC_{V4}$ since V4 is materialized. $UC(V4, M) = MC_4$ since V2 is materialized. Finally, consider V3. For V3, $Q(V3, M) = QC_3 + QC_1 + RC_{VB1}$ and $UC(V3, M) = MC_3 + MC_1$.

6.5.6.7   Genetic algorithm implementation

Visual C++ 6.0 was used to implement the view selection program for this project. The MIT GALib provided the GA implementation. This library performs all of the GA operations discussed, such as elitism, reproduction, and mutation. The calling software must provide a fitness function and specify some parameters to the GA. These parameters and the values used for this project are specified in Table 6.6. These values were based on those specified in Lee and Hammer (1999).

6.5.7   Resulting views

The view selection program was run against the view graphs presented in Figures 6.8 and 6.9. The small view graph in Figure 6.3 provided an example of the GA's ability to find an optimal solution that could be verified by inspection of the view graph and parameters used. These results are presented in the next section. Following the small OR view graph results, two sets of results for the complete view graph in Figure 6.9 are provided. These results are based on read, query, and maintenance cost figures collected from the data warehouse.

6.5.7.1   Small OR view graph

Table 6.7 contains the node and edge parameters for the small OR view graph that was used. The last column (cost constraint) denotes the lowest cost values.

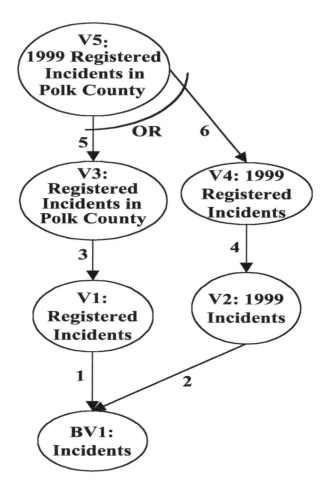

Figure 6.9 Small OR view graph.

Table 6.6 Genetic Algorithm Parameters

GA Parameter Name	Description	Value Used
Population size	Number of genomes in the population	30
Number of generations	Number of times to apply the GA to the population	400
P_c: probability of crossover	Probability of selecting a genome for crossover	0.9
P_m: probability of mutation	Probability of mutating a bit within a genome; each bit within each genome is considered	0.001

Table 6.7 Small OR View Graph Parameters

View	QF	UF	RC
B1	1	1	12
1	1	1	8
2	1	1	11
3	1	1	7
4	1	1	10
5	1	1	7

Edge	QC	MC	Cost Constraint = 4
1	0	4	
2	0	4	
3	0	0	
4	0	0	
5	0	0	

These values were selected based on an example from Gupta and Mumick (1999), and do not depend on the contents of the data warehouse. A value of 1 is used for all query and update frequencies, making them irrelevant. The query costs are all 0, indicating that there is no the cost to perform any query from any other view. This may not be far from reality as long as no complex calculations are occurring to create a view. Only the bottommost views have maintenance costs associated with them. It is assumed, then, that maintaining the remaining views from these base views is very cheap.

6.5.7.2   *Results from a small view graph*

Using the genetic algorithm for this small view graph helps to prove that it can find the optimal solution. Since there are only $2^5 = 32$ possible solutions, with a population of 30 it is quite possible that the optimal solution is present from the start. The results presented in Table 6.8 did not include the optimal solution initially, but it was included after only two generations.

Table 6.8 Small OR View Graph GA Results

GA Result Parameter	GA Result Value
Number of generations to convergence	20
Convergence percentage after 400 generations	99%
Fitness of best solution after 0 generations	10
Fitness of best solution after 2 generations	14
Fitness of best solution	14
Best solution	10100, M1 = {V1, V3} OR 10101, M2 = {V1, V3, V5}

This OR view graph had two solutions with equivalent fitness values that appeared in the final population. Both of these solutions had the same fitness since the only difference was in V5's query cost which was $QC_5 + RC_3 = 7$ or $RC_5 = 7$ for M1 and M2, respectively. If the query cost of edge 5 were greater than 0, materializing V5 would result in a higher fitness.

Proof that these are the optimal solutions is found upon closer inspection of the view graph parameters. Since the maintenance cost constraint is 4 and the cost of materializing either V1 or V2 is 4, only one of those views can be materialized in the optimal solution. Materializing both of these would increase the maintenance penalty too much. Since the QC and MC values of all other edges are 0, we can assume that all views on the path from V1 or V2 to V5 will be materialized in the optimal solution. This is due to the fact that materializing V3, V4, and V5 will not increase the maintenance cost or add additional query cost. Therefore, the optimal solution must either be M1 = {V1, V3, V5} or M2 = {V2, V4, V5}. The query cost of M1 is $RC_1 + RC_3 + RC_5 = 22$ and the query cost of M2 is $RC_2 + RC_4 + RC_5 = 33$. Since the query cost of M1 is less than the query cost of M2, the query benefit of M1 is greater than the query benefit of M2. Therefore, the optimal solution is M1. This basically indicates that it is more valuable to materialize V1 and V3 because they have fewer records than V2 and V4, or, since V2 and V4 are so similar to BV1, it is not useful to materialize these views.

6.5.7.3 Complete OR view graph

Table 6.9 contains the node parameters for the complete OR view graph. The number of records was calculated based on the actual data stored in the data warehouse. The read cost values were based on the percentage of records in each view compared with the base view. The query and update frequencies used were the same as those for the small OR view graph so that the impact of the realistic read cost could be seen more clearly.

Table 6.10 contains the edge parameters for the complete OR view graph. These values were obtained based on querying and materializing views on the data warehouse. The QC values are all 0 like the small OR view graph because the amount of time to execute a query from the lower view was

Table 6.9 Complete OR View Graph View Parameters

View	QF	UF	Number of Records	RC
B1	1	1	38,220	100.000
1	1	1	6,790	17.770
2	1	1	9,778	25.580
3	1	1	18,666	48.840
4	1	1	3,063	8.014
5	1	1	1,478	3.867
6	1	1	4,957	12.970
7	1	1	699	1.8290

Table 6.10 Complete OR View Graph Edge Parameters

Edge	QC	Time	MC
1	0	364	36.4
2	0	554	55.4
3	0	1018	101.8
4	0	180	18.0
5	0	85	8.5
6	0	80	8.0
7	0	190	19.0
8	0	297	29.7
9	0	298	29.8
10	0	40	4.0
11	0	40	4.0
12	0	40	4.0

negligible. This is due to the small number of records in the views. The maintenance costs represent the number of seconds it took to materialize a view from the lower view. This was done using Microsoft Access as a front-end tool; the query was executed in Access on the data in the Teradata database. Then, a table was created in the data warehouse based on the query results set. The MC values used were based on the time divided by ten.

6.5.7.4   Results from a complete view graph

Initially, the maintenance cost constraint was set to 180 (1800 seconds or 30 minutes). This value is greater than all of the edge maintenance cost values so it does not restrict any single view from being materialized. Results from the GA are presented in Table 6.11. Again, the best solution was found quite

Table 6.11 Complete OR View Graph GA Results (MC constraint = 180)

GA Result Parameter	GA Result Value
Number of generations to convergence	20
Convergence percentage after 100 generations	99%
Fitness of best solution after 0 generations	0.0350401
Fitness of best solution after 2 generations	0.229459
Fitness of best solution after 5 generations	8.18146
Fitness of best solution	8.18146
Best solution	1010111
	M = {V1, V3, V5, V6, V7}

Table 6.12 Complete OR View Graph GA Results
(MC constraint = 210)

GA Result Parameter	GA Result Value
Number of generations to convergence	20
Convergence percentage after 100 generations	99%
Fitness of best solution after 0 generations	0.157848
Fitness of best solution after 2 generations	0.16189
Fitness of best solution after 5 generations	1.06542
Fitness of best solution	1.06542
Best solution	1111000
	M = {V1, V2, V3, V4}

rapidly after only 5 generations and convergence of the GA occurred after only 20 generations. It is more difficult to make observations about the best solution because of the number of parameters affecting the outcome. However, it can be noted that, if V1, V2, and V3 are materialized, the maintenance cost constraint is not satisfied. Therefore, it is logical that all three are not in the best solution. Additionally, V5, V6, and V7 are relatively cheap to materialize so it makes sense that they are included in the optimal solution. The GA was run again with the same parameters except for the maintenance cost constraint, which was changed to 210. This would allow V1, V2, and V3 to be materialized. The results are presented in Table 6.12.

As suspected, V1, V2, and V3 are materialized in the best solution when the maintenance cost constraint allows it. Adding V2 and the additional maintenance cost allowance also has the effect of making V4 more attractive than V5, V6, and V7.

6.5.8   Summary of the case study

This case study has shown how a genetic algorithm can be used to solve the view selection problem for the data warehouse. For the small OR view graph, it was argued that the GA found the optimal solution. For the complete OR view graph, the GA selected views to materialize that would also provide the optimal query benefit for the data warehouse, based on the queries considered, while staying under the specified maintenance cost constraint.

Since the GA was able to find these optimal solutions so quickly, it is easy to see that it would be useful for OR view graphs with many more nodes. The only drawback to using this approach in the real world would be the time and effort required to collect the OR view graph parameters. This requires actually materializing each view under consideration, possibly in multiple ways. For large OR view graphs containing 20 to 25 views, this can be a daunting task. Techniques could be developed to estimate these parameters based on view record counts and knowledge of the database being used. With these techniques, the GA solution could be used in automatic data cube generation.

6.6   Summary

In this chapter, some basic features of data warehousing have been examined as materialized views. In particular, data cubes have been emphasized. Examples and case studies included in this chapter are simple implementations of some known approaches. These were described in detail, mainly for pedagogical reasons. In the next chapter, some more advanced studies related to materialized views will be reviewed.

References

Bischoff, J. and T. Alexander, *Data Warehouse: Practical Advice from the Expert,* Prentice Hall, Upper Saddle River, NJ, 1997.

Chaudhuri, S. and U. Dayal, An overview of data warehousing and OLAP technology, *Proceedings ACM SIGMOD Int. Conf. Manage. Data,* March 1997.

Chen, M., Aggregates calculation using preconstructed data structures in data cubes, in *Advances in Database and Knowledge-Based Systems: Data Mining and Data Warehousing* (G. E. Lasker and Z. Chen, Eds.), 37–42, 2000.

Chen, M., Data cube and its implementation, M.S. Thesis, Southeast University, Nanjing, China, 1999 (in Chinese).

Engebretson, C. J., View selection, project term paper, Department of Computer Science, University of Nebraska at Omaha, 2000.

Feige, U., A threshold of ln n for approximating set cover, *Proc. ACM Symp. Theory Comput. (STOC),* 1996, 314–318.

Garcia, Y-G., M. A. Lopez, and Scott, T. Leutenegger, On optimal node splitting for R-trees, *Proc. 24th Intl. Conf. on Very Large Data Bases,* 334–344, 1998.

Gatziu, S., M. Jeusfeld, M. Staudt, Y. Vassiliov, Design and management of data warehouses, *SIGMOD Record,* 28(4), 7–10, 1999.

Gupta, H. and I. S. Mumick, Selection of views to materialize under a maintenance cost constraint, *Proc. ICDT 1999,* 453–470.

Gupta, A. and I. S. Mumick, What is the data warehousing problem? (Are materialized views the answer?). (Panel) *Proc. 22nd Very Large Data Bases,* 1996, 602.

Gupta, H., Selection of views to materialize in a data warehouse, in *Proc. Int. Conf. Database Theory,* Delphi, Greece, 1997.

Han, J., *Data Mining: Concepts and Techniques,* Morgan Kaufmann, San Mateo, California, 2001.

Harinarayan, V., A. Rajaraman, and J. Ullman, Implementing data cubes efficiently, in *Proc. ACM SIGMOD Int. Conf. Manage. Data,* Canada, June 1996, 205–216.

Ho, C.-T., Range queries in OLAP data cube, *Proc. ACM SIGMOD Int. Conf. Manage. Data,* May 13–15, 1997.

Kong, Q., A simple implementation of data cubes, term project paper, Department of Computer Science, University of Nebraska at Omaha, 2001.

Lee, M. and J. Hammer, Speeding up warehouse design using a randomized algorithm, Technical report TR 99-12, Dept of Computer and Information Science and Engineering, University of Florida, Gainesville, April 1999.

Raab, F. , Ed., TPC Benchmark™ D (Decision Support), Proposed Revision 1.0. Transaction Processing Performance Council, San Jose, CA, 4 April 1995.

Roussopoulos, N., The logical access path schema of a database, *IEEE Trans. Software Eng.*, SE-8(6):563–573, November, 1982.

chapter seven

Advances in materialized views

7.1 Overview

Continuing the discussion begun in Chapter 6, this chapter addresses various aspects of and summarizes advanced work related to materialized views, including various algorithms related to view selection and maintenance. The main purpose is to illustrate which issues need to be considered and the basic ideas of how to deal with these problems. Therefore, the survey does not intend to provide complete solutions. In addition, focus will be on the ideas of problem solving instead of technical details. Whenever possible, research problems will be identified. Sample issues that need to be addressed and the basic ideas of dealing with these issues will also be provided.

To summarize existing work in progress in materialized views is somewhat challenging, because there have been many activities. Although there are many interrelated aspects, presentation is restricted to a sequential, linear format. Therefore, readers may need to read this chapter more than once, and study the original materials cited in the reference list.

Several sample warehousing projects have been conducted from research institutions. For example, the goal of the Architecture for Database Management Systems (ADMS) project (Roussopoulos et al., 1995) is to create a framework for caching materialized views, access paths, and experience obtained during query execution. The rationale behind this project is to amortize database access cost over an extended time period and adapt execution strategies based on experience. ADMS demonstrates the versatility of the views and their role in performance, data warehousing, management, and control of data distribution and replication.

A better known system prototype for warehouse view maintenance and performance analysis of WHIPS (WareHousing Information Project at Stanford University) incremental maintenance has been conducted at Stanford

(Wiener et al., 1996; Zhuge et al., 1996). It collects, transforms, and integrates data for the warehouse. The required functionality can be divided among cooperating distributed Common Object Request Broker Architecture (CORBA) objects, providing both scalability and the flexibility needed for supporting different application needs and heterogeneous sources. The WHIPS prototype is a functioning system implemented at Stanford and performance studies have been carried out.

Several important issues related to materialized views are examined next. Basic design and maintenance issues (including those related to integrity constraints) are discussed in Sections 7.2 to 7.5.

7.2   Data warehouse design through materialized views

7.2.1   Data warehouse design

Although, from an MIS perspective, warehouse design is largely concerned with conceptual modeling, many issues also need to be addressed at the logical or physical implementation level. Most researchers from the computer science perspective address the issue of designing a data warehouse (in the context of the relational model) by selecting a set of views to materialize. Theodoratos and Sellis (1999) proposed a theoretical framework for the data warehouse design problem with the following considerations: 1. the selected views should fit in the space allocated to the data warehouse; 2. the selected views should be able to answer all the queries of interest; and 3. the total query evaluation and view maintenance cost is minimum. The data warehouse design problem is formalized as a state space search problem by taking into account multiquery optimization over the maintenance queries (i.e., queries that compute changes to the materialized views) and the use of auxiliary views for reducing the view maintenance cost. In addition, incremental algorithms and heuristics for pruning the search space are presented. In the remaining part of this section several aspects of basic data warehouse design are examined. In Section 7.6 the design problem will be revisited, with an emphasis on the dynamic environment.

7.2.2   View selection problem

As indicated earlier, the data warehouse design problem through materialized views is usually stated as the view selection problem. When designing a warehouse, it is extremely important to minimize the cost of answering queries because the warehouse is very large, queries are often ad hoc and complex, and decision support applications require short response times. The determination of the optimal collection of views for available storage space and minimum query cost is referred to as the view selection problem. This view selection problem is totally different from the view selection problem under the disk space constraint. With numerous numbers of base tables (with schemas in hundreds of attributes) from dozens of data sources, it would be very challenging to decide which views should be materialized. Theodoratos and Sellis (1997) provided a theoretical framework for this problem in terms of the relational model. Yang et al. (1997) also presented a framework for analyzing the issues in selecting views to materialize. A heuristic algorithm was developed to provide a feasible solution based on individual optimal query plans. The materialized view design problem was mapped as a 0 to 1 integer programming problem whose solution could guarantee an optimal solution. Liang et al. (2001) investigated the view selection problem under the maintenance time constraint. Two heuristic algorithms are proposed. The key underlying these algorithms is to define good heuristic functions and to reduce the problem to some well-solved optimization problems. As a result, an approximate solution of the known optimization problem should efficiently give a feasible solution of the original problem.

Appropriate data structures are needed for view selection. Design problems using views typically select a set of views to materialize in order to optimize either the query evaluation cost, view maintenance cost, or both, with certain constraints. For example, greedy algorithms have been provided for queries represented as AND/OR graphs (Gupta et al., 1997). In another proposal, view selection algorithms when aggregation and grouping are present can be handled by constructing view graph structures (Akinde and Bohlen, 1999). The view graphs express how source data is materialized into views. The algorithm basically creates the search space of possible configurations of materialized views. Ad hoc rules are used to limit the size of the generated view graphs. An important research issue is how to incorporate a pruning strategy for the algorithm with specialized view selection algorithms.

A very important factor for the view selection problem is the constraints used for selection. For example, Theodoratos and Bouzeghoub (1999) refined the view selection problem to accommodate both source availability constraints (which are concerned with frequency of a data source accessed for view maintenance) and currency constraints (which are concerned with the aging of old data elements in the data warehouse). If constraints were not satisfactory, the source relation which caused the constraint violation would be identified. Otherwise, an algorithm was used to compute the minimal update frequencies to achieve the desired data currency. This work also concerned data quality in a warehousing environment.

There have been many discussions on selection of common views. A data warehouse may contain multiple views which can be defined over overlapping portions of data. Data warehouses may contain multiple views with different query frequencies. When these views are related to each other and defined over overlapping portions of the base data, then it may be more efficient to materialize certain shared portions of the base data, from which the warehouse views can be derived. Identifying the shared views or shared parts of a particular view can therefore improve data warehouse performance by diminishing the number of views which have to be materialized, as well as reducing the amount of data requiring frequent refreshment. Theodoratos et al. (1999) provided a generic method that, given a set of SPJ queries to be satisfied by the DW, generates all the "significant" sets of materialized views that satisfy all the input queries. This process is complex since common subexpressions between the queries need to be detected and exploited. In addition, algorithms have been developed so that a materialized view set selected in this way fits in the space allocated to the DW for materialization and minimizes the combined overall query evaluation and view maintenance cost. Yang et al. (1997) addressed some issues related to determining this set of shared views to be materialized in order to achieve the best combination of good performance and low maintenance. Indulska (1998) discussed the concept of attribute hierarchy and presented how the hierarchy concept improves the view selection method.

The complexity of the design problem has encouraged the use of artificial intelligence (AI) techniques for view selection. In order to optimize the view maintenance cost, given a materialized SQL view, an exhaustive approach is presented in Ross et al. (1996). Heuristics for selecting additional views that optimize the total view maintenance cost are also proposed. The same problem has been studied by Labio et al. (1997), with a focus on select-join views and the use of indices. It applies an A* algorithm (as sketched in Section 2.6.2) and provides rules of thumb under certain assumptions for search in the space of candidate views. Another example is use of genetic algorithms. Heuristics have been used to search a small fraction of the space to get a near optimal solution. Zhang et al. (1999) explore the use of a genetic algorithm for the selection of materialized views based on multiple global processing plans for many queries.

Although a majority of work related to the view selection problem takes an "add a view to the warehouse" approach, a different perspective in view selection is to define redundant views and eliminate them, as discussed in Kotsis and McGregor (2000).

7.2.3   View data lineage problem

The inverse of the view selection problem is equally interesting because, in many cases, not only are the view data useful for analysis, but knowing the set of source data that produced specific pieces of view information also can be useful. Given a data item in a materialized view, determining the source data that produced it and the process by which it was produced is termed the data lineage problem. The view data lineage problem in a warehousing environment (Cui and Widom, 1998, 2000) is concerned with how to identify the set of source data items that produced a given data item in a materialized view. For example, a tuple (a1, b1, c1) in warehouse view V(ABC) could be produced by tuple (a1, b1) from relation r(ABEF) in data source S1 and tuple (b1, c1) from relation s(BCD) in data source S2. This problem is closely related to the question of propagating changes in the warehouse back to the data sources. The problem has been formally defined and lineage tracing algorithms for relational views with aggregation have been developed. Based on these results, a lineage tracing package was implemented in the WHIPS data warehousing system prototype at Stanford. With this package, users can select view tuples of interest, then efficiently drill through to examine the exact source tuples that produced the view tuples of interest.

7.3 Maintenance of materialized views

In order to keep the contents of a data warehouse consistent, the materialized views in the warehouse have to be updated in response to changes in the source data. This process is referred to as view maintenance. Because a data warehouse consists of materialized views, maintaining these views can effectively maintain data warehouses as well.

7.3.1 Snapshot differential problem

The first issue to be addressed in view maintenance is detecting and extracting modifications from data sources. In some cases it is known that changes have occurred. (In some applications changed data become the working copy and overwrite old data. An application that changes the source of data notices is referred to as using the push technology.) For example, in sophisticated sources, such as a relational database system with triggers, this process is relatively easy to handle. Otherwise, it is often necessary to infer modifications by periodically comparing snapshots of data from the source. This is referred to as the snapshot differential problem. There are three ways to detect and extract modifications: 1. the application running on top of the source is altered to send the modification to the warehouse; 2. a system log file is parsed to obtain the relevant modification; and 3. the modification is inferred by comparing a current source snapshot with an earlier one. Labio and Garcia-Molina (1996) presented algorithms that perform compression of records, as well as a window algorithm that works very well if the snapshots are not very different. A related issue of large scale information monitoring in the Internet environment was addressed by Liu et al. (1996).

7.3.2 Using full and partial information for view maintenance

The problem of efficiently maintaining materialized views is the most extensively studied problem in all studies related to materialized views. In terms of information used for view maintenance, there are two major approaches:

- Full information approach. This approach assumes that all base relations and materialized views are available during the maintenance process; the focus has been on efficient techniques to maintain views expressed in different languages (relational algebra, SQL, Datalog), considering features like aggregations, duplicates, recursion, and so on. The techniques all work on all database instances for both insertions and deletions.

- Partial information approach. This approach handles view maintenance using only a subset of the underlying relations involved in the view. Unlike view maintenance using full information, a view is not always maintainable for a modification using only partial information. Whether the view can be maintained may also depend upon whether the modification is an insertion, deletion, or update. Algorithms using partial information focus on checking whether the view can be maintained and then on how to maintain it. In particular, a view is self-maintainable if it can be maintained without accessing the source data. Because the source data for the materialized views are often remote and difficult to access, the concept of self-maintainable has been identified as a key concept in data warehousing and view maintenance.

There is a need first to identify which problems need to be addressed, particularly in the case of using partial information. In order to reduce maintenance costs, we try to maintain the views, in response to a base update, using information that is local to the warehouse. This is referred to as self-maintenance. Only if the local view definitions and local view contents cannot achieve this maintenance will we have to access a subset of base relations. Without full use of the base data, maintaining a view unambiguously is not always possible. The two critical questions that must be addressed are to determine, in a given situation, whether a view is maintainable and, if it is, how to maintain it (Huyn, 1997a). In fact, Huyn (1996) addressed the issue of finding a maximal test that guarantees that a view is self-maintainable under a given update to the base relations. An observation made is that self-maintenance evaluation can be separated into two parts: a view definition-time portion where a maximal test is generated solely based on the view definition, and an update-time portion where the test can be efficiently applied to the view and the update.

7.3.3   Using incremental techniques

As for the actual techniques in view maintenance, an effective technique is to use an incremental approach, namely, to compute the changes to a view in response to changes to the underlying source data rather than recomputing the view from scratch. This approach is appealing because, usually, incremental computation is cheaper than recomputation. Gupta et al. (1998) defined the metrics for measuring the generality and efficiency of incremental maintenance algorithms, thereby outlining the framework for studying different view maintenance algorithms proposed in the literature. They presented a taxonomy of the view maintenance problems based upon language used to express a view, resources used to maintain the view, type of modification to the base data, and whether the algorithm applied to all instances of the view and modifications. Incremental maintenance of aggregate and outer-join expressions was also discussed (Gupta et al., 1999).

The idea behind incremental maintenance is to avoid recomputation and therefore reduce the amount of computation involved in maintenance. Nevertheless, recomputation may not always be completely avoided. In these cases, recomputation itself can be conducted in an incremental manner. In fact, since database updates are small and incremental compared to database contents, it is desirable that recomputations of active relational expressions (such as views, derived data, integrity constraints, active queries, and monitors) be performed incrementally as well. An efficient algorithm for the incremental recomputation of active relational expressions based on finite differencing techniques has been developed by Qian and Wiederhold (1991). Database updates are modeled as incremental changes to database relations, and the algorithm derives, by update propagation, the minimal incremental relational expressions that need recomputation. The algorithm has applications in the maintenance of materialized views and derived data, checking of integrity constraints, and evaluation of active queries and monitors.

Incremental techniques are pervasive in the entire data warehousing lifecycle. The next sections offer other applications of incremental techniques, such as incremental refresh or incremental deferred view maintenance (Colby et al., 1996), incremental design of data warehousing (Theodoratos and Sellis, 2000), and incremental view adaptation (Nica and Rundensteiner, 1999). In addition, knowledge patterns discovered on the warehouse data (discussed in Chapter 8) can also be incrementally maintained when warehouse data have been updated. In that case, the change detected in materialized views is further propagated to the resulting rules or other mined knowledge patterns.

7.3.4 Using auxiliary data and auxiliary views

Both self-maintenance and incremental techniques play important roles in materialized view maintenance. In order to improve efficiency of maintenance, some kinds of auxiliary data may be needed. For example, Bailey et al. (1998) considered the problem in a distributed database environment, with communication cost minimization as the primary objective. The views considered are defined based on the relational join operation. The approach is to use "yes/no" tags as auxiliary data on tuples in the base relations to indicate whether the tuples participate in joins. These tags will help avoid sending irrelevant data over the network and thus reduce the communication cost. Two basic view maintenance algorithms are proposed using the tags. In addition to reducing communication costs, an important feature of these algorithms is that they derive the "exact change" to views without looking at the old views. This feature allows maintenance of certain aggregates on views without actually materializing the views.

Ross et al. (1996) investigated the problem of incremental maintenance of an SQL view in the case of database updates, and showed that it is possible to reduce the total time cost of view maintenance by materializing (and maintaining) additional (auxiliary) views. The problem of determining the

optimal set of additional views to materialize is formulated as an optimization problem over the space of possible view sets (which includes empty
set). Mohania and Kambayashi (2000) also showed that warehouse views
can be made self-maintainable if some auxiliary relations, which are additional relations derived from the intermediate results of the view computation, can be materialized in the warehouse. An algorithm was developed to
determine which auxiliary relations need to be materialized in order to make
a materialized view self-maintainable.

7.3.5　Dealing with irrelevant update

Although much attention has been put on propagation of changes, an equally
interesting problem is how to optimize view maintenance by determining
when a modification leaves a view unchanged. This is known as the irrelevant update problem (or query independent of update). Blakeley et al. (1986,
1989) proposed a method in which all database updates to base relations are
first filtered to remove from consideration those that cannot possibly affect
the view. The conditions given for the detection of updates of this type, called
irrelevant updates, are necessary, sufficient, and independent of database
contents. For remaining database updates, a differential algorithm can be
applied to re-evaluate the view expression. The proposed algorithm exploits
the knowledge provided by both the view definition expression and database
update operations.

　　As an example of irrelevant update, look at an irrelevant deletion: consider two relation schemas R(ABC) and S(DE) and the derived relation AD
under conditions $(B > C)$, $(C = D)$ and $(D > 12)$. Now consider deleting from
r(R) all tuples with $B < 5$. Since the selected tuples should satisfy $B > 12$, the
delete operation will not have any impact on the result.

　　Sufficient and necessary conditions have been developed (on SPJ queries) for detecting when an update of a base relation cannot affect a derived
relation (an irrelevant update), and for detecting when a derived relation
can be correctly updated using no data other than the derived relation itself
and the given update operation (an autonomously computable update).
Continuing this direction of research, Levy and Sagiv (1993) considered more
expressive views in the deductive database context.

7.3.6　Incremental maintenance of materialized views
　　　　with duplicates

The problem of efficient maintenance of materialized views containing duplicates is particularly important when queries against such views involve aggregation functions, which need to consider duplicates to produce the correct
result. An algebraic approach was proposed in Griffin and Libkin (1995),
which provided a framework for deriving incremental view maintenance
expressions for a view with duplicate semantics where the view can be defined
using any number of bag-algebra operations such as select, project, join, or

bag union. (Note that a bag or a multiset is similar to a set, except for allowing duplication of elements.) The problem of efficient maintenance of materialized views that may contain duplicates has been studied, and an extension of the relational algebra operations to bags was used as the basic language, an algorithm was presented that propagates changes from base relations to materialized views, based on reasoning about equivalence of bag-valued expressions. Quass (1996) extended the framework to include maintaining views with aggregation in the general case, where aggregation can include group-by attributes and a view can include several aggregate operators.

Gupta et al. (1993) also conducted research work along this direction. Later, Gupta et al. (1995) introduced generalized projections, and extension of duplicate-eliminating projections that capture aggregations, group-bys, duplicate-eliminating projections, and duplicate-preserving projections in a common unified framework.

7.3.7   Externally materialized views

Chapter 2 discussed the relationship between data warehousing and the Internet. Since a data warehouse consists of a set of materialized views, this leads to considering the relationship between materialized views and the Internet. With the advent of the Internet, access to database servers from autonomous clients becomes increasingly popular. Client applications usually hold derived subsets of the database contents under their control. The incremental maintenance of such externally materialized views is an important open problem. In addition to some necessary changes in the known view maintenance procedures, the issue of translating updates through an API and a way for clients to accept such updates have to be defined. Staudt and Jarke (1996) proposed a monitoring service to be offered by such database servers, and presented algorithms for its implementation without the following assumptions: 1. the server has access to the original materialization when computing differential view changes to be notified; and 2. database capabilities exist on the client side that can compute precisely the required differentials rather than just an approximation, as is done by cache coherence techniques in homogeneous client-server databases. The method has been implemented in the deductive and object-oriented database system called ConceptBase, which is a metadata management system supporting an Internet-based, client-server architecture, and tried out in some cooperative design applications. Staudt et al. (1998) further discussed the properties of an incremental view maintenance procedure able to handle externally materialized views. The issue of large scale information monitoring in the Internet environment was also addressed by Liu et al (1996).

7.3.8   Views and queries

One of the most important reasons to use materialized views is for efficient query answering. Query equivalence and transformation have been studied in the database community for many years. Materialized views inside the data warehouse can potentially be reused during query evaluation. The question of using materialized views to answer queries has two components: 1. if the given query can be reformulated to use the available views, and 2. if the reuse of views saves resources like computation time. Levy et al. (1995) addressed the first problem for SPJ queries. The theoretical investigation involved in their work was based on the observation that all possible rewritings of a query can be obtained by considering so called containment mappings from the bodies of the views to the body of the query. Chaudhuri et al. (1995) addressed both problems for SPJ queries. They solved the first problem by presenting a relational query optimizer (for SPJ queries) which is able to choose one of the possible alternatives for reusing views.

One emphasis in the research of query rewriting in the data warehousing environment is the rewriting of queries involving sum, count, min, and max aggregations. Various algorithms have been proposed, including Cohen et al. (1999). Query rewriting forms the basis for a data warehousing query optimizer. Open questions are the handling of negation, functional dependencies, and queries with SQL's "having" clauses (Gatziu et al., 2000).

Srivastava et al. (1996) presented algorithms for the problem of using materialized views to compute answers to SQL queries with grouping and aggregation in the presence of bag (multiset) tables. Some interesting aspects of this study are

- In the case where the query has grouping and aggregation but the views do not, a view is usable in answering the query only if there is an isomorphism between the view and a portion of the query.
- When the views also have grouping and aggregation, it is necessary to identify conditions under which the aggregation information present in a view is sufficient to perform the aggregation computations required in the query.
- Previous work attempted to perform syntactic transformations on the query such that the definition of the view would be a subpart of the definition of the query; consequently, these methods could only detect usages of views in limited cases. In contrast to this, the proposed approach is complete, because it can always (under a set of reasonable assumptions) detect when information existing in the views is sufficient to answer the query.

In addition, the problem of optimizing the combined query evaluation and view maintenance cost was studied by Yang et al. (1997). The proposed approach differs from previous approaches in that it requires all queries of interest to be answerable using this view set exclusively.

7.3.9 Unified view selection and maintenance

For convenience of discussion, Section 7.2 and this section have discussed view selection and view maintenance separately. Due to the complex structure of the warehouse and the different profiles of the users who submit queries, tools are needed to automate the selection and management of the materialized data. Kotidis and Roussopoulos (1999) present DynaMat, a system that not only dynamically materializes information at multiple levels of granularity in order to match the demand (workload) but also takes into account the maintenance restrictions for the warehouse, such as downtime to update the views and space availability. DynaMat unifies view selection and view maintenance problems under a single framework, using a novel "goodness" measure for the materialized views. DynaMat constantly monitors incoming queries and materializes the best set of views, subject to space constraints.

7.3.10   Other work

Design and maintenance of materialized views are closely related to logical design issues that are discussed in Chapter 5. More recent work on logical design of various forms of data warehousing (including data cubes) can be found in Cabibbo and Torlone (2000) and Golfarelli et al. (2000). Schrefl and Thalhammer (2000) have examined the issue of making data warehouses active. Scalable maintenance of multiple interrelated data warehousing systems has been discussed by Ding et al. (2000), and maintaining horizontally partitioned warehouse views by Xu and Ezeife (2000). Recent work on warehouse data creation (and, to a certain degree, maintenance) and other issues includes Zhang and Rundensteiner (2000) and Liefke and Davidson (2000).

7.4   Consistency in view maintenance

7.4.1   Immediate and deferred view maintenance

The discussion on view maintenance in the previous section is largely conducted at a "macro" level. The mechanism of view maintenance or maintenance view policy is now examined in a little more detail. Materials presented in this section are closely related to DBMS implementation, particularly transaction processing.

Maintenance of a view involves two major steps (Gupta and Mumick, 1998): 1. propagate: compute changes to the view that result from changes to the base data and 2. refresh: apply the computed changes to bring the materialized view table up to date.

Concurrency control problems may arise in the presence of materialized views (Kawaguchi et al., 1997). Consider a database system supporting materialized views to speed up queries. For a range of important applications (e.g., banking, billing, and network management), transactions that access materialized views would prefer some consistency guarantees — if a transaction reads a base relation after an update, and then reads a materialized view derived from the base relation, it expects to see the effect of the base update on the materialized view. If a transaction reads two views, it expects that the two views reflect a single consistent database state. However, such guarantees are not easy to obtain because materialized views may become inconsistent upon updates to base relations.

Therefore, maintenance policies should be established to make decisions in regard to view refreshment. Two important issues are how and when refreshment occurs. When the policy called immediate view maintenance is used, a view is refreshed within the transaction that updates the base tables. In contrast, in deferred view maintenance, the refreshment is delayed.

In immediate view maintenance, the view is refreshed immediately upon an update to a base table used to derive the view as a part of the transaction that updates the base table. Immediate maintenance involves a potential refreshment of the view after every update to the deriving tables. Immediate maintenance reestablishes consistency within the transaction that updates the base relation, but this consistency comes at the cost of delaying update transactions. It allows fast querying, at the expense of slowing down update transactions. Immediate maintenance imposes a significant overhead on update transactions that cannot be tolerated in many applications.

When staleness of views can be tolerated, a view may be refreshed periodically or (on demand) when it is queried; a deferred policy may be appropriate in this case. In deferred view maintenance, the view is refreshed in a separate transaction T', outside the transaction T that updates a base table used to derive the view. In addition, the refreshing transaction T' must be serialized after the updating transaction T. Deferred maintenance does not significantly slow down update transactions. Therefore, the basic idea of deferred maintenance is to avoid penalizing update transactions by shifting maintenance into a different transaction; however, doing so causes a materialized view to become temporarily inconsistent with its definition. A refreshment operation is needed to reestablish consistency. Colby et al. (1996) presented algorithms to refresh a view incrementally during deferred maintenance. Incremental deferred view maintenance requires auxiliary relations (tables) that contain information recorded since the last view refreshment. With proper choice of auxiliary tables, it is possible to lower both per-transaction overhead and view refreshment time.

As a consequence of a materialized view becoming temporarily inconsistent with its definition, transactions that read multiple materialized views, or that read a materialized view and also read and/or write base relations, may execute in a nonserializable manner even when they are running under a strict two-phase locking (2PL) protocol. Kawaguchi et al. (1997) formalized the concurrency control problem systems supporting materialized views. A serializability theory based upon conflicts and serialization graphs in the presence of materialized views is thus developed.

There are several variants of deferred view maintenance policies, such as lazy deferred (the view is refreshed as late as possible), periodic deferred, or forced delay (the view is refreshed after a predetermined number of changes have occurred on the base tables used).

Maintenance policies chosen for views have implications on the validity of the results of queries and affect the performance of queries and updates. Colby et al. (1997) investigated a number of issues related to supporting multiple views with different maintenance policies. Formal notions of consistency for views with different maintenance policies were developed, a model based on view groupings for view maintenance policy assignment was introduced, and algorithms based on the viewgroup model were proposed to allow the consistency of views to be guaranteed.

7.4.2 Dealing with anomalies in view maintenance

Due to inconsistencies mentioned above, anomalies could occur for view maintenance in a warehousing environment. We need to take a closer look at this issue. A key point here is the prompt and correct propagation of updates at the sources to the views at the warehouse. However, materialized view maintenance algorithms developed in earlier DBMS literature may not work correctly in a warehousing environment. These algorithms assume that each source understands view management and knows the relevant view definitions. Consequently, when an update occurs at a source, the source knows exactly which data are needed for updating the view. However, in a warehousing environment, the sources can be legacy or unsophisticated systems that do not understand views. To answer a query, the warehouse may have to issue (sub)queries to some of the sources; these queries are evaluated at the sources later than the corresponding updates, so the source states may have changed. This decoupling between the base data on the sources and the view definition and view maintenance machinery on the warehouse can lead the warehouse to compute incorrect views. Zhuge et al. (1995) discussed this issue in detail.

As an example, consider two base relations, r1 and r2, with the following initial contents:

R1			R2	
W	X		X	Y
1	2		2	3

The view at the warehouse is defined by $V = \Pi_{W,Y}$ (r1 join r2). Initially the materialized view MV at the warehouse contains the single tuple {1,3}. Now suppose the source deletes the only tuple in r1, and then deletes the only tuple in r2. Apparently, the new result should be empty; however, deletion anomaly may occur. The steps shown in Table 7.1 will take place.

As a possible solution to this kind of anomaly, the warehouse can recompute the full view either whenever an update occurs at the source or periodically. Alternatively, one can store the warehouse copies of all relations involved in views. As a better approach, the eager compensating algorithm (ECA) and its more advanced siblings were proposed to avoid the overhead

Table 7.1 An Example Illustrating Deletion Anomaly

Data Source	Warehouse
a. The source updates u1 = delete(r1, {1,2}) and notifies the warehouse.	
	b. The warehouse receives u1 and emits q1 = $\Pi_{W,Y}$ ({1,2} join r2).
c. The source updates u2 = delete(r1, {2,3}) and notifies the warehouse.	
	d. The warehouse receives u2 and emits q1 = $\Pi_{W,Y}$ (r1 join r2).
e. The source receives q1. The answer it returns is A1 = empty since both relations are now empty.	
	f. The warehouse receives A1 and replaces the view by MV – A1 = ({1,3}).
g. The source receives q2. The answer it returns is A2 = empty since both relations are now empty.	
	h. The warehouse receives A2 and replaces the view by MV – A2 = ({1,3}). This is the final answer.

of recomputing the view or storing copies of base relations. ECA is based on previous incremental view maintenance algorithms, but extra "compensating" queries are used to eliminate anomalies.

Zhuge et al. (1996) further examined the consistency problem in multiple source environments. The following is an example of a view maintenance anomaly over multiple sources. Let view V be defined as the natural join of relation r1 on source x, relation r2 on course y, and relation r3 on source z, respectively. Assuming the initial relations are

r1

A	B
1	2

r2

B	C
—	—

r3

C	D
3	4

The materialized view at the warehouse is MV = Ø. Now consider two source updates: u1 = insert (r2, {2,3}) and u2 = delete (r1, {1, 2}). The final answer of join apparently should be empty. However, using a conventional incremental view maintenance algorithm, one may not be able to get this answer, as shown in the following steps:

1. The warehouse receives u1 from source y. It generates query q1 = r1 join {2, 3} join r3. To evaluate q1, the warehouse first sends subquery r1 join {2,3} to source x.
2. The warehouse receives A_1^1 = {1, 2, 3} from source x. A new subquery q_1^2 = {1, 2, 3} join r3 is then sent to source z for evaluation.

3. The warehouse receives u2 = delete(r1, {1,2}) from source x. Since the current view is empty, no action is taken for this deletion.
4. The warehouse receives A_1^2 = {1,2,3,4} from source z, which is the final answer for q1. Since there are no pending queries or updates, the answer is inserted into MV and MV = {1,2,3,4}. This final view is apparently not correct.

To avoid such inconsistency, the Strobe family of algorithms was proposed. The basic idea behind these algorithms is to process updates as they arrive, sending queries to the sources when necessary, but not to perform updates immediately on the materialized view MV. Instead, a list of actions, Action List (AL), is generated to be performed on the view. The MV is updated only when applying all of the actions in AL (as a single transaction at the warehouse) will bring the view to a consistent state. This is carried out when there are no outstanding queries and all received updates have been processed.

When the basic Strobe algorithm is applied to the previous example, it works in the following manner:

1. AL = {}. The warehouse receives u1 from source y. It generates query q1 = r1 join {2, 3} join r3. To evaluate q1, the warehouse first sends subquery r1 join {2,3} to source x.
2. The warehouse receives A_1^1 = {1, 2, 3} from source x. A new subquery q_1^2 = {1, 2, 3} join r3 is then sent to source z for evaluation.
3. The warehouse receives u2 = delete(r1, {1,2}) from source x. It first adds u2 to a list called pending(q1) and then adds an item key-delete(MV, u2) to AL, which becomes AL = {key-delete(MV, u2)}.
4. The warehouse receives A_1^2 = {1,2,3,4} from source z. Since pending(q) is not empty, the warehouse applies key-delete(MV, u2) and generates resulting answer A2 = Ø. Nothing is added to AL. Since now there are no more pending queries, the warehouse updates MV by applying AL = {key-delete(MV, u2)}. The final answer is correct.

Zhuge et al. (1996) identify three fundamental transaction processing scenarios for data warehousing and define four levels of consistency for warehouse data. All of the algorithms in the Strobe family are incremental and can handle a continuous and overlapping stream of updates from the sources. The implementation shows that the algorithms are practical and realistic choices for a wide variety of update scenarios.

Ling and Sze (1998) also described a new compensation algorithm of incremental computation for updating the view that is used in removing anomalies caused by interfering updates at the base relations. Unlike existing methods on view maintenance, however, the algorithm does not assume that messages from a data source will reach the view maintenance machinery in the same order as they are generated, nor that one is able to detect update notification messages lost in their transit to the view, which would otherwise cause the view to be updated incorrectly. Anomalies are avoided by introducing version numbers that reflect the states of the base relations. The algorithm does not require that the system be quiescent before the view can be refreshed; therefore, the problem is handled in a more realistic setting.

The approaches described here put emphasis on ensuring that each view reflects a consistent state of the base data. In fact, the problem of ensuring data consistency at the warehouse can be divided into two components: one ensures that each view reflects a consistent state of the base data as discussed above, and the other ensures that multiple views are mutually consistent. Zhuge et al. (1997) studied the problem of guaranteeing multiple view consistency (MVC), identified and defined three layers of consistency for materialized views in a distributed environment, and presented a scalable architecture for consistently handling multiple views in a data warehouse implemented in the WHIPS prototype.

7.4.3 *Concurrent updates in distributed environment*

As another aspect of consistency in view maintenance, recent research work in data warehousing has also addressed the problem of view maintenance of data warehouses under concurrent data updates of different sources. A problem that must be addressed here is that different maintenances of the same materialized global view for different local updates may interfere with each other. As a result, the view may be incorrectly maintained. This is view maintenance anomaly in a distributed environment. In order to correct the problem, one needs to detect the occurrence of each anomaly precisely. In a distributed environment, the departure order of a set of messages from one site may be different from the arrival order of these messages at another site due to unpredictable network routings and delays. In such an environment, precise detection of the occurrence of each anomaly is difficult. A method for precisely detecting the occurrence of each maintenance anomaly for global views defined by SPJ queries has been proposed by Chen and Meng (1997).

Agarwal et al. (1997) presented incremental view maintenance algorithms for a data warehouse derived from multiple distributed autonomous data sources. A framework has been developed for analyzing view maintenance algorithms for multiple data sources with concurrent updates. Earlier approaches for view maintenance in the presence of concurrent updates typically require two types of messages: one to compute the view change due to the initial update, and the other to compensate the view change due to interfering concurrent updates. The algorithms developed based on this framework perform the compensation locally by using information already available at the data warehouse. An algorithm, termed SWEEP, ensures complete consistency of the view at the data warehouse in the presence of concurrent updates. However, its performance is limited due to enforcing a sequential ordering on the handling of data updates from data sources by the view maintenance module. Zhang and Rundensteiner (1999) tried to overcome this limitation by developing a parallel algorithm for view maintenance, called PSWEEP, that still incorporates all the benefits of SWEEP while offering substantially improved performance. In order to perform parallel view maintenance, two issues need to be resolved: 1. detecting maintenance-concurrent data updates in a parallel mode, and 2. correcting the problem that the data warehouse commit order may not correspond to the update processing order due to parallel maintenance handling.

The algorithms described above offer several significant advantages over previous solutions, such as high performance, no potential for infinite waits, and reduced remote queries (thus reduced network and data/information source loads). However, similar to many other algorithms, they still have the restricting assumption that each data or information source can be composed of just one single relation. This is unrealistic in practice. To deal with this, Ding et al. (1999) presented a solution to overcome this restriction. The proposed multirelation encapsulation (MRE) wrapper supports multiple relations in data or information sources in a manner transparent to the rest of the environment. The MRE wrapper treats one data or information source composed of multiple relations as if it were a single relation from the data warehousing point of view; thus, any existing incremental view maintenance algorithms can be applied even to complex data or information sources without any changes.

7.5   Integrity constraints and active databases

7.5.1   Integrity constraints

So far the relationship between warehouse data (namely, materialized views) and base data has been examined. When a base relation is not available for use in maintaining a view, we have to turn to integrity constraints that the relation is known to satisfy. Constraints are often available in practice, yet very little is known about how they can be exploited fully to enhance view self-maintainability (Huyn, 1997).

Chapter 3 defined an integrity constraint (IC) as a condition specified on a database schema that restricts data that can be stored as an instance of the database. Note that integrity constraints are closely related to views. As an example, consider the referential integrity constraint in a database of a retail change, which requires that every item ID in the OrderTable must occur in the ItemsTable. Also consider the view out_of_stockID:

> Define VIEW out_of_stockID as
> Select itemID from OrderTable
> Where itemID not in (select itemID from ItemsTable).

The constraint is violated whenever the view out_of_stockID is not empty. In general, an IC can be expressed using a view such that the view is not empty whenever the constraint is violated. Realizing the constraint as a materialized view then becomes similar to materializing an empty view. Checking the constraint when the underlying relations change corresponds to maintaining the view and indicating a violated IC whenever the view becomes not empty (Gupta and Mumick, 1995).

Self-maintenance of materialized views can be achieved by using key and referential integrity constraints (Quass et al., 1996). It has been shown that, by using key and referential integrity constraints, one often can maintain a select-project-join view when there are insertions, deletions, and updates to the base relations, without going to the data sources or replicating the base relations in their entirety in the warehouse. A set of auxiliary views can be derived so that the warehouse view and the auxiliary views together are self-maintainable. The problem of determining view self-maintenance in the presence of functional dependencies has been studied, and self-maintenance of conjunctive query view can be reduced to a problem of query containment in the context of a deductive database language, Datalog (Huyn, 1997b).

Section 7.3.2 distinguished view maintenance using partial information vs. full information. Maintaining materialized views using partial information is an important issue for integrity constraint checking. It is well known that, for relational databases in which keys are the only ways to identify objects, efficient incremental view maintenance using partial information is only possible under certain conditions and for certain modifications of the base data. Essentially, the information needed for view maintenance cannot be sufficiently represented in the derived relation itself so that the view can be updated autonomously. Shu (1997) showed that more information can be converted into the derived relation if variables are introduced to represent values in both the base and the derived relations which can be considered as a modest step towards combining relations and objects. The derived relations can be represented using conditional tables, which are more expressive in representing information needed for view maintenance than conventional tables.

7.5.2   *Active databases*

The examination of integrity constraints leads us to a discussion of the relationship between materialized views and triggers in active databases in many ways. Active databases contain production rules that specify when to carry out actions, and which actions to carry out. In fact, materialized views, integrity constraints, and rules or triggers are examples of different types of active elements in databases and are strongly correlated. Active elements are inherently recursive in nature and are important to the issue of scalability (Gupta and Mumick, 1998).

It is widely recognized that production rules in database systems can be used to maintain derived data such as views automatically. However, writing a correct set of rules for efficiently maintaining a given view can be a difficult and ad hoc process. Ceri and Widom (1991) provided a facility whereby a user defines a view as an SQL select expression and from which the system automatically derives set-oriented production rules that maintain a materialization of that view. The maintenance rules are triggered by operations on the view's base tables. Generally, the rules perform incremental maintenance: the materialized view is modified according to the sets of changes made to the base tables, which are accessible through logical tables provided by the rule language. However, for some operations substantial recomputation may be required. Algorithms have been developed to use key information to perform syntactic analysis on a view definition to determine whether efficient maintenance is possible.

7.6   Dynamic warehouse design

7.6.1   Dynamicity of warehouse design

In Section 7.2 data warehousing design through materialized views was discussed. Subsequent sections addressed related issues, such as view maintenance. To simplify this discussion, it has been implicitly assumed that the static structure of data warehousing, such as database schema, will always stay the same. However, this assumption is often not realistic. Therefore, the next aspect to be examined is the dynamicity involved in warehouse design. The basic idea for dealing with the dynamic nature of data warehouses is addressed by Rundensteiner et al. (2000). The dynamicity lies in the fact that many data and information sources, particularly Web-based data sources, may change not only their data, but also their capabilities, without cooperating with users. Assuming the relational model as a common integration paradigm, the types of changes visible at the middleware can be categorized as: 1. data updates, such as adding tuples or change values; 2. schema changes, such as adding columns or deleting tables; 3. constraint modifications, such as removing key constraints or adding containment constraints; and 4. statistics and metadata adjustments, such as selectivity of attributes and size of relations.

Data warehousing issues for dynamic sources include: 1. adapting to data or information source changes at the level of wrappers of the information sources; 2. adapting the definition of the data warehouse; and 3. adapting the data content in the data warehouse. The next section details some specific aspects.

7.6.2   Warehouse evolution

Since a data warehouse consists of materialized views, research in data warehouses addresses the evolution problem from two different perspectives, namely, the schema evolution of base relations and views, or the maintenance of the extent of the view (i.e., the actual tuples satisfied by the view).

Adaptation has played an important role in the study of schema evolution. A taxonomy of view adaptation has been established (Rundensteiner et al., 2000) based on the types of changes to the view, the desired level of view adaptability in the context of changes, and the changes related to the base information system, such as data updates, capability changes, or metadata changes. A related issue is the view synchronization problem, which is concerned with updating the views when base tables are updated. One solution is to design an environment so that view definition adaptation is triggered by capability changes of information systems. Balschka (1999) described a framework for the evolution of conceptual multidimensional schemas in which each evolution operation at the conceptual level of the warehouse has well-defined semantics and is mapped to a physical implementation level.

7.6.3   From static to dynamic warehouse design

Recall that the dynamicity of a data warehouse means that, when user query requirement changes, the existing materialized views should evolve to meet the new requirement. This aspect has a profound impact on data warehouse design because the changes of user query requirement will demand schema changes at the warehouse as discussed above and should be handled with as little disruption or modification to other components of the warehousing system as possible. Zhang and Yang (1998) proposed a framework to determine if and how existing materialized views will be affected by requirement changes. Algorithms are proposed to deal with the situation when a new query is added, the aim of which is to get the new materialized views efficiently by analyzing relationships among queries using a specification for the query processing plan called MVPP.

The data warehouse design problem discussed in Section 7.2 can be referred to as the static data warehouse design problem (Theodoratos and Sellis, 2000) because it does not emphasize that data warehouses are dynamic entities in that they evolve over time and new queries need to be answered. Although some of the new queries can be answered by views already materialized in the data warehouse, other new queries necessitate the materialization of new views. The static data warehouse design problem deals with this issue by reimplementing the warehouse from scratch. However, selecting the appropriate set of views for materialization (as needed in this reimplementation) could be time consuming. To deal with the problems faced by the static approach, the dynamic data warehouse design problem has been proposed, and can be stated as follows:

> Given a set of materialized views consisting of the data warehouse, a set of new queries to be answered by the warehouse, and, possibly, some extra space allocated for materialization to the warehouse, select a set of new views to additionally materialize, such that: 1. new materialized views fit in the extra allocated space; 2. all new queries can be answered using exclusively the old and new materialized views; and 3. the combination of the cost of evaluating new queries over the materialized views and the view maintenance cost of new views is minimal.

Using an AND/OR directed acyclic graph (DAG) representation of multiple queries, the dynamic data warehouse design problem can be modeled as a state space search problem. States are multiquery AND/OR DAGs representing old and new materialized views and complete rewritings of all the new queries over the materialized views. State transformation rules have been defined and proved to be sound, nonredundant, and complete, so that, from an initial state, a goal state (which is an optimal solution) can be reached by applying transformation rules. In addition, algorithms have been developed to compute incrementally the cost and size of a state when moving from one state to another. The efficiency of algorithms is improved by applying proposed pruning methods in the search space. Since the approach can be applied to statically designing a data warehouse, it is compatible and subsumes the previously proposed approach.

A different, but related problem of data warehousing dynamics is that, after some time, some of the data may no longer be needed or may not be of interest. Garcia-Molina et al. (1998) deal with this problem by expiring or removing unneeded materialized view tuples. A framework supporting such expiration is presented; within it, a user or administrator can declaratively request expirations and specify what type of modifications are expected from external sources. The latter can significantly increase the amount of data to be expired. Efficient algorithms are presented for determining which data can be expired (data not needed for maintenance of other views), taking into account the types of updates that may occur.

7.6.4 View redefinition and adaptation

Traditional view maintenance tries to maintain the materialized view in response to modifications to the base relations; however, one can try to "adapt" the view in response to changes in the view definition (Gupta et al., 2001). Such techniques are needed for applications where the user can change queries dynamically and quickly see the changes in the results. Data archeology, data visualization, and dynamic queries are examples of such applications. Gupta et al. (2001) have considered possible redefinitions of SQL select-from-where-groupby, union, and minus views, and have shown how these views can be adapted using the old materialization for cases in which it is possible to do so. Extra information that can be kept with a materialization to facilitate a redefinition has been identified. Multiple simultaneous changes to a view without necessarily materializing intermediate results can also be handled. Guidelines that can be used to facilitate efficient view adaptation have been provided for users and database administrators.

The evolvable view environment (EVE) project conducted by Nica and Rundersteiner (1999) addresses the dynamicity problem by evolving the view definitions affected by source schema changes, referred to as view synchronization. In EVE, the view synchronizer rewrites the view definitions by replacing view components with suitable components from other data sources. After such a view redefinition process, the contents of the view (i.e., the view extents), if materialized, are also brought up to date. Strategies have been proposed to address this incremental adaptation of the view extent after view synchronization.

7.7   Implementation issues and online updates

7.7.1   Physical implementation

The issue of data warehouse implementation has already been addressed in Chapter 5 (Section 5.4). Since a data warehouse consists of materialized views, here one aspect related to implementation of materialized views is reexamined. It is possible and desirable to separate the process of warehouse refreshment from the process of warehouse use. Baekgaard and Roussopoulos (1996) described and compared view refreshment algorithms based on different combinations of materialized views, partially materialized views, and pointers. These algorithms and data structures are designed to minimize network communication and interactions between the warehouse and the source databases. The minimal set of data necessary for both warehouse refreshment and warehouse use is stored in the warehouse. An experiment comparing these methods with respect to storage overhead and I/O has been carried out.

7.7.2   Indexing techniques

As already discussed in Section 3.7, materialized views have a close relationship with indexing. The read-mostly environment of data warehousing makes it possible to use more complex indices to speed up queries than in situations where concurrent updates are present. Indexing technology has been widely studied in the data warehousing environment (O'Neil and Quass, 1997).

A particular problem related to indexing selection can be described as follows. In most commercial OLAP systems a two-step process occurs; namely, the summary tables to be precomputed are picked first, followed by the selection of appropriate indices on them. A trial-and-error approach can be used to divide the space available between the summary tables and the indices, but this two-step process can perform poorly. Since both summary tables and indices consume the same resource (i.e., space), their selection should be done together for the most efficient use of space (Gupta et al., 1997). A family of algorithms has been developed to automate the selection of summary tables and indices.

7.7.3   Online updates

The warehouse is often kept only loosely consistent with sources: it is periodically refreshed with changes sent from the source. When this happens, the warehouse is taken off-line until local relations and materialized views can be updated. Clearly, users would prefer as little downtime as possible; often downtime can be reduced by adding carefully selected materialized views or indices to the physical schema.

Labio et al. (1999) addressed the issue of reducing the time taken for updating warehouse views. The time needed for update, referred to as the update window, can be reduced by minimizing the work required to compute and install a batch of updates. Various strategies have been proposed in the literature for updating a single warehouse view. These algorithms typically cannot be extended to come up with good strategies for updating an entire set of views. An efficient algorithm was developed to select an optimal update strategy for any single warehouse view. Based on this algorithm, algorithms for selecting strategies to update a set of views were also developed. The performance of these algorithms was studied with experiments involving warehouse views based on TPC-D queries.

In different research, Labrinidis and Roussopoulos (1998) proposed, for online incremental view updates, a MAUVE algorithm that uses timestamps and allows consistent read-only access to the warehouse while it is being updated. The algorithm propagates the updates to the views more often than the typical once a day in order to reduce view staleness. MAUVE has been implemented on top of the Informix Universal Server, and a synthetic workload generator has been used to experiment with various update workloads and different view update frequencies. Results show that all kinds of update streams benefit from more frequent view updates.

Data warehouses store materialized views over base data from external sources. Clients typically perform complex read-only queries on the views. The views are refreshed periodically by maintenance transactions, which propagate large batch updates from the base tables. Note that, in current warehousing systems, maintenance transactions usually are isolated from client read activity, limiting availability and/or size of the warehouse. Multiple materialized summary tables are often related in that they are defined over the same fact table, so it would be possible to take advantage of their interrelationships when maintaining them in a batch process. Quass and Widom (1997) described an algorithm called "two version no locking (2VNL) that allows warehouse maintenance transactions to run concurrently with readers. By logically maintaining two versions of the database, no locking is required and serializability is guaranteed. The relationship to other multiversion concurrency control algorithms, as well as an implementation on top of a conventional relational DBMS using a query rewrite approach, were described.

7.8 Data cubes

The importance of data cubes can be justified by the various reasons why materialized views play a very important role in OLAP (Gupta and Mumick, 1998):

- Warehouses are very large and computing results on the fly may be slow, so materialization is desirable.
- Unlike operational databases, warehouse data may not always reflect up-to-date data. However, decision support queries submitted to data warehouses do not require exact answers and can tolerate some out-of-date data. Therefore, previously acquired data can be materialized for later use.
- Queries by analysts are frequently interrelated, making reusing intermediate queries possible; these intermediate queries can be materialized.
- The result of a query may need substantial off-line preprocessing for viewing in a visualization tool, and views enable this kind of processing

Multidimensional data cubes are a particular form of materialized views and their design deserves special attention. Chapter 6 already provided a discussion on materialized views; this section presents some research results related to data cubes. In a multidimensional database, views are selected from the multidimensional lattice whose elements represent the solution space of the problem. Several techniques have been proposed in the past to perform the selection of materialized views for databases with a reduced number of dimensions. When the number and complexity of dimensions increase, the proposed techniques do not scale well. The technique proposed by Baralis and Paraboschi (1997) reduces the solution space by considering only the relevant elements of the multidimensional lattice. An additional statistical analysis allows a further reduction of the solution space.

Harinarayan et al. (1996) investigated the issue of which cells of a data cube (views) to materialize when it is too expensive to materialize all views. A lattice framework is used to express dependencies among views. Greedy algorithms are developed that work off this lattice and determine a good set of views to materialize. The optimization criterion can be either the space available for storing the views or the number of views that may be materialized. A simplified implementation of this work has been described in Chapter 6. Furthermore, methods have been proposed to compute a data cube in which all the different nodes in the lattice may not necessarily need to be materialized. Sort and hash-based methods with optimization techniques were proposed (Agarwal et al., 1996).

A method called the summary-delta table method was proposed by Mumick et al. (1997) to maintain aggregate views. The authors further investigate how to use this method to solve two problems in maintaining summary tables in a warehouse: how to maintain a summary table efficiently while minimizing the batch window needed for maintenance, and how to maintain a large set of summary tables defined over the same base tables. It has been shown that much of the work required for maintaining one summary table by the proposed method can be reused in maintaining other summary tables, so that a set of summary tables can be maintained efficiently.

Another interesting method is concerned with dynamically assembling views in multidimensional data cubes in order to support data analysis and querying involving aggregations more efficiently (Smith et al., 1998). The proposed method decomposes the data cubes into an indexed hierarchy of view elements. These view elements differ from traditional data cube cells in that they correspond to partial and residual aggregations of the data cube. The view elements provide highly granular building blocks for synthesizing the aggregated and range-aggregated views of the data cubes. A strategy for selecting and materializing the view elements based on the frequency of view access was proposed, which allows the dynamic adaptation of the view element sets to patterns of retrieval. A fast and optimal algorithm was presented for selecting nonexpansive view element sets that minimize processing costs for generating a population of aggregated views. Also presented was a greedy algorithm for selecting redundant view element sets in order to reduce processing costs further. It has been demonstrated that the view element approaches perform better in terms of lower processing and storage costs than methods based on materializing views.

OLAP applications use precomputation of aggregate data to improve query response time. However, all aggregates are usually computed from a single cube (in a star schema, this corresponds to existence of a single fact table). Many real world applications require aggregates over multiple fact tables. Performance issues on the precomputation problem for multicube systems also need to be considered. This problem is significantly more complex than the single cube precomputation problem, and algorithms and cost models developed for single cube precomputation must be extended to deal well with the multicube case (Shukla et al., 1998).

A perspective concerning relationships among data cubes in data cube design can be described as follows. To reduce maintenance cost, which is related to the number of cubes materialized, some cubes can be merged, but the resulting larger cubes will increase the response time of answering some queries. In order to satisfy both maintenance and response time bounds given by the user, one may have to sacrifice some queries by not taking them into consideration. The optimization problem in the data cube system design is to optimize an initial set of cubes such that the system can answer a maximum number of queries and satisfy the bounds. This is an NP-complete problem; greedy algorithms have been proposed (Hung et al., 2000).

Shukla et al. (1998) studied the structure of the precomputation problem and presented an improved algorithm under certain broad conditions on the multidimensional data. An interesting aspect distinguishing this work from previous work is that previous work assumed that all aggregates were either precomputed in their entirety or not at all. By allowing aggregates to be partially precomputed, it is possible to find solutions better than those found by previous algorithms, and, in some cases, to find solutions better than the optimal solution by the previous definition.

OLAP systems support data analysis through a multidimensional data model, according to which data facts are viewed as points in a space of application-related dimensions, organized into levels which conform to a hierarchy. Although the usual assumption is that these points reflect the dynamic aspect of the data warehouse while dimensions are relatively static, in practice, dimension updates are often necessary to adapt the multidimensional database to changing requirements. These updates can take place either at the structural level (e.g., addition of categories or modification of the hierarchical structure) or at the instance level (elements can be inserted, deleted, merged, etc.). They are poorly supported (or not supported at all) in current commercial systems and have not been addressed in the literature. Hurtado et al. (1999) extended a formal model supporting dimension updates introduced earlier by adding a set of semantically meaningful operators which encapsulate common sequences of primitive dimension updates in a more efficient way. Normalized and denormalized mappings from the multidimensional to the relational model have been defined, and a comparison of an implementation of dimension updates using these two approaches has been carried out.

In different research, Pourabbas and Rafanelli (1999) proposed and discussed some different types of hierarchies within a single dimension of a cube. These hierarchies are organized into different levels of aggregation in a single dimension. The characterization of some OLAP operators that refer to hierarchies in order to maintain the data cube consistency can then be defined. Moreover, a set of operators was proposed for changing the hierarchy structure. The issues discussed provide modeling flexibility during the scheme design phase, as well as correct data analysis.

In another study dealing with dynamic contents, Liang et al. (2000) investigated the particular problem of range queries in data warehouses consisting of dynamic OLAP data cubes. A range query applies an aggregation operation (such as sum) over all selected cells of an OLAP data cube where the selection is specified by providing ranges of values for numeric dimensions. Range queries are often tied with the dynamicity of data warehousing because many application domains require that data cubes be updated often and the information provided by analysis tools be current or near current. Other work on OLAP system design and query analysis includes Bauer et al. (2000). Meta queries and OLAP query evaluation have been discussed in Ben-Eliahu and Gudes (1999) and Ben-Eliyahu-Zohary and Gudes (2000).

Finally, an issue related to physical implementation of data cubes should be examined. Data warehousing applications cope with enormous data sets in the range of gigabytes and terabytes. Queries usually either select a very small set of this data or perform aggregations on a fairly large data set. Although materialized views storing precomputed aggregates are used to process queries with aggregations efficiently, this approach increases resource requirements in disk space and slows down updates because of the view maintenance problem. Multidimensional hierarchical clustering (MHC) of OLAP data was introduced by Markl et al. (1999) to overcome these problems while offering more flexibility for aggregation paths. In-clustering was introduced as a way to speed up aggregation queries without additional storage cost for materialization. Performance and storage cost of this access method were investigated and compared to current query processing scenarios. Performance measurements on real world data for a typical star schema were also presented.

7.9   Materialized views in advanced database systems

Although data warehousing typically employs relational techniques, it is not necessarily restricted to such an environment. Next, issues related to materialized views in these more advanced database systems are discussed.

7.9.1   Materialized views and deductive databases

Some approaches discussed earlier require deductive database techniques due to the inference power residing in these systems. Below is a summary of some additional work related to materialized views in deductive databases. Motivated by integrating data and knowledge from multiple heterogeneous sources for answering certain queries, Lu et al. (1995) proposed a framework for defining mediated views spanning multiple knowledge bases by a set of constrained rules. Materialization of these views was investigated by unfolding the view definition and the efficient maintenance of the resulting materialized mediated view in case of updates. Therefore, two kinds of updates needed to be considered: updates to the view and updates to the underlying sources. For each of these two cases several efficient algorithms maintaining materialized mediated views were given.

Huyn (1996) addressed the problem of incrementally maintaining a materialized view using the view instance and the update but with only limited access to the base data. Necessary and sufficient conditions were given for self-maintainability (handling updates without looking at all base data) for conjunctive-query (CQ) views. These conditions were generated at view-definition time and expressed as safe, nonrecursive Datalog queries.

To reduce maintenance costs, Huyn (1997) tried to maintain the views in response to a base update, using information strictly local to the warehouse: the view definitions and the view contents. Only when failing to do so is it necessary to resort to accessing a subset of the base relations. However, there may be situations in which, under a specific base update and given a specific state of the views and subset of base relations used, no way to maintain a view unambiguously exists. Gupta and Mumick (1999) have more recently attempted to deal with the cost issue.

Gupta et al. (1992) presented an incremental evaluation algorithm for materialized views in relational and deductive database systems. Counting solutions to the view maintenance problem were provided. The algorithm computes, in an incremental fashion, the changes to the materialized view in response to changes (insertions, deletions, and updates) to the base relations. The view may be defined in SQL or in Datalog, and may use UNION, negation, aggregation (e.g., SUM, MIN), linear recursion, and general recursion. The algorithm is optimal in that it computes exactly those view tuples that are inserted or deleted. The algorithm works by tracking the number of derivation trees for each tuple in the view, which corresponds to the count of a tuple in the duplicate semantics used in relational systems such as those based on SQL. For deductive databases using set semantics, the number of derivation trees for nonrecursive queries can be computed at little or no cost above the cost of evaluating the query.

The issue of irrelevant update for materialized views in general was discussed in Section 7.3.5. Levy and Sagiv (1993) studied queries independent of updates in the deductive database context: views with stratified negation and order constraints. Detecting independence is important for several reasons. It can be used in view maintenance to identify that some views are independent of certain updates. In transaction scheduling, it can provide greater flexibility by identifying one transaction that is independent of updates made by another. It can also use independence in query optimization by ignoring parts of the database for which updates do not affect a specific query.

7.9.2   *Materialized views in object-oriented databases*

Another direction of extension in the study of materialized views is from relational databases to relational-object databases or object-oriented databases. Whether a view can be maintained incrementally depends on the types of involved database objects, their update operations, and the properties of the functions that the view computation process applies to these objects. Gluche et al. (1997) discussed the CROQUE approach to the maintenance problem for materialized views. In a CROQUE database, application-specified collections (type extents or classes) themselves need not be materialized. In exchange, the system maintains (redundant) views of the application data that help to minimize query response time. Views are treated as functions of database objects and examine algebraic properties of these functions, in particular linearity, to derive incremental update plans. The result is that it is feasible to employ ODMG OQL as a view definition language in such an environment, since the majority of its clauses represent linear functions.

A group of expressions for incrementally evaluating query expressions in the nested relational model were derived by Liu et al. (1999). It is important to note that there are several significant differences between the relational and object-oriented paradigms that can be exploited when addressing the object-oriented view materialization problem. Kuno and Rundensteiner (1996, 1999) proposed techniques that prune update propagation by exploiting knowledge of the subsumption relationships between classes to identify branches of classes to which updates need not be propagated and by using derivation ordering to eliminate self-canceling propagation.

7.10   Relationship with mobile databases

Recently, database aspects of mobile computing have received increased attention. Wolfson et al. (1995) provided an outline of the major issues related to maintaining personalized views in a network of fixed and mobile computers. Although the issue of view maintenance has been studied extensively in the literature, new problems have been introduced by distribution and mobility. These problems are introduced by the fact that the connection between the materialized view at the mobile computer and the online database may vary widely in terms of cost, reliability, and capacity. Specifically, wide-area wireless networks are costly and unreliable, and have a small bandwidth, whereas local-area wireless networks suffer much less from these limitations. A software system for view maintenance in mobile computing has been built to address these problems.

Specific efforts have been made to invent methods for developing mobile client-server database applications by utilizing materialized views and understanding their correctness requirements. For example, Lauzac (1999) and Lauzac and Chrysanthis (1998) proposed a notion called view holder within the fixed network whose job is to maintain versions of the views required by a particular mobile host.

In a mobile environment, querying the database at a stationary server by a mobile client is expensive due to the limited bandwidth of a wireless channel and the instability of the wireless network. Lee et al. (1998) addressed this problem by maintaining a materialized view in the client's local storage that contains results of common queries in which the mobile client is interested. Such a materialized view is termed a mobile data warehouse. The view update problem for maintaining a mobile data warehouse is studied. It has been noted that existing view update mechanisms are push-based because the server is responsible for notifying all clients whose views might be affected by database changes. This is not appropriate in a mobile environment due to the frequent disconnection of a wireless channel. A pull-based approach was proposed to allow a materialized view to be incrementally updated at the client's site. This approach requires a client to request changes to its view from the server when needed.

7.11   Other issues

The following sample issues illustrate the diversity of research in materialized views.

7.11.1   Temporal view self-maintenance

A data warehouse is a time-varying data collection, consequently, the views in a data warehouse belong to two categories: temporal and nontemporal (i.e., only the current state of the data is available). Yang and Widom (1998a, 1998b) examined the use of data warehousing for providing temporal views over the history of source data that may itself be nontemporal. An architecture for a temporal data warehouse, as described in this study, automatically maintains temporal views over nontemporal source relations, and allows users to ask temporal queries using these views. Temporal views need to be maintained during change propagation (when source relations are updated) and view refresh (when the current time of the temporal database advances). An eager approach is taken for change propagation: changes at sources are immediately propagated through all the affected views. A lazy approach is taken for view refresh: a materialized view is refreshed with respect to advanced time only when the view is required for computation.

7.11.2   Real-time warehousing

The issue of real-time warehousing was briefly examined in Chapter 2. Next is an example of research work concerning real-time data warehousing for importing a view. To import a view, i.e., to install a stream of updates, a real-time database system must process new updates in a timely fashion to keep the database fresh, but at the same time must process transactions and ensure they meet their time constraints. Adelberg et al. (1995) discussed the various properties of updates and views (including staleness) that affect this tradeoff. Through simulation, four algorithms were examined for scheduling transactions and installing updates in a soft real-time database.

7.11.3   Materialized views in Oracle

Although there has been a significant gap between data warehouse research and practice, recently the concept of using materialized views has been incorporated into commercial products. Oracle Materialized Views are designed for data warehousing and replication. For data warehousing, materialized views based on inner/outer equijoins with optional aggregation can be refreshed on transaction boundaries, on demand, or periodically. Refreshes are optimized for bulk loads and can use a multimaterialized views scheduler. Materialized views based on subqueries on remote tables support bidirectional replication. Optimization with materialized views includes transparent query rewrite based on cost-based selection methods. The ability to rewrite a large class of queries based on a small set of materialized views is supported by using a new Oracle object called Dimensions, and by using losslessness of joins, functional dependencies, aggregate rollup, etc. (Bello et al., 1998).

Using Oracle8i's materialized views can simplify data-warehouse summary management and speed query processing. At the same time, summary tables can help improve the performance of queries that summarize data. However, summary tables introduce some new challenges:

- The database administrators (DBAs) must manually update each summary table and associated indices after loading new data into the corresponding detail tables. This keeps the summary data synchronized with underlying detail tables and ensures accurate query results.

- Developers and ad hoc analysts must be aware of all available summary tables and understand when to target a summary table explicitly for a specific query.

To help solve the problems of managing summary tables while preserving the corresponding performance benefits, Oracle8*i* introduces several new features: a new schema object, the materialized view, that can be used for summary-table data; enhancements to the optimizer, which enable it to automatically rewrite queries to use materialized views; a built-in package, DBMS_MVIEW, that provides refresh and other procedures to manage materialized views; and facilities for analyzing the effectiveness of existing and potential materialized views. More details about Oracle can be found in Bobrowski (2000).

7.12 Summary

This chapter summarized various research work on materialized views. The main purpose has been to illustrate the diversity of this direction of research, showing what kinds of problems should be considered and basic ideas behind these approaches. Wrap-up of this chapter provides several research problems related to materialized views, including those that have not been addressed in this text (Gupta and Mumick, 1998):

- There are many approaches to maintaining materialized views. But how should a set of views be maintained together? A very important example of such views is that of the aggregation lattice in a roll-up hierarchy of a multidimensional data source.
- How should different kinds of updates be treated?
- How should views be maintained in the presence of incomplete information?
- How should semantic information and metadata be used? Often, a database system has available integrity constraints (such as functional dependencies). This information is useful in view maintenance because it helps identify irrelevant updates and optimize computations. For example, primary key information is used to handle updates efficiently and to propagate deletions to views.

Solutions to these problems, as well as many other problems, will have significant impact on the future development of data warehouses.

References

Adelberg, B., H. Garcia-Molina, and B. Kao, Applying update streams in a soft real-time database system, *Proc. SIGMOD*, 245–256, 1995.

Agarwal, S., R. Agrawal, P. M. Deshpande, A. Gupta, J. F. Naughton, R. Ramakrishnan, and S. Sarawagi, On the computation of multidimensional aggregates, *Proc. Very Large Databases 1996.* (Reprinted as Chap. 24 in A. Gupta and I. S. Mumick (Eds.), *Materialized Views,* 1998, pp. 361–386.)

Agrawal, D., A. El Abbadi, A. Singh, and T. Yurek, Efficient view maintenance at data warehouses, *Proc. SIGMOD,* 1997, 417–427.

Akinde, M. and M. H. Bohlen, Constructing GPSJ view graphs, *Proc. DMDW 1999 (online),* Chap. 8, 1999.

Baekgaard, L., Event-entity-relationship modeling in data warehouse environments, *Proc. ACM Second Intl. Workshop on Data Warehousing and OLAP (DOLAP),* 1999, 9–14.

Baekgaard, L. and N. Roussopoulos, Efficient refreshment of data warehouse views, Technical Report, Dept. of Computer Science, Univ. of Maryland, College Park, May 1996.

Bailey, J., G. Dong, M. K. Mohania, and X. S. Wang, Incremental view maintenance by base relation tagging in distributed databases, *Distributed Parallel Databases,* 6(3), 287–309, 1998.

Balschka, M., FIESTA: A framework for schema evolution in multidimensional information systems, *Proc. 6th CAiSE Doctoral Consortium,* 1999.

Baralis, E. and S. Paraboschi, Materialized view selection in a multidimensional database, *VLDB J.,* 156–165, 1997.

Bauer, A., W. Hummer, and W. Lehner, An alternative relational OLAP Modeling approach, *Proc. DaWak,* 189–198, 2000.

Bello, R. G., K. Dias, A. Downing, J. Feenan Jr., W. D. Norcott, H. Sun, A. Witkowski, and M. Ziauddin, Materialized views in Oracle, *Proc. 24th VLDB,* 659–664, 1998.

Ben-Eliyahu-Zohary, R. and E. Gudes, Meta-queries — computation and evaluation, *Proc. DaWaK,* 265–275, 2000.

Ben-Eliyahu-Zohary, R. and E. Gudes, Towards efficient meta-querying, *Proc. IJCAI-99,* 800–805, 1999.

Blakeley, J. A., P.-Å. Larson, and F. W. Tompa, Efficiently updating materialized views, *SIGMOD,* 61–71, 1986.

Blakeley, J. A., N. Coburn, and P.-Å. Larson, Updating derived relations: detecting irrelevant and autonomously computable updates, *ACM Trans. Database Sys.,* 14(3), 369–400.

Bobrowski, S., Using materialized views to speed up queries, 1999. Available at http://www.oracle.com/oranag/oracle/99-sep/index.html?59bob.html.

Boehnlein, M. and A. U.-v. Ende, Deriving initial data warehouse structures from the conceptual data models of the underlying operational information systems, *Proc. DOLAP,* 15–21, 1999.

Bouzeghoub, M. and Z. Kedad, A logical model for data warehouse design and evolution, *Proc. DaWaK,* 178–188, 2000.

Cabibbo, L. and R. Torlone, The design and development of a logical system for OLAP, *Proc. DaWak,* 1–10, 2000.

Ceri, S. and J. Widom, Deriving production rules for incremental view maintenance, *Proc. 1991 Very Large Databases Conf.,* 577–589, 1991.

Chaudhuri, S., R. Krisjnamurthy, S. Potamianos, and K. Shim, Optimizing queries with materialized views, *Proc. 11th ICDE,* 190–200, 1995.

Chen, J., X. Zhang, S. Chen, A. Koeller, and E. A. Rundensteiner, DyDa: data warehouse maintenance in fully concurrent environments, *Proc. SIGMOD,* 2001.

Chen, R. and W. Meng, Precise detection and proper handling of view maintenance anomalies in a multidatabase environment, *Proc. Intl. Conf. on Cooperative Info. Syst.*, 110–119, 1997.

Cohen, S., W. Nutt, and A. Serebrenik, Algorithms for rewriting aggregate queries using views, *Proc. DMDW,* 1999.

Cohen, S., W. Nutt, and A. Serebrenik, Rewriting aggregate queries using views, *Proc. 18th ACM Symp. Principles Database Syst.*, 1999.

Colby, L. S., T. Griffin, L. Libkin, I. S. Mumick, and H. Trickey, Algorithms for deferred view maintenance, *Proc. SIGMOD,* 469–480, 1996. (Reprinted MV 16, 209-228)

Colby, L. S., A. Kawaguchi, D. F. Lieuwen, I. S. Mumick, and K. A. Ross, Supporting multiple view maintenance policies, *SIGMOD Conf.*, 405–416, 1997.

Cui, Y. and J. Widom, Practical lineage tracing in data warehouses, *Proc. 16th Int. Conf. Data Eng.*, 367–378, 1998.

Cui, Y., J. Widom, and J. L. Wiener, View data in a data warehousing environment, *ACM Trans. Database Syst. (TODS)*, 25(2), 179–227, 2000.

Ding, L., X. Zhang, and E. A. Rundensteiner, The MRE wrapper approach: enabling incremental view maintenance of data warehouses defined on multi-relation information sources, *Proc. DOLAP,* 30–35, 1999.

Ding, L., X. Zhang, and E. A. Rundensteiner, Scalable maintenance of multiple inter-related data warehousing systems, *Proc. DaWaK,* 104–113, 2000.

Dong, G., Incremental maintenance of recursive views: a survey, Chap. 12 in A. Gupta and I. S. Mumick (Eds.), *Materialized Views,* 159–162, 1998.

Franconi, E. and U. Sattler, A data warehouse conceptual data model for multidimensional aggregation, *Proc. DMDW,* 1999.

Garcia-Molina, H., W. Labio, and J. Yang, Expiring data in a warehouse, *Proc. 24th Int. Conf. Very Large Data Bases,* 1998.

Gatziu, S., M. Jeusfeld, M. Staudt, and Y. Vassiliou, Design and management of data warehouses (Report on the DMDW'99 Workshop), *SIGMOD Rec.,* 2000.

Gluche, D., T. Grust, C. Mainberger, and M. H. Scholl, Incremental updates for materialized OQL views, *Proc. Deductive Object-Oriented Databases (DOOD97),* 1997.

Golfareli, M., D. Maio, and S. Rizzi, Applying vertical fragmentation techniques in logical design of multidimensional databases, *Proc. DaWak,* 11–23, 2000.

Griffin, T. and L. Libkin, Incremental maintenance of views with duplicates, *Proc. SIGMOD,* 1995, 328–339. (Reprinted in *Materialized Views,* A. Gupta and I. S. Mumick, Eds., 191–208.)

Gupta, A. and I. S. Mumick, Maintenance of materialized views: problems, techniques, and applications, *IEEE Data Eng. Bull.,* 1995. (Reprinted as Chap 11 in A. Gupta and I. S. Mumick (Eds.), *Materialized Views,* 145–158.)

Gupta, A. and I. S. Mumick, Challenges in supporting materialized views, in *Materialized Views,* A. Gupta and I. S. Mumick, Eds., 39–52.

Gupta, A., I. S. Mumick, and V. S. Subrahmanian, Maintaining views incrementally, *Proc. SIGMOD,* 157–167, 1993. (Reprinted as in A. Gupta and I. S. Mumick (Eds.), *Materialized Views,* 177–190.)

Gupta, A., D. Katiyar, and I. S. Mumick, Counting solutions to the view maintenance problem, Workshop on Deductive Databases, *JICLSP,* 1992.

Gupta, A., I. S. Mumick, and V. S. Subrahmanian, Maintaining views incrementally, *Proc. ACM SIGMOD Int. Conf. Manage. Data,* 157–166, 1993.

Gupta, A., I. S. Mumick, and K. A. Ross, Adapting materialized views after redefinitions, *Proc. SIGMOD,* 211–222, 1995.

Gupta, A. and I. S. Mumick, What is the data warehousing problem? (Are material-ized views the answer?), *Proc. Very Large Databases 96*, 602 (Panel).

Gupta, A. and I. S. Mumick, Maintenance policies, in *Materialized Views*, A. Gupta and I. S. Mumick, Eds., MIT Press, Cambridge, MA, 1998, 9–12.

Gupta, A., I. S. Mumick, J. Rao, and K. A. Ross, Adapting materialized views after redefinitions: techniques and a performance study, *Inf. Syst.*, Special issue on data warehousing (to appear, 2001). (Preliminary version appeared in *Proc. ACM SIGMOD Conf.*, May 1995, 211–222; also in *Materialized Views*, A. Gupta and I. S. Mumick, Eds., 1998, 107–124.)

Gupta, A., V. Harinarayan, and D. Quass, Aggregate-query processing in data ware-housing environments, *Proc. 21st Very Large Databases Conf.*, 358–369, 1995.

Gupta, A. and I. S. Mumick, Maintenance of materialized views: problems, tech-niques, and applications, in *Materialized Views*, A. Gupta and I. S. Mumick, Eds., 1998, 145–158.

Gupta, H., Selection of views to materialize in a data warehouse, *Proc. ICDT*, 1997.

Gupta, H., V. Harinarayan, A. Rajaraman, and J. D. Ullman, Index selection for OLAP, *Proc. 13th Int. Conf. Data Eng.*, 208–219, 1997.

Gupta, H. and I. S. Mumick, Incremental maintenance of aggregate and outerjoin expressions, Technical Report, Stanford University, 1999.

Gupta, H., V. Harinarayan, A. Rajaraman, and J. D. Ullman, Index selection for OLAP, *Proc. ICDE*, 1997.

Harinarayan, V., A. Rajaraman, and J. D. Ullman, Implementing data cubes efficiently, *SIGMOD*, 205–216, 1996. (Reprinted in *Materialized Views*, A. Gupta and I. S. Mumick, Eds., 1998, 343–360.)

Hung, E., D. W. Cheung, B. Kao, and Y. L. Liang, An optimization problem in data cube system design, *Proc. Pacific-Asia Conf. Knowledge Discovery Data Mining*, 74–85, 2000.

Hurtado, C. A., A. O. Mendelzon, and A. A. Vaisman, Updating OLAP dimensions, *Proc. DOLAP*, 60–66, 1999.

Huyn, N., Efficient view self-maintenance, *Proc. ACM Workshop Materialized Views*, 1996, 17–25.

Huyn, N., Multiple-view self-maintenance in data warehousing environments, *Proc. 23rd VLDB Conf.*, 26–35, 1997.

Huyn, N., Exploiting dependencies to enhance view self-maintainability, Technical note, Stanford University, 1997b, available at
http://www.db.stanford/edu/warheousing/publications.html.

Huhn, N., Efficient view self-maintenance, *Proc. ACM Workshop on Materialized Views*, 17–25, 1996.

Indulska, M., Shared result identification for materialized view selection, *Proc. 11th Australasian Database Conf.*, 49–56, 1998.

Kambayashi, Y., M. K. Mohania, and A. M. Tjoa, Eds., Data warehousing and knowl-edge discovery, *Proc. 2nd Int. Conf. (DaWaK 2000), Lecture Notes in Computer Science*, Vol. 1874, Springer-Verlag.

Kawaguchi, A., D. Lieuwen, I. S. Mumick, D. Quass, and K. A. Ross, Concurrency control theory for deferred materialized views, *Proc. ICDT*, 306–320, 1997.

Koeller, A. and E. A. Rundensteiner, History-driven view synchronization, *Proc. DaWaK*, 168–177, 2000.

Kotidis, Y. and N. Roussopoulos, DynaMat: a dynamic view management system for data warehouses, *Proc. SIGMOD*, 371–382, 1999.

Kotsis, N. and D. R. McGregor, Elimination of redundant views in multidimensional aggregates, *Proc. DaWaK*, 146–161, 2000.

Kuno, H. A. and E. A. Rundensteiner, Using object-oriented principles to optimize update propagation to materialized views, *Proc. ICDE96*, 1996.

Kuno, H. A. and E. A. Rundensteiner, Incremental maintenance of materialized object-oriented views in multiview: strategies and performance evaluation, *IEEE Trans. Knowledge Data Eng.*, 10(5), 768–792, 1998.

Labio, W. J. and H. Garcia-Molina, Efficient snapshot differential algorithms for data warehousing, *Proc. Very Large Databases*, 1996, 63–74.

Labio, W., D. Quass, and B. Adelberg, Physical database design for data warehousing, *Proc. 13th Int. Conf. Data Eng. (ICDE)*, 277–288, 1997.

Labio, W. J., R. Yerneni, and H. Garcia-Molina, Shrinking the warehouse update window, *Proc. SIGMOD*, 383–394, 1999.

Labio, W. J., J. Yang, Y. Cui, H. Garcia-Molina, and J. Widom, Performance issues in incremental warehouse maintenance, *VLDB J.*, 461–472, 2000.

Labrinidis, A. and N. Roussopoulos, Reduction of materialized view staleness using online updates, Center for Satellite and Hybrid Communications Networks (CSHCN), TR 98-3, University of Maryland, College Park.

Lauzac, S. W., Utilizing materialized views: methods for creating database facilities suitable for mobile database applications, Ph.D. proposal, University of Pittsburg, PA, 1999.

Lauzac, S. W. and P. K. Chrysanthis, Utilizing versions of views within a mobile environment, *Proc. 9th Int. Conf. Comput. Inf.*, 1998.

Lee, K. C. K., A. Si, and H. V. Leong, Incremental view update for a mobile data warehouse, *Proc. SAC '98*, 1998.

Levy, A. Y. and Y. Sagiv, Queries independent of updates, *Proc. 19th Very Large Databases*, 171–181, 1993. (Reprinted in *Materialized Views*, A. Gupta and I. S. Mumick, Eds., 323–338, 1998.)

Levy, A. Y., A. O. Mendelzon, Y. Sagiv, and D. Srivastava, Answering queries using views, *Proc. 14th ACM SIGACT-SIGMOD-SIGART Symp. Principles Database Syst.*, 1995, 95–104. (Reprinted in *Materialized Views*, A. Gupta and I. S. Mumick, Eds., 93–106, 1998.)

Liang, W., H. Wang, and M. E. Orlowska, Range queries in dynamic OLAP data cubes, *Data Knowledge Eng.*, 34 (1), 21–38, 2000.

Liang, W., H. Wang, and M. E. Orlowska, Materialized view selection under the maintenance time constraint, *Data Knowledge Eng.*, 37, 203–216, 2001.

Liefke, H. and S. B. Davidson, View maintenance for hierarchical semistructured data, *Proc. DaWaK*, 114–125, 2000.

Ling, T. W. and E. K. Sze, Materialized view maintenance using version numbers, *Proc.e 6th IEEE Int. Conf. Database Syst. Adv. Appl.*, 1998.

Liu, J., M. Vincent, and M. Mohania, Incremental maintenance of nested relational views, *Proc. 1999 Int. Database Eng. Appl. Symp.*, 197–205.

Liu, L., C. Pu, R. Barga, and T. Zhou, Differential evaluation of continual queries, *Proc. Int. Conf. Distributed Comput. Syst.*, 458–465, 1996.

Lu, J., G. Moerkotte, J. Schu, and V. Subrahmanian, Efficient maintenance of materialized mediated views, in *ACM SIGMOD Int. Conf. Manage. Data Proc.*, 345–351, 1995. (Reprinted in *Materialized Views*, A. Gupta and I. S. Mumick, Eds., 1998, 275–294.)

Markl, V., F. Ramsak, and R. Bayer, Improving OLAP performance by multidimensional hierarchical clustering, *Int. Database Eng. Appl. Symp.*, 1999.

Mohania, M. and Y. Kambayashi, Making aggregate views self-maintainable, *Data Knowledge Eng.*, 32, 87–109, 2000.

Mumick, I. S., D. Quass, and B. S. Mumick, Maintenance of data cubes and summary tables in a warehouse, *Proc. SIGMOD,* 100–111, 1997. (Reprinted in *Materialized Views,* A. Gupta and I. S. Mumick, Eds., 1998, 387–408.)

Nica, A. and E. A. Rundensteiner, View maintenance after view synchronization, *Proc. 1999 Int. Database Eng. Appl. Symp.,* 1999.

Nuynh, T. N., B. Nguyen, J. Schiefer, and A. M. Tjoa, BEDAWA — a tool for generating sample data for data warehouses, *Proc. DaWaK,* 83–93, 2000.

O'Neil, P. and D. Quass, Improved query performance with variant indexes, *Proc. SIGMOD,* 38–49, 1997.

Pourabbas, E. and M. Rafanelli, Characterization of hierarchies and some operators in OLAP environment, *Proc. DOLAP,* 54–59, 1999.

Qian, X. and G. Wiederhold, Incremental recomputation of active relational expressions, *IEEE Trans. Knowledge Data Eng.,* 3(3), 337–341, 1991.

Quass, D., Maintenance expressions for views with aggregation, *ACM Workshop Materialized Views: Techniques and (VIEWS 1996),* 110–118, 1996.

Quass, D., A. Gupta, I. S. Mumick, and J. Widom, Making views self-maintainable for data warehousing, *Proc. Conf. Parallel Distributed Inf. Syst.,* 1996.

Quass, D. and J. Widom, On-line warehouse view maintenance for batch updates, *Proc. SIGMOD 1997,* 393–404.

Ross, K. A., D. Srivastava, and S. Sudarshan, Materialized maintenance and integrity constraint checking: trading space for time, *Proc. ACM SIGMOD Int. Conf. Manage. Data,* 447–458, 1996.

Roussopoulos, N., C.-M. Chen, S. Kelley, A. Delis, and Y. Papakonstantinou, The ADMS project: view R us, *Data Eng. Bull.,* 18(2), 19–28, 1995.

Rundensteiner, E. A., A. Koeller, and X. Zhang, Maintaining data warehouses over changing information sources, *Comm. ACM,* 43(6), 57–62, 2000.

Rundensteiner, E. A., A. J. Lee, and A. Nica, On preserving views in evolving environments, *Proc. 4th Knowledge Representation Meets Data Bases (KRDB) Workshop,* 1997.

Schrefl, M. and T. Thalhammer, On making data warehouses active, *Proc. DaWak,* 34–46, 2000.

Shu, H., Incremental view maintenance using active database rules based on conditional tables, 1997.

Shukla, A., P. M. Deshpande, and J. F. Naughton, Materialized view selection for multi-cube data models, *Proc. Advances in Database Tech. LNCS 1777,* 269–284, 2000.

Shukla, A., P. M. Deshpande, and J. F. Naughton, Materialized view selection for multidimensional datasets, *Proc. Very Large Databases,* 488–499, 1998.

Smith, J. R., C.-S. Li, V. Castelli, and A. Jhingran, Dynamic assembly of views in data cubes, *Proc.,* 274–283, 1998.

Srivastava, D., S. Dar, H. V. Jagadish, and A. Y. Levy, Answering queries with aggregation using views, *Proc. Very Large Databases,* 318–329, 1996.

Staudt, M. and M. Jarke, Incremental maintenance of externally materialized views, *Proc. Very Large Databases,* 75–86, 1996.

Staudt, M., C. Quix, and M. A. Jeusfeld, View maintenance and change notification for application program views, *Proc. ACM Symposium Applied Computing,* 220–225, 1998.

Theodoratos, D. and T. K. Sellis, Data warehouse configuration, *Proc. Very Large Databases,* 126–135, 1997.

Theodoratos, D., S. Ligoudistianos, and T. Sellis, Designing the global data warehouse with SPJ views, *Conf. Adv. Inf. Syst. Eng.,* 180–194, 1999.

Theodoratos, D. and M. Bouzeghoub, Data currency quality factors in data warehouse design, *Proc. DMDW,* 1999.

Theodoratos, D. and T. Sellis, Designing data warehouses, *Data Knowledge Eng.,* 31, 279–301, 1999.

Theodoratos, D. and T. Sellis, Incremental design of a data warehouse, *J. Intel. Info. Sys.,* 15, 7–27, 2000.

Tryfona, N., F. Busborg and J. G. B. Christiansen, StarER: a conceptual model for data warehouse design, *Proc. DOLAP,* 3–8, 1999.

Uchiyama, H., K. Runapongsa, and T. J. Teorey, A progressive view materialization algorithm, *Proc. DOLAP,* 36–41, 1999.

Wiener, J. L., H. Gupta, W. J. Labio, and Y. Zhuge, A system prototype for warehouse view maintenance, *VIEWS,* 1996.

Wolfson, O., P. Sistla, S. Dao, K. Narayanan, and R. Raj, View maintenance in mobile computing, *SIGMOD Rec.,* 24(4), 22–27, 1995.

Xu, M. and C. I. Ezeife, Maintaining horizontally partitioned warehouse views, *Proc. DaWaK,* 126–133, 2000.

Yang, J. and J. Widom, Maintaining temporal views over non-temporal information sources for data warehousing, *Proc. 6th Int. Conf. Extending Database Technol.,* 389–403, 1998b.

Yang, J., K. Karlapalem, and Q. Li, Algorithms for materialized view design in data warehousing environment, *Proc. 23rd Int. Conf. Very Large Data Bases,* 136–145, 1997.

Zhang, C. and J. Yang, Materialized view evolution support in data warehouse environment, *Proc. 6th IEEE Int. Conf. Database Syst. Adv. Appl.,* 1998.

Zhang, C., X. Yao, and J. Yang, Evolving materialized views in data warehouse, *Proc. Congr. Evol. Computation,* Vol. II, 823–829, 1999.

Zhang, X. and E. A. Rundensteiner, PSWEEP: parallel view maintenance under concurrent data updates of distributed sources, 1999.

Zhang, X. and E. A. Rundensteiner, DyDa: dynamic data warehouse maintenance in a fully concurrent environment, *Proc. DaWaK,* 94–103, 2000.

Zhuge, Y., H. Garcia-Molina, and J. L. Wiener, The strobe algorithms for multi-source warehouse consistency, *Proc. PDIS,* 1996.

Zhuge, Y., H. Garcia-Molina, and J. L. Wiener, Consistency algorithms for multi-source warehouse view maintenance, *Distributed Parallel Databases,* 1–36, 1998.

Zhuge, Y., J. L. Wiener, and H. Garcia-Molina, Multiple view consistency for data warehousing, *Proc. ICDE,* 1997.

Zhuge, Y. and H. Garcia-Molina, Performance analysis of WHIPS incremental maintenance, Computer Science Department, Stanford University, CA.

Zhuge, Y., H. Garcia-Molina, J. Hammer, and J. Widom, View maintenance in a warehousing environment, *Proc. SIGMOD 95,* 316–327, San Jose, CA, June 1995.

Part III

---

chapter eight

Intelligent data analysis

8.1 Overview

Data warehouses contain consolidated data in which data have been restructured. Since data in warehouses are summary tables or other kinds of materialized views, they are ready for analysis. This chapter discusses how to perform intelligent data analysis in the data-warehousing environment, mainly focusing on data mining techniques. A concise description of several selected data analysis techniques (such as rough set theory) is provided and illustrated by case studies. Several typical data mining functionalities (such as clustering, classification, and association) conducted in data warehousing environment are also summarized. These functionalities are illustrated by examples and case studies.

A popular viewpoint in regard to intelligent data analysis is the integration of data warehousing and data mining, ranging from loose coupling to tight coupling. In the case of loose coupling, a data mining system (also called a data miner) uses some facilities of a data warehouse, while in tight coupling, the data miner is smoothly integrated into the data warehouse. The data miner is treated as one functional component of the integrated system. An important advantage of tight coupling is that it provides an environment for integration of data mining and other data analysis tasks, such as OLAP. As a quick example of the relationship between data mining and OLAP operations in data warehousing environment, Boulicaut et al. (1999) studied data mining processes on multidimensional data from a query point of view. Focusing on association rule mining, they consider typical queries to cope with the preprocessing of multidimensional data and the postprocessing of the discovered patterns as well. They use a model and rule-based language stemming from the OLAP multidimensional representation, and demonstrate that such a language fits well for writing KDD queries on multidimensional data. Using a homogeneous data model and language for expressing queries at every phase of the process appears to be a valuable step toward a better understanding of interactivity during the whole process. A recent progress report on data mining in data warehousing environments can be found in Palpanas (2000).

8.2   Basics of data mining

8.2.1   Categories of data mining

One criterion for categorizing data mining is based on what is discovered. The following are some typical cases:

- Regularity. In many cases there is interest in knowledge patterns or regularity of data. This is the most popular case and will be further examined in the next section.
- Single datum. In other cases, one may be interested in specific items of data or single pieces of information (singular datum). Note that this is not simply to discover the outliers; the purpose of this kind of analysis is to increase the efficiency of knowledge works.

Data mining problems can also be divided into two general categories: prediction and knowledge discovery. Arguably the strongest goal of data mining, prediction has the greatest potential payoff and the most precise description. Knowledge discovery is an all-encompassing label for many topics related to decision support. Knowledge discovery problems usually describe a stage prior to prediction, where information is insufficient for prediction. Knowledge discovery is complementary to predictive mining, but is closer to decision support than decision making. The two central types of prediction problems are classification and regress. Time series is a specialized type of a regression or, occasionally, a classification problem, in which measurements are taken over time for the same features. Knowledge discovery includes deviation detection, database segmentation, clustering, association rules, summarization, visualization, text mining, etc.

Predictive data mining requires data modeling (which is different from data reduction). There is also a concern related to timelines in predictive data mining. From the perspective of database systems, the efficient storage and query of time-stamped information is a complex task. From a predictive data-mining perspective, the time-stamped data greatly increase the dimensions of problem solving in a completely different direction. Instead of cases with one measured value for each feature, cases have the same feature measured at different times. Predictive data-mining methods prefer the classical sample and case model of data but have difficulties reasoning with time and its greatly increased dimensions. Many data mining techniques have a close relationship with machine learning. Just like machine learning algorithms, data mining techniques could be based on symbolic, connectionism (i.e., artificial neural networks), evolutionary, or other forms. For example, there has been a growing interest in data mining using evolutionary algorithms.

As pointed out by Chen, Han, and Yu (1996), data mining techniques can be classified by different criteria, such as the kinds of databases to be worked on (such as relational, object-oriented, etc.), the kind of knowledge to be mined (such as association or characteristic rules), or the kind of techniques to be utilized (such as data-driven or query-driven).

In terms of the kind of knowledge to be mined, data mining functionalities consist of the following:

- Association rules (to be discussed in the next section);
- Data generalization and summarization tools: the most popularly used data mining and data analysis tools;
- Data classification: the process that finds the common properties among a set of objects in a database and classifies them into different classes according to a classification model. The objective of the classification is first to analyze the training data and then to develop an accurate description or model for each class using the features available in the data. Some machine learning techniques, such as ID3, are closely related to discovery of classification knowledge;
- Data clustering: the process of grouping physical or abstract objects into classes of similar objects. Clustering analysis helps construct meaningful partitioning of a large set of objects based on a divide and conquer methodology which decomposes a large scale system into smaller componets to simpify design and implementation. The task of clustering is to maximize intraclass similarity and to minimize interclass similarity. It has a close relationship with spatial data mining (see below);
- Spatial/temporal data mining: concerned with data mining involving spatial and/or temporal data. There is an interesting relationship between spatial and temporal data mining (for example, the problem of temporal data mining can be converted to spatial data mining); and
- Mining path traversal patterns: there is an interesting relationship between data mining and the Internet that has several aspects. The Internet provides a huge resource for data mining. Note also that, recently, there have been various efforts to apply data mining for Web page analysis.

In addition, three types of knowledge discovery have also been identified: pattern-based similarity search, data mining query languages and graphical user interface, and sequential patterns.

8.2.2   Association rule mining

Association rules, usually called market basket analysis (MBA), or affinity analysis in business applications, are intended to discover associations between various attributes or transactions. (Note that in the literature of association rule mining, a transaction refers to a list of items purchased by a customer in one shipping activity; a transaction database usually is a relation consisting of such transactions.)

Discovery of association rules between sets of items over basket data was introduced in Agrawal et al. (1993). Since then, discovery of association rules has become an important goal of data mining. Typically, basket data are a set of transactions in which a list of items, their quantity, prices, etc. are recorded. These data are usually collected by bar code scanning (e.g., at supermarket checkout counters).

As one of the data mining goals, a conventional association rule was originally defined as $X \Rightarrow Y$, where $X \subseteq I$, $Y \subseteq I$, $X \cup Y = \varnothing$, and I (I_1, I_2, ..., $I_n \in I$) is a set of transaction items (Agrawal et al., 1993). In a set of transactions T, the rule $X \Rightarrow Y$ has a support s ($s\%$ of transactions in T contain X) with a confidence c ($0 \leq c \leq 1$), if at least $c\%$ of transactions in T that satisfy X also satisfy Y. Item set X is denoted antecedent and item set Y is denoted consequent.

For instance, 10% of customers at checkout counters of a grocery store purchase bread and, among the customers who purchase bread, 70% of them also purchase butter. There exists an association between bread and butter. Item bread is antecedent and item butter is consequent. The association rule *Bread $\Rightarrow$ Butter* has support $s(Bread \Rightarrow Butter) = 10\%$ and confidence $c(Bread \Rightarrow Butter) = 0.7$.

Inherently, discovery of association rules over a set of records would be *NP*-hard if constraints had not been considered. For instance, if there are total n items in a set of transactions, the length of antecedent or consequent item set could be any number from 1 to ($n - 1$) for all possible association rules. Together with permutation of items in a given length of antecedent or consequent, the computation of association discovery is *NP*-hard if all possibilities were considered.

The widely accepted constraints in discovery of association rules are minimum support and minimum confidence (Agrawal and Srikant, 1994). Minimum support requires that the occurring frequency of the antecedents of all association rules be greater than a certain user-defined value. A frequent set is the set of items whose occurring frequency in the whole set of transaction records is greater than minimum support. Minimum confidence is for the discovery of meaningful associations in terms of frequently occurring association patterns.

For an item set S, $SUPPORT(S)$ is defined as the percentage of transactions containing item set S in all transactions considered. The item set S is a frequent set if $SUPPORT(S)$ is larger than or equal to the predefined minimum support. For a frequent set $\mathcal{F}$, all subsets of $\mathcal{F}$ are also frequent sets. Association rule $X \Rightarrow Y$, where $X \subset \mathcal{F}$, $Y \subset \mathcal{F}$, and $X \cap Y = \varnothing$, can be computed as:

> *support* $s(X \Rightarrow Y) = SUPPORT (X)$
> *confidence* $c(X \Rightarrow Y) = SUPPORT(X \cup Y)/SUPPORT (X)$
> where $s \geq$ minimum support and $c \geq$ minimum confidence

Thus, there are two computation steps for candidate association rules. The first step, computation of frequent sets, is time-consuming and expensive. The next step, derivation of candidate association rules from a frequent set, is straightforward. Most research on discovery of association rules pays much attention to the design of efficient and scalable algorithms for frequent set computation.

8.2.3   Data classification and characterization

Data classification is the process which finds the common properties among a set of objects in a database and classifies them into different classes, according to a classification model. To construct such a classification model, a sample database E is treated as the training set, in which each tuple consists of the same set of multiple attributes (or features) as the tuples in a large database W. Additionally, each tuple has a known class identity (label) associated with it. The objective of the classification is first to analyze the training data and then to develop an accurate description or model for each class using features available in the data. Such class descriptions are then used to classify future test data in the database W or to develop a better description (called classification rules) for each class in the database. Applications of classification include medical diagnosis, performance prediction, and selective marketing, to name a few. Data classification has been studied substantially in statistics, machine learning, neural networks, and expert systems and is an important theme in data mining.

A decision-tree-based classification method has been influential in machine learning studies. This is a supervised learning method that constructs decision trees from a set of examples. The quality (function) of a tree depends on both classification accuracy and size of the tree. The method first chooses a subset of the training examples (a window) to form a decision tree. If the tree does not give the correct answer for all the objects, a selection of the exceptions is added to the window and the process continues until the correct decision set is found. The eventual outcome is a tree in which each leaf carries a class name, and each interior node specifies an attribute with a branch corresponding to each possible value of that attribute.

There have been many other approaches to data classification, including statistical approaches. Linear regression and linear discriminant analysis techniques are classical statistical models. Methods have also been studied for scaling machine learning algorithms by combining base classifiers from partitioned data sets. Some studies of classification techniques in the context of large databases have been conducted. An interval classifier has been proposed to reduce the cost of decision tree generation. The artificial neural network approach for classification and rule extraction in databases has also been studied extensively. A current study explores how to incorporate the rough set theory to implement data classification, specifically, by focusing on the uncertainty reasoning.

In contrast to classification, characterization means to discover the common features of a concept independently of the characteristics of other concepts. Hence, a characterization may discover commonalities not unique to a given concept.

8.3   Case study: stock food chain analysis

8.3.1   Overview of the case study

The stock food chain is the relationship between large companies and the companies from which they buy goods and services. Chapter 4 presented a case study of preparing stock food chain data for analysis. Once this relationship and the corresponding stock prices of the participating companies are stored in a prototype data warehouse, it can be used to analyze the stock price data for companies within a food chain to find strongly connected stocks. This provides good insight on when to buy or sell a stock. The Apriori algorithm lends itself to this analysis by finding stocks that have strong support for increasing in the same weeks. Once the item set of stocks with strong supports is created, rules can be created to find those with the strongest confidence.

The case study described next deals with analysis of data in the warehouse created during one project. The Apriori algorithm was implemented to find members of the stock food chain that have the strongest support. After the algorithm has found the item set with the strongest support, the rules and confidence for an item set can be found. Using these rules provides some verification that the stock food chain concept is valid. This project does not intend to show that the stock food chain is the only influence on a company's stock, but instead to show that it does have an influence on that stock.

8.3.2   Implementing the Apriori algorithm

The Apriori algorithm (Agrawal and Srikant, 1994) marks a milestone in the study of association rule mining. This algorithm is used to find members of the stock food chain that have the strongest support; it is run through a geographical user interface (GUI) interface that allows the user to select the "parent" stock on which to run the Apriori algorithm. The parent stock is the root of the stock food chain. After this stock is selected, the program runs the Apriori algorithm on all members of the food chain with the parent stock at the root. For each iteration of the algorithm, C_i and L_i are displayed on the GUI screen.

The data analysis tool was created using Visual Basic and Microsoft Access. Microsoft Access provides the required database functionality. Its integration with Visual Basic allows for GUI screens to be built, as well as for manipulation of the data within the Visual Basic code.

First, the candidates (C_k) are created by joining L_{k-1} with itself. This is done in two steps:

Items in L_{k-1} are listed in order.
Step 1: self-joining L_{k-1}
> insert into C_k
> select $p.item_1, p.item_2, ..., p.item_{k-1}, q.item_{k-1}$
> from $L_{k-1}\ p, L_{k-1}\ q$
> where $p.item_1 = q.item_1, ..., p.item_{k-2} = q.item_{k-2}, p.item_{k-1} <$
> $q.item_{k-1}$

The condition "$p.item_{k-1} < q.item_{k-1}$" is used to remove duplicate values. This condition works because the items are listed in order.

Any (k–1)-item set that is not frequent cannot be a subset of a frequent k-item set and is "pruned" from the candidate set.

Step 2: pruning
> forall item sets c in C_k do
> > forall (k–1)-subsets s of c do
> > > if (s is not in L_{k-1}) then delete c from C_k

Pseudocode for the Apriori algorithm is shown below.

C_k: Candidate item set of size k
L_k: frequent item set of size k
L_1 = {frequent items};
for (k = 1; L_k != NULL; k++) do begin
> C_{k+1} = candidates generated from L_k;
> for each transaction t in database do
> increment the count of all candidates in C_{k+1} that are contained in t
> L_{k+1} = candidates in C_{k+1} with min_support
> end
return Union L_k

An example of using the Apriori algorithm is depicted in Figure 8.1.

The implementation of the Apriori algorithm used in this project bases the transactions on whether the stock price increased or decreased during the same week/year. The end result of using this as the definition of a transaction is that one obtains an item set of stocks that have strong support for increasing or decreasing in the same week. This information is exactly what the analysis of the stock food chain intended to glean from the data warehouse. From this information, the program allows one to generate rules that show the confidence that the stocks will increase or decrease in relation to other stocks in the item set.

8.3.3 Graphical user interface

The GUI for the stock food chain Apriori algorithm was designed to resemble the example of the Apriori algorithm in Section 3.2 and also in the class

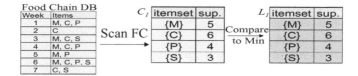

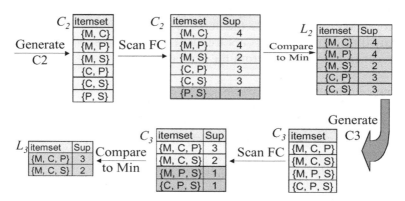

Figure 8.1 Example of the Apriori algorithm applied to the stock food chain.

textbook. The GUI allows tables to be displayed for the food chain database, C_k item sets, and L_k item sets. The food chain database contains stocks involved in the stock food chain relationship for the current parent stock and their corresponding week and year.

8.3.4 Analysis

The analysis of the stock food chain used the Apriori algorithm to find item sets within a stock food chain that contained the strongest support. The rules and confidence for those item sets were then generated. This provided a great deal of insight into the strength of the relationships of the stocks within the food chain.

Many of the stocks analyzed contained rules with better than 65% confidence; some were around 90%. Given the volatile nature of the stock market, such high confidence, combined with the traditional research necessary when purchasing a stock, could provide a potent formula for earning purchasing stocks that will increase their value.

There is an overwhelming amount of information to be gained from these rules. For example, for AOL we can obtain rules for its stock when the price is either increased (UP) or decreased (DOWN) in value:

Up
AOL ^ COMS ^ ERTS — > INTU with 68% confidence

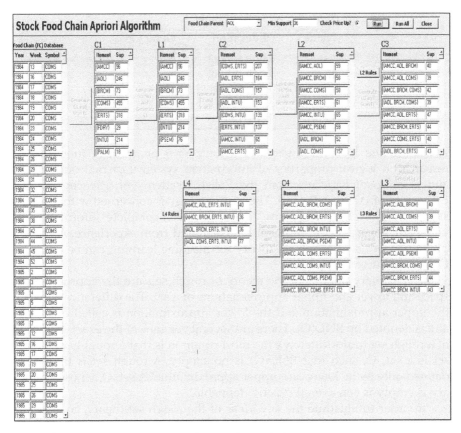

Figure 8.2 Stock food chain Apriori algorithm panel.

Down
AOL ∧ COMS ∧ ERTS — > INTU with 66% confidence

This rule implies that when AOL, COMS, and ERTS increase, INTU also increases with 68% confidence. But when AOL, COMS, and ERTS decrease, INTU decreases with 66% confidence. This implies that these stocks are strongly related and helps to validate the stock food chain concept. As the rules for the stock food chains were being generated and analyzed, this type of scenario occurred numerous times for all of the stock food chains.

8.4 Case study: rough set data analysis

8.4.1 Basics of rough set theory

The theory of rough sets has been under continuous development for the past three decades, and a fast growing group of researchers and practitioners are interested in this methodology. The theory was originated by Zdzislaw

Table 8.1 A Decision Table

Name	Education	Good Job
Joe	High School	No
Mary	High School	Yes
Peter	Elementary	No
Paul	University	Yes
Cathy	Doctorate	Yes

Pawlak in the 1970s as a result of a long term program of fundamental research on logical properties of information systems, carried out by him and a group of logicians from the Polish Academy of Sciences and the University of Warsaw, Poland. The methodology is concerned with the classificatory analysis of imprecise, uncertain, or incomplete information or knowledge expressed in terms of data acquired from experience. A concise discussion of using rough set theory for machine learning can be found in Gryzmala-Busse (1991).

The primary notions of the theory of rough sets are the approximation space and lower and upper approximations of a set. The difference between the upper approximation and the lower approximation is called boundary and is denoted by BND(O). There are several versions of the exact definition of a rough set (unfortunately); the most common is that a roughly definable set is a set, O, such that BND(O) is nonempty. A rough set is thus a set defined only by its lower and upper approximation. A set, O, whose boundary is empty is considered exactly definable.

In order to illustrate the key ideas of the rough set theory, an example using the data in Table 8.1 is presented. Many researchers have used rough set theory for inductive learning systems, generating rules of the form:

So, the set of positive examples of people with good job prospects, O, consists of three elements:

O = {Mary, Paul, Cathy}
The set of attributes:
A = AT = {Education}
The equivalence classes:
R(A)* = {{Joe, Mary}, {Peter}, {Paul}, {Cathy}}
The lower approximation and positive region is:
POS(O) = LOWER(O) = {Paul, Cathy}
The negative region is:
NEG(O) = {Peter}
The boundary region is:
BND(O) = {Joe, Mary}
The upper approximation is:
UPPER(O) = POS(O) + BND(O) = {Paul, Cathy, Joe, Mary}. Decision
     rules to be derived:
description(POS(O)) $\rightarrow$ Yes

description(NEG(O)) → No
description(BND(O)) → Yes (equivalently ~~ No)

Inductive rules can be generated in the following manner:

description(POS(O)) — > positive decision class
description(NEG(O)) — > negative decision class
description(BND(O)) — > probabilistically positive decision class

Back to our example, we have:

(Education, University) or (Education, Doctorate) → Good prospects
(Education, Elementary) → No good prospects
(Education, High School) → Good prospects (possible)

This example indicates that the starting point of using rough sets to perform uncertain reasoning is somewhat different from that in reasoning using probability theory or fuzzy set theory. Both of these approaches are intended to deal with a certain kind of uncertainty: probability theory deals with randomness while fuzzy set theory deals with vagueness. For rough sets, the uncertainty is due to the method used: suppose one is interested in set X; instead of investing X itself, one investigates its two sets (called approximations) and uses these approximations to characterize X. Important concepts related to rough set theory include the following:

- A decision table is a flat table containing attributes and decisions as columns, and actual data elements as rows. A decision table consists of several condition attributes, as well as one or more decision variables. It is actually a relation, although it has somewhat different semantics.
- An indiscernibility relation partitions domains into equivalence classes and the concept of lower and upper approximation regions to allow the distinction between certain and possible, or partial, inclusion in a rough set. The indiscernibility relation allows one to group items based on some definition of equivalence as it relates to the application domain. This partitioning may be used to increase or decrease the granularity of a domain, to group items together that are considered indiscernible for a given purpose, or to "bin" ordered domains into range groups.
- An indiscernibility class is tuples (rows) with certain properties grouped together.
- An indispensable attribute is a significant attribute in the indiscernibility class.

The next group of definitions is related to the concept of approximation space A, which is an ordered pair A = (U, R), where U is the universe (a nonempty set), while R is an indiscernibility relation (which is an equivalence relation) on U. Rough set theory employs the concept of equivalent class to reduce the information. The following definitions are related to this:

$[x]_R$: for any element of U, the equivalence class of R in which x is contained.
Elementary sets in A: there are equivalence classes of R.
Definable set in A: it refers to any finite union of elementary sets in A.

Another two important concepts in rough set theory are lower and upper approximations. They can be formally defined as following the

Lower approximation of X in A: the greatest definable set in A that is contained in X: $\underline{R}X = \{x \in U \mid [x]_R \subseteq X\}$, and
Upper approximation of X in A: the least definable set in A containing X: $\overline{R}X = \{x \in U \mid [x]_R \cap X \neq \Phi\}$.

In order to perform reduction in rough data analysis, two fundamental concepts, namely, reduct and core, play a central role. Intuitively, a reduct of knowledge is its essential part, which suffices to define all basic concepts occurring in the considered knowledge, whereas the core is, in a certain sense, its most important part. Attribute reduction technique aims at removing superfluous attributes and finding minimal subsets of attributes, each of which has the same discriminating power as all the attributes. Attribute reducts, denoted as RED(D), are the minimal subsets of condition attributes C with respect to decision attributes D. None of the attributes of any minimal subsets can be eliminated without affecting essential information. These minimal subsets can discern decision classes with the same discriminating power as all the condition attributes. Any reduct, $RED_i \in RED(D)$, can be used instead of the original system S.

The core can be defined as: $CORE(P) = \cap RED(P)$, where RED(P) is the family of all reducts of P. So, if one finds all the reduction of the set P, one can get the core. Another way to compute the core is that, if the two objects differ at only one attribute, that attribute is core.

In the RSDA approach, the matrix approach is used to compute the core, based on the second definition. Following is an example to explain the matrix approach in the core computation:

Consider a decision table consisting of eight objects. To handle this table, it is necessary to have an 8×8 matrix (M[x, y], x = y = 8). The value of M(a, b) is the set of all attributes which make object a and object b different, if the value of M(a, b) is only one condition attribute a1. This means that, if only one attribute makes the objects a, b different, then condition attribute a1 is the core.

8.4.2 Applying RSDA methodology for bankruptcy analysis

Rough set data analysis takes a reduction approach. There are two important concepts related to reduction; one is related to reduction of rows, and the other to reduction of columns.

Ultra large data, redundant and dynamic data, and uncertainty in data are generally thought to be appropriate to be mined using the rough set theory.

Below, rough set data analysis (RSDA) methodology is described. We also describe the data set used in a comprehensive example to illustrate RSDA.

8.4.2.1 Description of the RSDA methodology
The main idea of RSDA can be summarized in the following steps:

1. Creating target data set: whatever the original data are, they need to be loaded and parsed into a table in a database. In this step, the text file will be read and parsed into a table in an access database.
2. Categorizing attributes: to facilitate the mining method, it is essential to associate numeric value with appropriate category sets. In this step, an algorithm needs to be designed for automatic generation of categories based on the numeric values in the table.
3. Removing the reduct attributes: attribute reduction technique is aimed at removing superfluous attributes and finding minimal subsets of attributes. An algorithm will be developed to remove the reduct attributes. In this step, some attributes will be removed from the original table based on the reduct concept presented by the rough set theory.
4. Finding core attributes: in this step, the decision matrix approach presented by rough set theory will be used to find core attributes among the condition attributes.
5. Analysis step: first, a decision table will be constructed based only on the core attribute. Then, the partition, low approximation, and high approximation approach presented in the rough set theory will be used in the analysis. On the basis of low approximation, certain rules can be derived, while the uncertain rule can be derived based on both high and low approximations.

From the uncertain list produced, a new decision table with more attributes will be generated. By using the same method used in the last step, new rules will be generated in which certain other attributes will affect the uncertain rules generated from the previous step. This analysis will be recursively continued until the uncertain list is empty or no rule can be generated.

8.4.2.2 Source data used in the case study
The data used in this case study are from a text file obtained from a financial institution. The original data contain information on approximately 3000

customers. The data are customer credit information. In order to analyze these data, clustering analysis has been performed; in total, 196 clusters have been obtained. However, it is well known that results of clustering analysis are subject to appropriate interpretation, and finding this interpretation may not be straightforward. In order to further interpret the results obtained from clustering analysis, rough set data analysis has been used. RSDA is appropriate for this task because the data are inconsistent and uncertain. The result of RSDA can be further compared with other analytical approaches, such as using neural networks.

As indicated above, the input of this case study is the set of 196 clusters. This input will be treated as a decision table. There are nine attributes in this table, which include:

1. rowid: id from 0 to 196, which means there are 196 rows in this table (one row represents one cluster);
2. row-number: representing certain number of objects in this cluster;
3. bankrupt-flag: 1 or 0;
4. line98: credit line at month 11/97–10/98;
5. avg-cash98: average cash advance at month 11/97–10/98;
6. avg-sale98: average purchase at month 11/97–10/98;
7. avg-pay98: average payment at month 11/97–10/98;
8. avg-balance98: average balance at month 11/97–10/98; and
9. sum-delinquency98: sum delinquency at month 11/97–10/98.

A portion of the decision table is shown in Table 8.2, where the second column (Bkrupt) is the decision variable. After applying an appropriate categorization algorithm, original values are converted to qualities such as "low" or "high."

Table 8.2 A Portion of the Data to be Analyzed

Num	Bkrupt	Rownum	Line98	Avgcash	Avgsale	Avgpay	Avgbala	Sumdelinq
0	0	94	8.33	0.35	1.33	1.33	13.59	0.79
1	0	233	13.81	0.10	1.81	1.76	10.62	0.86
2	0	120	15.58	1.66	1.13	1.37	17.73	1.11
3	0	67	5.31	0.71	0.85	1.04	12.56	1.84
4	0	161	15.08	0.10	1.97	1.65	9.24	0.46
5	0	295	19.61	0.47	3.47	3.62	16.88	0.55
6	0	252	23.47	0.48	4.36	3.14	12.85	0.38
7	0	8	11.61	4.00	2.52	3.54	14.56	0.29
8	0	246	22.05	0.32	3.86	3.85	12.93	0.27
9	0	36	19.95	0.93	2.86	2.57	13.72	0.49
10	0	6	6.55	0	0.0052	0.14	11.80	38.49
11	0	92	16.57	1.34	3.98	2.36	21.43	2.18
12	0	114	14.60	0.47	1.79	2.14	12.01	0.62
13	0	62	17.65	1.39	2.41	3.74	19.85	1.50
14	0	117	17.19	1.15	3.43	3.98	16.51	0.82
15	0	39	24.98	1.67	1.65	1.33	10.38	0.85

Table 8.3 Records with the Categorized Data

Obj.	Avg_Cash98	Avg_Pay98	Avg_Sales98	Avg_Balance98	Bankrupt
1	Medium	Low	Medium	Medium	No
2	High	High	High	Low	Yes
3	Low	Medium	Low	Low	Yes
4	High	High	High	High	No
5	Medium	High	Low	Medium	Yes
6	Low	Low	Low	High	No
7	High	Medium	Medium	High	No
8	Low	Low	Low	Low	Yes

Note: Avg_Cash98: average cash advance at month 11/97–10/98; Avg_Pay98: average payment at month 11/97–10/98; Avg_Balance98: average balance at month 11/97–10/98; and Avg_Sales98: average purchases at month 11/97–10/98.

Table 8.3 includes eight objects (data records) with categorized data. For convenient discussion, only four of eight attributes are used. The RSDA method was applied in this decision table.

If one concerns the object with the three attributes Avg_Cash98, Avg_Pay98, and Avg_Balance98, we can see that these eight objects are different. Therefore the partition set {1} {2} {3} {4} {5} {6} {7} {8} exists. Since these eight objects are different, the indiscernibility relation in this case is empty.

If one concerns the object only with the attributes Avg_Cash98, Avg_Pay98, and ignore Avg_Balance98 and Avg_Sales98, there will be a different partition set as shown in the above table: {1} {2, 4} {5} {6, 8} {7}. The objects 2 and 4 are identical; 6 and 8 are identical objects. In this case, the indiscernibility relation is {{2, 4}, {6, 8}}.

The decision matrix approach presented by the rough set theory will be used to find the core attributes among the condition attributes. The basic idea of the matrix approach is to compare any combinations of two objects inside the decision table to see whether or not these objects are the same and to see which and how many attributes contribute to this difference. If any one of the attributes makes these two objects different, this attribute is called the core. The core of a set Q is the intersection of all reducts of Q; attributes in the core of Q are said to be indispensable for Q. The core of Q may be empty.

Table 8.4 is an example of using the matrix approach to compute the core. The numbers 1, 2, 3, 4, 5, 6, 7, and 8 represent object 1, object 2, object 3, object 4, object 5, object 6, object 7, and object 8. The attributes are a1 = Avg_Cash98, a2 = Avg_Pay98, a3 = Avg_Sale98, and a4 = Avg_Balance98.

From this matrix, one can find that

difference(2, 4) = {a4} and
difference(6, 8) = {a4}

which means that the difference between objects 2 and 4 is in attribute 4, and the difference between objects 6 and 8 is in attribute 4. So the core (Avg_Cash98, Avg_Pay98, Avg_sales98, Avg_Balance98) = {Avg_Balance98}.

Table 8.4 Using a Matrix Table to Compute the Core

δ	1	2	3	4	5	6	7	8
1		a1, a2, a3, a4	a1, a2, a3, a4	a1, a2, a3, a4	a2, a3	a1, a2, a3	a1, a2, a4	a1, a3, a4
2			a1, a2, a3	a4	a1, a3, a4	a1, a2, a3, a4	a2, a3, a4	a1, a2, a3
3				a1, a2, a3, a4	a1, a2, a4	a3, a4	a1, a3, a4	a2, a4
4					a1, a2, a3, a4	a1, a2, a3	a2, a3	a1, a2, a3, a4
5						a1, a2, a4	a1, a2, a3, a4	a1, a2, a4
6							a1, a2, a3	a4
7								a1, a2, a3, a4

It is now necessary to compute the reducts (for class Bankrupt = YES). The previous step taught that the Avg_Balance98 is the core. Assuming that the reduction of the condition attribute existed, then the reduction must contain the Avg_Balance98 with one or more condition attributes.

> For attribute Avg_Cash98, The POS(Avg_cash98) = (A3, A6, A8),
> POS(Avg_Balance98) = (A2, A3, A8).
>   POS (Avg_Balance98) $\not\subset$ POS(Avg_cash98)
> So, Avg_Cash98.

In this case, objects will be partitioned by looking into three attributes as shown in Table 8.5: Avg_Cash98, Avg_Pay98, and Avg_Sales98.

Table 8.5 Object Partitioning

Object	Avg_Cash98	Avg_Pay98	Avg_Sales98	Avg_Balance98	Bankrupt
1	Medium	Low	Medium	Medium	No
2	High	High	High	Low	Yes
3	Low	Medium	Low	Low	Yes
4	High	High	High	High	No
5	Medium	High	Low	Medium	Yes
6	Low	Low	Low	High	No
7	High	Medium	Medium	High	No
8	Low	Low	Low	Low	Yes

The partition result is {1} {2, 4} {5} {6, 8} {7}.

If one compares the partition result by looking into Avg_Cash98, Avg_Pay98, and Avg_Sales98, with the partition result by looking into the

Avg_Cash98 and Avg_Pay98, one can find that these two partition results are the same. One can then conclude that {Avg_Cash98, Avg_Pay98} is a reduct of {Avg_Cash98, Avg_Pay98, Avg_Sales98}.

(Recall that A set $P \subseteq Q$ is a reduct of Q if P is the minimum set such that $\theta(P) = \theta(Q)$).

8.4.2.3 Applying RSDA on sample data

The following example demonstrates how to apply rough set theory in data analysis, step-by-step.

Step 1:
Table 8.6 shows a decision table that has eight objects. In this decision table there are four condition attributes: avg_cash98, avg_pay98, avg_sales98, and avg_balance98, and one decision attribute: bankrupt.

Table 8.6 An Initial Decision Table

Object	Avg_Cash98	Avg_Pay98	Avg_Sales98	Avg_Balance98	Bankrupt
1	Medium	Low	Medium	Medium	No
2	High	High	High	Low	Yes
3	Low	Medium	Low	Low	Yes
4	High	High	High	High	No
5	Medium	High	Low	Medium	Yes
6	Low	Low	Low	High	No
7	High	Medium	Medium	High	No
8	Low	Low	Low	Low	Yes

The indiscernibility relation θ{bankrupt} yields two classes: Decision1 = {1, 4, 6, 7}; Decision2 = { 2, 3, 5, 8}. The indisceribility relation θ{avg_balance98} yields three classes: B1 = {1, 5}, B2 = {2, 3, 8}, B3 = {4, 6, 7}. The result is indicated in Table 8.7.

Table 8.7 Partitioning Based on Decision

Decision	Lower Approximation	Upper Approximation	Difference
Decision1 (bankrupt = NO)	B3	B1∪B3	B1
Decision2 (bankrupt = yes)	B2	B1∪B2	B1

Analysis results: Table 8.5 shows that B1 is nondeterministic, so an uncertain rule is generated: rule1: if Avg_Balance98 = medium, then Bankrupt True or False. Since B2 and B3 are deterministic, positive rules can be generated from there. Rule2: if Avg_Balance98 = Low, then Bankrupt True. Rule3: if Avg_Balance98 = High, then Bankrupt False.

Step 2:
From the step 1, it is known that B is uncertain, so for B one cannot generate positive rule if only by looking at the values of Avg_balance98. If one builds a new decision table based on set B, then Table 8.8 is created.

Table 8.8 A Decision Table Involving Avg_Balance98

Obj	Avg_Cash98	Avg_Pay98	Avg_Sales98	Avg_Balance98	Bankrupt
1	Medium	Low	Medium	Medium	No
5	Medium	High	Low	Medium	Yes

Since the value of the condition attribute Avg_Balance98 is the same in all the objects in the decision table above, this column can be removed from the decision table, as shown in Table 8.9.

Table 8.9 A Decision Table without Avg_Balance98

Obj	Avg_Cash98	Avg_Pay98	Avg_Sales98	Bankrupt
1	Medium	Low	Medium	No
5	Medium	High	Low	Yes

The indiscernibility relation $\theta\{Bankrupt\}$ yields two classes: decision1 = {1}, and decision2 = {5}. The indiscernibility relation $\theta\{Avg\_Sales98\}$ yields two classes: S1 = {1}, and S2 = {5}. The result is shown in Table 8.10.

Table 8.10 New Partitioning for Decision

Decision	Lower Approximation	Upper Approximation	Difference
Decision1	S1	S1	Φ
Decision2	S2	S2	Φ

The following rules are thus obtained: rule 4: if Avg_Balance98 = Medium, then if Avg_Sales98 = Medium, then Bankrupt NO, and rule 5: if Avg_Balance98 = Medium, then if Avg_Sales98 = Low, then Bankrupt Yes.

The rules obtained serve as classifiers for customer bankruptcy. The rules are classification rules because they can be used for predicating purpose. The rules also have a flavor of characterization because they capture important traits of bankrupcy.

In this study, a group of attributes was found using an approach based on the rough set theory. This study was mainly focused on performing an evaluation of attribute ability to approximate bankrupt classification.

8.5   Recent progress of data mining

The previous two case studies demonstrated data mining steps in detail. Next, some recent progress of data mining is summarized to illustrate the diversity of this active research area.

8.5.1 Mining the metadata

Although most of the time metadata are used for data mining, the metadata can be mined also. This is an interesting issue that refers to conducting data mining on metadata. Data in the database may be incomplete, inaccurate, or unstructured, so metadata could provide more meaningful information. Issues to be considered are when to mine metadata and what kinds of technique are appropriate. Metadata (such as metadata in repository) can be mined to extract useful information in cases where the data are not analyzable. For example, one can find characterizing rules that characterize an unstructured Web document and store the mined features as a description of the document in the metadata repository.

8.5.2 User expectations

To prevent the user of data mining from being overwhelmed by the large number of patterns, techniques are needed to rank the discovered knowledge patterns according to the interest that they arouse. Liu et al. (1999) proposed using the user-expectation method to deal with this problem. When this technique is applied, the user is first asked to provide expected patterns according to past knowledge or intuitive feelings. Given these expectations, the system uses a fuzzy matching technique to match the discovered patterns against the user's expectations, and rank the discovered patterns according to the matching results. A variety of ranking methods can be performed for different purposes, such as to confirm the user's knowledge or to identify unexpected patterns.

8.5.3 Discovery of low-support rules

In general, association rule mining has mainly relied on the condition of high support to do its work efficiently. This is typically demonstrated in the Apriori algorithm. However, there are a number of applications, such as identification of similar Web documents, clustering, and collaborate filtering, where the rules of interest have few instances in the data. In these cases, one must examine highly correlated items, or possibly even causal relationships between infrequent items. Cohen et al. (2001) developed a family of algorithms for solving this problem by employing a combination of random sampling and hashing techniques.

8.5.4 Dynamics of data mining

As noted in Ganti et al. (2001), in practice, the input data to a data mining process usually reside in a large data warehouse whose data are kept up to date through periodic or occasional addition and deletion of blocks of data. Most existing data mining algorithms have either assumed that the input data are static, or have been designed for arbitrary insertions and deletions of data records. Ganti et al. (2001) considered a dynamic environment that evolved through systematic addition or deletion of blocks of data; an approach called DEMON (data evolution and monitoring) was proposed. The authors introduced the concept of data span dimension, which allows user-defined selections of a temporal subset of the database. Taking this new concept, the authors described efficient model maintenance algorithms for frequent item sets (two new algorithms were developed for dynamically maintaining the set of frequent item sets) and clusters (an existing clustering algorithm called the BIRCH algorithm, was extended). A generic algorithm was developed which takes any traditional incremental model maintenance algorithm and transforms it into an algorithm that allows restrictions on the data span dimension. Another algorithm was developed for automatic discovery of a specific class of interesting block selection sequences.

8.6   Summary

In this chapter, a discussion on basic data mining techniques for intelligent data analysis was provided. Since the main purpose of this book is to examine the entire process of intelligent data warehousing, and since data mining is only a portion of this entire process, the discussion on data mining has been very brief. Interested readers are referred to Han and Kamber (2000) for detailed algorithms of data mining, Cios et al. (1998) for a discussion from a computational intelligence perspective, and Chen (2001) for a more holistic treatment on data mining, with an emphasis on uncertain reasoning.

This chapter also provided two case studies to illustrate how to use these techniques to analyze real-world data. Note that these methods can be applied to a wide range of applications and are not restricted to the data warehousing environment. The next chapter examines data mining techniques which take advantage of the data warehousing environment so that integrated data mining and OLAP can be achieved.

References

Agrawal, R., C. Faloutsos, and A. Swami. Efficient similarity in sequence databases, *Proc 4th Int. Conf. Found. Data Organ. Algorithms*, 1993.

Agrawal, R. and R. Srikant, Fast algorithms for mining association rules, presented at *Proc. 21st Int. Conf. Very Large Databases*, Santiago, Chile, 1994.

Boulicaut, J.-F., P. Marcel, and C. Rigotti, Query driven knowledge discovery in multidimensional data, *Proc. DOLAP*, 87–93, 1999.

Chen, M. S., J. Han, and P. S. Yu, Data mining: an overview from a database perspective, *IEEE Trans. Knowledge Data Eng.*, 8: 866–883, 1996.

Chen, Z., *Data Mining and Uncertain Reasoning: An Integrated Approach*, Wiley Interscience, New York, 2001.

Cios, K. J., W. Pedrycz, and R. Swiniarski, *Data Mining Methods for Knowledge Discovery*, Kluwer, Boston, 1998.

Cohen, E., M. Datar, S. Fujiwara, A. Gionis, P. Indyk, R. Motwani, J. D. Ullman, and C. Yang, Finding interesting associations without support pruning, *IEEE Trans. Knowledge Data Eng.*, 13(1), 64–78, 2001.

Deogun, J. S., V. V. Raghavan, A. Sarkar, and H. Sever, Data mining: in research and development, in *Rough Set and Data Mining. Analysis of Imprecise Data,* Kluwer, Boston, 1997.

Ganti, V., J. Gehrke, and R. Ramakrishnan, DEMON: mining and monitoring evolving data, *IEEE Trans. Knowledge Data Eng.,* 13(1), 50–63, 2001.

Gryzmala-Busse, J. W., *Managing Uncertainty in Expert Systems,* Kluwer, Boston, 1991.

Han, J., Y. Cai, and N. Cercone, Knowledge discovery in databases: an attribute-oriented approach, in *Proc. 18th Int. Conf. Very Large Data Bases,* 1992.

Han, J. and Y. Fu, Mining multiple level association rules in large databases, *IEEE Trans. Knowledge Data Eng.,* 11; 5: 1999.

Han, J. and M. Kamber, *Data Mining: Concepts and Techniques,* Morgan Kaufman Publisher, Palo Alto, CA, 2001.

Hu, X., N. Cercone, and W. Ziarko, Generation of multiple knowledge from databases based on rough sets theory, in *Rough Set and Data Mining. Analysis of Imprecise Data,* T. Y. Lin and N. Cerone (Eds.), Kluwer, Boston, 1997.

Liao, L., Rough Set Data Analysis, M.S. thesis-equivalent, University of Nebraska at Omaha, 2001.

Liu, B., W. Hsu, L.-F. Mun, and H.-Y. Lee, Finding interesting patterns using user expectations, *IEEE Trans. Knowledge Data Eng.,* 11(6), 817–832, 1999.

Palpanas, T., Knowledge discovery in data warehouses, *SIGMOD Rec.,* 29(3), 2000.

Pawlak, Z., Bough sets, in *Rough Set and Data Mining. Analysis of Imprecise Data,* T. Y. Lin and N. Cerone (Eds.), Kluwer, Boston, 1997, 3–7.

Plum, D., Preparation and Mining for Stock Food Chain Analysis, Term project paper, Department of Computer Science, University of Nebraska at Omaha, 2001.

Stefanowski, J. and K. Slowinski, Rough sets as a tool for studying attribute dependencies in the urinary stones treatment data set, in *Rough Set and Data Mining. Analysis of Imprecise Data,* Kluwer, Boston, 1997.

Yao, Y. Y., S. K. M. Wong, and T. Y. Lin, A review of rough set models, in *Rough Set and Data Mining. Analysis of Imprecise Data,* T. Y. Lin and N. Cerone (Eds.), Kluwer, Boston, 1997.

chapter nine

Toward integrated OLAP and data mining

9.1   Overview

This last chapter of the book examines the issue of integrated OLAP and data mining, beginning with a discussion on the need for such integration. The rest of the chapter is devoted to a particular approach for integrated OLAP and data mining, namely, mining of influential association rules. This encompasses a detailed discussion because, although it is an important issue, discussion is not available elsewhere. Also, since this is the last chapter, a detailed discussion offers a chance to wrap up by reviewing several useful techniques discussed earlier for intelligent data warehousing, such as association rule mining, search space pruning, and bitmap indexing.

9.2   Integration of OLAP and data mining

There are significant semantic differences between data mining and OLAP (Chen, 1998). Although both OLAP and data mining deal with analysis of data, the focus and methodology are quite different. This section provides much needed discussion on this issue and uses several examples to illustrate these differences. The differences of data mining carried out at different levels, including how different types of queries can be handled, how different semantics of knowledge can be discovered and how different heuristics may be used, will be pointed out.

First, note that different kinds of analysis can be carried out at different levels. For example, what are the features of products purchased along with promotional items? The answer for this query could be association rule(s) at the granularity level because one needs to analyze actual purchase data for each transaction involved in promotional items (assuming information about promotional items can be found in product price). As another example, what kinds of products are most profitable? This query involves aggregation and can be answered by OLAP alone. Finally, what kinds of customers buy the most profitable products? This query can be answered in different ways. One is to analyze individual transactions and obtain association rules between products and customers at the granularity level. An alternative way is to select all most profitable products, project the whole set of customers who purchased them, and then find out the characteristics of these customers. In this case, one tries to answer the query by discovering characteristic rules at an aggregation level. (For example, customers can be characterized by their addresses.)

The preceding discussion further suggests that data mining at different levels may have different semantics. Since most people are familiar with semantics of knowledge discovered at the granularity level, this discussion emphasizes what kind of difference is made by the semantics of knowledge discovered at aggregation levels (which will be referred to as aggregation semantics). However, since they are complementary to each other, it would be ideal to integrate these two directions of data analysis. For this purpose, On-Line Analytical Mining (OLAM) has been proposed (Han and Kamber, 2000).

9.3 Influential association rules

A particular approach to achieving integrated OLAP and data mining is the mining of influential association rules. The primary goal of discovering influential association rules is to reveal the relationship between the influencing factors (dimensions) and the influenced target (numeric measures). Note that, in a data warehouse, the term dimension usually refers to a detail table that may contribute one or more attributes to the fact table of a data warehouse. In an influential association rule, a dimension refers to a specific attribute in the fact table, which is derived from a detail dimension table (Parsaye, 1997). Influential association rules represent the influence pattern of influencing items X on influenced targets Y, which can be viewed as a special form of conventional association rules. In the form of $X \Rightarrow Y$, an influential association rule is expressed as: condition part X has an influential association relationship with assertion part Y and $X \cap Y = \varnothing$ (Chen et al., 1999). The condition part X is composed of a set of dimension items and the assertion part Y is composed of a set of measure items. Influential association rules concern data patterns in two levels, granularity level and aggregation level. In granularity level, the frequency of X and $X \cup Y$ is concerned. In aggregation level, the summarized value of Y in the transactions $X \cup Y$ is concerned. The support s of the rule in granularity level is the percentage $s\%$ of item sets in the whole analytical scope containing the set X. The confidence c of the rule in granularity level is the fraction c in item sets containing X that also contain item set Y. The aggregation value v of the rule in aggregated level is the sum on Y for all item sets containing both X and Y.

Thus, to an analytical target of relation view R, influence association rules are stated as $X \Rightarrow Y$ with support s, confidence c, and aggregation value

v, where X is the condition part composed of a dimension item set and Y is the assertion part composed of a measure item set. There are at least $s\%$ tuples of all tuples in view R containing X, and a fraction c of all tuples containing X falls into the category of Y. The aggregated value v is the accumulation on measure attributes for all tuples containing X and falling into category Y (Parsaye, 1997; Chen, 1998; Chen et al., 1999). Item set Y is derived from these measure attributes.

In addition to frequent set computation, another challenge for discovery of association rules is to prune and refine the discovered candidate rules so that only meaningful rules are presented and maintained. Redundancy should be removed. Pruning and refining is also time consuming and expensive for analysis of a massive data set. Constraints imposed in candidate association rule computation will greatly reduce the computation cost and rule redundancy. Influential association rules can be considered as conventional association rules in a special format and restricted with quantitative measurement constraints. Thus, influential association rules present useful information with less redundancy.

In the data warehouse environment where a multidimensional data model is used, the association patterns along dimensions may not be a primary target for analysis in decision support processing. Only when the dimension context plays a significant role on numeric measure, are the association patterns of dimensions and their impacts on target numeric measures meaningful to a decision support system. Therefore, discovery of influential association rules is of great interest to decision support processing in the context of data warehouses.

Due to the massive data volume and multiple dimensions of a data warehouse, the following issues must be dealt with for discovery of influential association rules in the data warehouse environment.

- Multiple dimensions of data warehouses suggest that multiple dimensions are very common for data mining of influential association rules.
- Influence of dimensions on numeric measures is expressed in the association patterns of dimensions with categories of the numeric measures considered. The effects of categorization of the target numeric measures on discovery of influential association rules must be scrutinized.
- In addition to the granularity level in which occurring frequencies of association patterns are considered, the influence of dimensions on aggregation of numeric measures is an integral part of influential association rules.
- The massive volume of data warehouses suggests that algorithms for discovery of influential association rules be efficient and scalable.

Conventional association rules are the association patterns of items in a set of records. The main difference between influential association rules and conventional association rules is that influential association rules emphasize the influential effects of a set of dimensions on a set of numeric measures. The set of dimensions are, to some extent, equivalent to the frequent sets of conventional association rules. Therefore, it is necessary to review the strategies used to discover conventional association rules before discussing methodology of discovering influential association rules.

Discovery of influential association rules can be applied for a decision support system in two types of context. First, a conventional association rule is carried over further to analyze the influential effects of this association pattern on numeric measure. In this situation, each item in the frequent set of the association rule is considered a dimension. Association rule *Bread* ⇒ *Butter* can be used as an example. The frequent set of this association rule is {*Bread, Butter*}. In the context of influential association rules, *Bread* and *Butter* are two dimensions. The influential effects of the two dimensions on numeric measures, such sale quantity and profitability, are analyzed to discover influential association patterns.

In the other situation in which data warehouses and OLAP are integral parts of decision systems, influential association rules are computed on selected dimensions and numeric measures within a multidimensional data model. In addition to the influential associations of different items as dimensions with target numeric measures, one item and its features and characteristics can also be considered dimensions. For instance, one may be interested in the sale patterns of television sets with other dimensions such as store location, brand name, model, and size.

Given a set of dimensions and a set of numeric measures, the problem of mining influential association rules is to discover the influential association patterns between the two such that the set of dimensions has the highest influential effect on the set of numeric measures. The final rules must have support and confidence greater than the user-specified support (minimum support) and confidence (minimum confidence). Highest influential effects means that the final rules have the highest confidence and highest absolute aggregation value among all candidate rules with the same value of dimension set.

9.4   *Significance of influential association rules*

Discovering the association patterns hidden within data in the form of conventional association rules, which is an important and successful data mining technique, helps marketing managers design information-driven marketing processes and strategies. For instance, associated items can be arranged on the same shelf in a supermarket. The convenience for customers provides better service and may potentially increase sales.

However, conventional association rules only concern the association patterns between items or attributes and do not provide information with regard to the quality of the association patterns. The quality of association rules can be defined as the impacts of the association rules on primary

Table 9.1 A Simple Relation

Product	Manufacturer	Profit
P1	M1	100
P1	M2	−50
P2	M1	−100
P2	M2	50

business goals, such as sale quantity and profitability. The quality of association patterns may play a crucial role when choices have to be made rather than when all options are examined.

Discovering convention association rules merely considers the occurring frequency of association patterns in transaction and ignores the "weight" of the individual transaction. For instance, one transaction contains item 1 and item 2 and another transaction contains item 1 and item 3. In conventional association rules, the two transactions are equivalent in considering whether item 1 associates with item 2 or item 3. However, in some numeric measures, such as quantity, value, and profitability, the two transactions are not equivalent. Assume that:

Transaction 1: item 1 (price $10.99 and quantity 10) and item 2 (price $20.99 and quantity 8)

Transaction 2: item 1 (price $10.99 and quantity 4) and item 3 (price $12.99 and quantity 5)

Transaction 1 is more important than transaction 2 in terms of quantity, which may result in more profit. If a choice has to be made between associations item 1–item 2 and item 1–item 3, the association item 1–item 2 is the choice in terms of profitability. Association rules concern not only occurring frequency but also the influential effects of item association patterns on analytical numeric measures.

In a multidimensional data model, the values of numeric measures depend on a set of dimensions. OLAP operations are not capable of satisfying analysis of the influence of a set of dimensions on target numeric measures. Results based on OLAP may sometimes be misleading (Parsaye, 1997).

An example appears in Table 9.1. These data show that the products P1 of manufacturer M1 and P2 of manufacturer M2 are profitable and the products P1 of manufacturer M2 and P2 of manufacturer M1 are not profitable.

After OLAP roll-up operations, the results shown in Table 9.2 can be obtained. The result shows that product P1 is profitable, product P2 is in debt, and products of all manufacturers are not profitable.

These results are contradictory and misleading because OLAP is not capable of analyzing synergic effects of multiple dimensions. Influential association rules integrated with OLAP address the issue well.

Table 9.2 Result of Rollup

Roll-up	Profit
P1	50
P2	−50
M1	0
M2	0

9.5   Reviews of algorithms for discovery of conventional association rules

Discovery of influential association rules can be divided into three major steps: 1. computation of condition part (a set of dimensions), 2. computation of occurring frequency of condition part and its influential association patterns on numeric measures, and 3. analysis of influence of condition part on aggregation values of numeric measures. The condition part of an influential association rule is a set of dimensions equivalent to a frequent set in conventional association rules. One can take advantage of experience and strategies used for frequent set computation in discovering conventional association rules to avoid reinventing the wheel.

The concept of association rules was first introduced in Agrawal et al. (1993). An algorithm, AIS algorithm, to find all association rules in transaction processing database was also proposed in Agrawal et al. (1993). Since then, most research on discovering association rules paid much attention to the computation of frequent set. In AIS algorithm, the transaction set is repeatedly scanned until no more new frequent sets can be found. In each scan, existing frequent sets found by previous scans are extended by one in each transaction to become new candidate frequent sets. A user-specified minimum support is used to filter the newly found candidate frequent sets to obtain new frequent sets. Then, the union of newly found frequent sets with pre-existing frequent sets is the total frequent sets found.

Since then, many algorithms for discovering association rules have been proposed. However, most research has been to discover association rules within "basket data." Little attention has been paid to the multidimensional data model, which is popular in data warehousing. Even less work has been done in discovering influential association rules.

In the search for algorithms for discovery of influential association rules, the Apriori Tid algorithm proposed by Agrawal and Srikant (1994) inspired the proposal of discovering influential association rules using bitmap indexing. In Chapter 8 we have already presented the basic Apriori algorithm. Before a discussion of bitmap indexing for influential association rule takes place, a brief review of the Apriori Tid algorithm is needed:

Let F_k be the set for all frequent sets whose length is equal to k

Let C_k be the set of candidate frequent set

C_k (where $k > 1$) is computed from F_{k-1} as follows:

$F_{k-1} \times F_{k-1}$, and delete all item sets whose length is not k

delete the item sets whose any $k - 1$ subset is not in F_{k-1}

For example, let $F_2 = \{\{1, 2\}, \{2, 3\}, \{1, 4\}\}$, then $F_2 \times F_2$ will be

$$\{\{1, 2\}, \{1, 2, 3\}, \{1, 2, 4\}, \{2, 3\}, \{1, 2, 3, 4\}, \{1, 4\}\}$$

Delete those item sets with length of not 3, and the result is $\{\{1, 2, 3\}, \{1, 2, 4\}\}$. Subset $\{1, 3\}$ of the set $\{1, 2, 3\}$ is not in F_2 and subsets $\{2, 4\}$ of the set $\{1, 2, 4\}$ are not in F_2. Deleting these two sets leaves an empty set C_3. That is, $C_3 = \emptyset$.

The feature of algorithm AprioriTid is to keep the recording of TID (transaction identifier). Only the transactions in the TID set of previous one pass are scanned in the next pass. As the process is going on, fewer transactions are needed for processing. This algorithm is shown in Figure 9.1.

For example (modified from Agrawal and Srikant, 1994), consider the database in Figure 9.2 and assume that minimum support is two transactions. One element frequent set is computed as F1. All item sets in F1 have at least two transaction supports. Then a candidate set with one more element extension is computed as C2. Minimum support of two transactions is applied to C2 to obtain frequent set F2. This process repeats until no frequent set is found or all items are computed.

Let F be the set of all frequent sets and $F = \emptyset$;

Let T_k be the transaction set after kth pass, then T_1 is the transactions set of the whole database;

F_1 is the set of all frequent sets of item sets with length one;

$F += F_1$;

for ($k = 2$; $F_{k-1} \neq \emptyset$; k++)

        Compute C_k from F_{k-1};

        Let $T_k = \emptyset$;

        for each entry t_i in T_{k-1}

        for all candidate item sets c, $c \in C_k$ and c is contained in t_i

                $c.count$ ++;

                $T_k += t_i$;

                End of for-loop

                $F_k += \{ c \in C_k \mid c.count \geq$ minimum support

                $F += F_k$;

        End of for-loop

End of for-loop

Return F;

Figure 9.1 Algorithm Apriori Tid. (From Agrawal and Srikant, 1994.)

Database

TID	Items
100	1 3 4
200	2 3 5
300	1 2 3 5
400	2 5

F_1

Item Set	Support
{1}	2
{2}	3
{3}	3
{5}	3

C_2

Item Set
{1 2}
{1 3}
{1 5}
{2 3}
{2 5}
{3 5}

F_2

{1 3}	2
{2 3}	2
{2 5}	3
{3 5}	2

C_3

Item Set
{2 3 5}

F_3

Item Set	Support
{2 3 5}	2

Figure 9.2 Demonstration example of the AprioriTID algorithm.

The main improvement of algorithm AprioriTID over AIS and Apriori algorithm (Agrawal, 1994) is that Apriori TID only processes the subset of transactions derived from previous passes. After each pass, the number of transactions requiring processing is quickly reduced within an operational database with the use of TID sets, as already illustrated in Figure 9.2.

9.6   Discovery of influential association rules

9.6.1   The IARM algorithm

In the data warehousing environment, results of OLAP operation are not enough — and even misleading for decision support systems. To tackle the mismatch between OLAP and data mining, integrating the two has gained much attention recently (Chen, 1998).

For association rule mining in the environment of integration of OLAP and data mining, two factors not present in classical association rule discovery of basket data require consideration. First, the semantics of association rules in the integration environment has been changed as compared to that for basket data. For example, one may want not only to find out purchase patterns but also to use measure attributes such as "profit" and "sell increase" to quantify these patterns. For example, a promotion (such as price dropping) of items (item set A) has increased the sale of those items price dropped, as well as for associated items (item set B), even though there has been no price drop for the associated items. That is, there exists an association between item sets A and B. This is what is expected and the association rule is trivial. What one may really want to find out is whether increased sales are large, fair, or small and whether the profit is large, fair, or small in terms of user-defined criteria. This phenomenon — the influence of promotion on profit and sell increase — is defined as "influence pattern" (Chen et al., 1999).

Recently, an algorithm termed influential association rule mining (IARM), for discovery of influential association rules, was proposed (Chen et al., 1999). In the IARM algorithm, the process of discovering influential association rules can roughly be divided into four steps. These steps are 1. computation of the support of condition part, which is similar to the computation of frequent sets in mining conventional association rules; 2. categorization and support calculation of assertion part; 3. mining candidate rules from supports of condition and assertion; and 4. refinement of candidate rules to obtain desired influential association rules. These four steps are described below.

9.6.2 Support counting of condition part item set

Let D be the set of dimensions in a given multidimensional data model. Then distinct item sets of dimension d_i, $d_i \in D$ and $0 < i \leq |D|$, are represented in the form of a pair $<d_i, v_p>$, where v_p is a distinct value of dimension d_i.

The target database is scanned with one pass and support of each distinct item set $<d_i, v_p>$ is calculated as:

$$S(<d_i, v_p>) = \text{(number of tuples containing } <d_i, v_p>) \times 100/\text{(total tuples } N)$$

Let R be the cardinality of dimension d_i and number of records analyzed be N. The time complexity of computing support all distinct item sets within dimension d_i will be $\theta(f(R)*N)$ rather than $\theta(N)$ as claimed by the author (Chen, 1998), where $f(R)$ is the time complexity to search the set of all distinct item sets ($<d_i, v_p>$) previously found and N is the linear search of N records.

9.6.3 Categorization and support counting of a numeric measure

To identify the influential effects of dimensions on a numeric measure in a multidimensional data model, the data domain of the numeric measure is categorized into several categories and the association patterns of the dimensions with each category are analyzed.

Let M be the set of numeric measures in a given multidimensional data model. The domain range of target numeric measure m_j, $m_j \in M$, and $0 < j \leq |M|$ is first divided into segments. The number of segments is user-specified. Then segments are merged into user-specified numbers of categories. Two rules apply in segmentation and mergence of segments into categories: 1. no segment or category covers both negative and positive values of m_j and 2. the difference of support count between any two categories should be as small as possible in segment merging.

Rule 1 makes sense when one considers the aggregation value [SUM ($m_i \mid <d_i, v_p> \cup <m_j, c_k>)$] for each candidate rule $<d_i, v_p> \Rightarrow <m_j, c_k>$ (refer to section 2.3.3). This will prevent data disappearance caused by compensation of negative values with positive values. Besides, non-profitable and profitable are obviously different, for instance, when one uses profitability as the numeric measure. Rule 2 normalizes the possibility of skew distribution of values of a numeric measure.

After categorization of numeric measure m_j, let C be the set of categories. Each distinct value within numeric measure m_j is represented in the form of $<m_j, v_q>$, and then mapped into $<m_j, c_k>$ based on the categorization, where $c_k \in C$. The target database is scanned with one pass and support of each distinct item set $<m_j, c_k>$ within m_j is calculated as:

$$S(<m_j, c_k>) = \text{(number of tuples mapping to } <m_j, c_k>)$$
$$\times 100/\text{(total tuples } N)$$

9.6.4   Mining candidate influential association rules

Once all $S(<d_i, v_p>)$ for dimension d_i are computed, candidate influential association rules for one dimension and one measure are computed. For dimension $d_i, d_i \in D$, and measure $m_j, m_i \in M$, influential association rule $<d_i, v_p> \Rightarrow <m_j, c_k>$ has support $s(<d_i, v_p> \Rightarrow <m_j, c_k>)$, confidence $c(<d_i, v_p> \Rightarrow <m_j, c_k>)$, and aggregation value $v(<d_i, v_p> \Rightarrow <m_j, c_k>)$:

$$s(<d_i, v_p> \Rightarrow <m_j, c_k>) = S(<d_i, v_p>)$$
$$c(<d_i, v_p> \Rightarrow <m_j, c_k>) = S(<d_i, v_p> \cup <m_j, c_k>)/S(<d_i, v_p>)$$
$$v(<d_i, v_p> \Rightarrow <m_j, c_k>) = SUM (m_i | <d_i, v_p> \cup <m_j, c_k>)$$

Letting R be the cardinality of dimension d_i and number of records analyzed be N, there will be $R*|C|$ candidate rules. The time complexity of computing all candidate rules for one dimension d_i and one numeric measure m_i will be $\theta(f(R*|C|)*N)$ rather than $\theta(N)$ as claimed by the author, where $f(R*|C|)$ is the time complexity to search the set of all candidate rules previously found and N is the linear search of N records. In the worst case, the dimension d_i has N distinct values in N tuples and sequential search is used for previously found candidate rules. The time complex of mining candidate rules should be $\theta(|C|*N^2)$ in the worst case.

9.6.5   Pruning and refining candidate influential association rules

In the set of candidate rules, there could be $R*|C|$ candidate rules, as discussed in a previous section (2.3.3). In this case, each distinct item set from dimension d_i has $|C|$ candidate rules, in which identical condition part item set associates with different categories from numeric measure m_j. The candidate rules with identical condition parts are pruned and refined as follows.

- If there are one or more candidate rules having the highest support s_h and the highest absolute aggregation value $|v_h|$, keep these rule(s) and delete all others.

- Otherwise, it is denoted as incompatible candidate rules, in which one or more candidate rules have the highest support s_h and some other rule(s) has (have) the highest aggregation value $|v_h|$.

The incompatible candidate rules are resolved as follows:

Keep the rules having the highest aggregation value $|v_h|$ and discard others

Let $<d_i, v_r>$ be the condition part item set of incompatible candidate rules

Let m_j be the target numeric measure

$\Sigma v = SUM\ (m_j\ |<d_i, v_r>)$

if Σv contains positive value only, **then** let $v_g = \Sigma v /$support count of $<d_i, v_r>$

  else let $v_g = \Sigma v$

if v_g falls within the boundaries of category c_s, $c_s \in C$ of numeric measure m_j

  then v_g is assigned the category c_s.

A new rule $<d_i, v_r> \Rightarrow <m_j, c_s>$ with aggregation value (summarized or average) v_g is obtained, associated with the context of tuples that contribute the most to v_g.

In the worst case that all distinct item sets from dimension d_i have incompatible candidate rules and that $(|C| - 1)$ candidate rules have the same greatest absolute aggregation value for each item set, the time complexity of pruning and refining will be $O(R^*(|C| - 1)^*N)$.

9.6.6   Problems of the IARM algorithm

The IARM algorithm effectively addressed the issue of incorporating OLAP considerations into data mining. Nevertheless, several issues need to be further examined. The first is the multiple dimensions and measures. The IARM algorithm did not explain well how to adopt the algorithm to apply it for multiple dimensions and measures. In the context of multiple dimensions and measures, an influential association rule will be

$$<d_1, v_{1p}> \cup <d_2, v_{2q}> \cup ... \cup <d_k, v_{kx}> \Rightarrow$$
$$<m_1, c_{1a}> \cup <m_2, c_{2b}> \cup ... \cup <m_j, c_{jy}>$$

Assuming that the average cardinality of K dimensions involved is R and the average number of category for J measures involved is C, the number of all possible condition part item sets will be R^K and the number of all possible assertion part item sets (categories) C^J. The resulting all possible candidate rules will be $R^K * C^J$. That is, the complexity of combination is exponential to both number of dimensions K and number of measures J. To process a large volume of data efficiently, a more efficient algorithm than IARM algorithm is necessary.

Another issue is the resolution of incompatible candidate rules. In mining conventional association rules, occurring frequency of an association pattern is the sole measurement to judge the importance of the pattern. In the context of a multidimensional data model, one should also consider the influencing effect of conditional item sets on the overall value (aggregation value) of target numeric measures. Occurring frequency of an influential association pattern and its influenced aggregation value should be considered relatively equally important unless users have specified the primary concern for further refinement of candidate rules.

These issues lead to designing more efficient algorithms and more reasonable pruning and refining schemes for mining influential association rules. The first strategy is filtration with minimum support and minimum confidence, which is widely applied in mining conventional association rules. The second strategy is to take advantage of the efficiency of bitmap indexing, which is gaining more popularity in indexing technology for large volumes of high read/update ratio data in the data warehousing environment (Wu and Buchanan, 1998; Winter, 1999).

In summary, influential association rules that address issues that conventional association rules ignore are significant in data mining. Well-designed algorithms have been developed for discovery of conventional association rules; however, they are not suitable to be applied directly in discovery of influential association rules. The IARM algorithm for discovery of influential association rules is not efficient in handling multiple dimensions, which are very common in discovery of influential association rules.

9.7   Bitmap indexing and influential association rules

9.7.1   Basic idea of bitmap indexing

In order to deal with the problem related to IARM, it is necessary to discuss the principles of bitmap index technology and why it is useful in discovery of influential association rules. The basic idea of using bitmap was already discussed in Chapter 5. Bitmap indexing has emerged as a promising technique in query optimization for large databases and data warehouses. Several commercial DBMSs, such as IBM DB2, Informix, and Oracle, have implemented bitmap indexing for support of DSSs and OLAP.

The major advantage of bitmap indices is that bitmap manipulations using bit-wise operators (AND, OR, XOR, NOT) are very efficiently supported by hardware. In various contexts of the environment, specially designed bitmap indexing schemes are much more efficient than traditional indices, such as B-tree index, for ad hoc and complicated queries that are frequently observed in the data warehousing environment (Chan and Ioannidis, 1998).

A bitmap index uses a bit vector to record the presence or absence of a value. For instance, one can use bitmaps to index the column "gender" of a table "employee" shown in Table 9.3.

Table 9.3 An Example of Bitmap Indexing

Emp_ID	Sex	...	Emp_ID	M_bitmap	F_bitmap	....
10001	Male		10001	1	0	
10002	Female	Bitmap	10002	0	1	
10003	Female	indexing on	10003	0	1	
10004	Male	Gender	10004	1	0	
10005	Male		10005	1	0	

M_bitmap is used to index gender on the value of male. If the tuple has the value of male, the corresponding position in M_bitmap is to set the bit on ("1"); otherwise it is to set the bit off ("0"). The same strategy is applied for the value of female.

The following sections briefly discuss bitmap index technology used in data warehouses. Two bitmap indexing schemes, simple bitmap indexing and binary encoded bitmap indexing, will then be discussed in more detail. Finally, the use of bitmap indexing in mining influential association rules to improve efficiency is investigated.

9.7.2   Bitmap indexing in data warehouses

A framework for various bitmap indexing schemes was proposed by Chan and Ioannidis (1998). In that framework, bitmap indices were within the design space from optimal time query performance to optimal space performance, as shown in Figure 9.3.

From Figure 9.3, one can see that, at the end of optimal time, bitmap indexing has the lowest space performance. Similarly, at the other end of

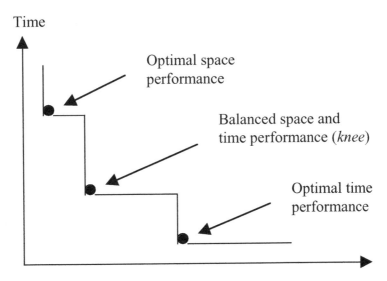

Figure 9.3 Bitmap indexing design space (modified from Chan and Ioannidis, 1998).

optimal space, bitmap indexing has the lowest time performance. This indicates that, when the most space is used to store bitmap indices, the best time performance is gained. On the other hand, the worst time performance occurs when least space is used to store the bitmap indices.

Simple bitmap indexing scheme is a typical optimal time bitmap index that takes the most space; binary encoded indexing is a typical optimal space bitmap index that takes the least space (Wu and Buchanan, 1998). In simple bitmap indexing, each distinct value occupies a bit vector within the bitmap. A simple bitmap for indexing an attribute is composed of the same number of bit vectors as the number of distinct values the indexed attribute contains. For example, attribute A of table T has distinct values $\{a, g, p, s\}$. The indexing bitmap for attribute A of table T is shown in Table 9.4.

Table 9.4 A Simple Bitmap Indexing

	Simple bitmap index for attribute A						
...	A	...		a	g	p	s
	a			1	0	0	0
	s			0	0	0	1
	a			1	0	0	0
	g			0	1	0	0
	p			0	0	1	0
	s			0	0	0	1
	p			0	0	1	0
	...			...	...	...	...

To make a query, for example with selection condition "WHERE $A = g$ OR $A = s$," one simply OR together vector g-$\{0\ 0\ 0\ 1\ 0\ 0\ 0\}$ and vector s-$\{0\ 1\ 0\ 0\ 0\ 1\ 0\}$ to obtain a new vector $\{0\ 1\ 0\ 1\ 0\ 1\ 0\}$. With the new bit vector, one can easily locate the tuples having a value of either g or s.

In binary encoded bitmap indexing, each distinct value is mapped to a binary value and the bitmap is composed of the bits of these binary values. Looking at the same example above, one sees that attribute A of table T has distinct values $\{a, g, p, s\}$. Assume the mapping functions are $\{a = 001, g = 010, p = 011,$ and $s = 100\}$. The bitmap to index attribute A will be as shown in Table 9.5.

To make a selection query with selection condition "WHERE $A = g$ OR $A = s$," one needs to OR together the two mapping functions for value g ($\overline{B_2}B_1\overline{B_0}$) and value s ($B_2\overline{B_1}\overline{B_0}$). A new mapping function for "$A = g$ OR $A = s$" is generated from the OR operation.

$$\text{New function: } f_{g+s} = \overline{B_2}B_1\overline{B_0} + B_2\overline{B_1}\overline{B_0} = (\overline{B_2}B_1 + B_2\overline{B_1})\overline{B_0}$$

Then this new mapping function is used to query the database to obtain relevant data.

Table 9.5 Binary Encoded Bitmap Indexing

Binary Encoded Bitmap index for attribute A			
... A ...	B_2	B_1	B_0
a	0	0	1
s	1	0	0
a	0	0	1
g	0	1	0
p	0	1	1
s	1	0	0
p	0	1	1
...	...	...	...

In the previous example, the number of vectors to be examined depends on the new function. For some queries, the new function can be further reduced to a simpler expression. In this case, fewer vectors are examined. For example, g OR p is f_{g+p} $\overline{B_2}B_1\overline{B_0} + \overline{B_2}B_1B_0 = \overline{B_2}B_1(\overline{B_0} + \overline{B_0}) = \overline{B_2}B_1$. In this case, only two bit vectors needed to be examined.

Assuming attribute A has cardinality C, simple bitmap indexing requires C bit vectors. However, only $\log_2(C + 1)$ bit vectors are needed for binary encoded bitmap indexing.

9.8   Mining influential association rules using bitmap indexing (IARMBM)

Mining influential association rules requires computing supports, confidences, and aggregation values. Queries similar to SQL statements can be used to express the computation. For example, to mining influential association rules $<d_i, v_p> \Rightarrow <m_j, c_q>$ from one dimension d_i and one measure m_j, where c_q is a category of m_j within the range of [*lower, upper*] and [*lower, upper*] means that lower boundary is inclusive and upper boundary is exclusive (the "inclusive" and "exclusive" meaning of [a, b] will be used throughout this thesis):

$S(<d_i, v_p> \Rightarrow <m_j, c_q>) = COUNT$ (tuples WHERE $d_i = v_p$)
$C(<d_i, v_p> \Rightarrow <m_j, c_q>) = COUNT$ (tuples WHERE $d_i = v_p$
        AND *lower* $\leq m_j <$ *upper*)/COUNT (tuples WHERE $d_i = v_p$)
$v(<d_i, v_p> \Rightarrow <m_j, c_q>) = SUM$ (m_j, WHERE $d_i = v_p$ AND *lower* $\leq m_j <$ *upper*)

These statements are straightforward and can be very efficiently processed by SQL query engines currently available. However, there are two challenges: one must efficiently compute all candidate influential rules and must repeatedly execute similar queries until all candidate rules are found; however, this is not efficient enough to process a large volume of data. As another challenge, one must consider multiple dimensions and multiple numeric measures for data mining influential association rules in the context of multidimensional data model.

In mining convention association rules, algorithm Apriori Tid (Agrawal and Srikant 1994) takes advantage of the transaction identifier set. As the length of frequency gets longer, the set of transactions gets smaller. This results in dramatic reduction of frequent set computation time. In mining influential association rules, a bitmap is an efficient data structure to locate the tuples within a multidimensional view for further processing.

In addition, the consideration of aggregation values in discovery of influential association rules makes things much more complicated. One consideration is to map the continuous values of measure attributes into binary values (e.g., categorization) and then apply the algorithms developed for conventional association rules to discover candidate influential association rules in the terms of support and confidence. Then, aggregation value is computed for each rule found to complete the process for mining candidate influential association rules. Even though the performance of this algorithm is acceptable, it can be greatly improved by using bitmap indexing.

First, in the mapping of continuous values to binary values (categorization), a bitmap index is constructed for each category. The aggregate value of each rule found in granularity level can be easily computed through this bitmap index. Furthermore, the computation of granularity level rules can also take advantage of the bitmap index. Second, a bitmap index for dimension attributes, together with the category bitmap index, converts the computation of granularity level rules into bit manipulations, thus greatly improving efficiency and discovering all candidate granularity level rules in one step.

As an example to demonstrate the strategy described above, consider that a bitmap is a bit vector used to represent data in a column of a table. For instance, use bit "1" can represent male and bit "0" can represent female. Then, the gender column of a table can be mapped into a bit vector as shown in Table 9.6.

If a column contains many distinct values, we each value can be assigned a unique binary value and be mapped into a bit vector using the binary values. For N distinct values, $\log_2(N + 1)$ bits are used for the bit vector if no value is assigned a binary value 0. This scheme is called binary encoded bitmap indexing (Wu and Buchanan, 1998). In the example of influential

Table 9.6 A Simple Mapping

RID	Gender		RID	Bit Vector
1	Male		1	1
2	Male	Mapping	2	1
3	Female	Male → 1	3	0
4	Male	Female → 0	4	1
5	Female		5	0

Table 9.7(a) Dimensions Bitmap

RID	Dimensions
1	010
2	101
3	001
4	010
5	110
6	011
7	101
8	100
9	010
10	111

Table 9.7(b) Categories Bitmap

Rid	Categories
1	001
2	101
3	110
4	011
5	100
6	111
7	110
8	001
9	010
10	101

association rules discovery, a unique binary value is assigned to each distinct dimension item set. If the tuple contains the item set, the bitmap is set to the binary value at this tuple position. Similarly, a bitmap of categories for measure attribute is built (for details on building the bitmaps, refer to related sections), as shown in Tables 9.7(a) and 9.7(b).

From the bitmap for dimensions, one can easily compute the frequency for each distinct dimension item set, defined SUPPORT for influential association rules. Shifting left three bits on dimension bitmap and then "oring" it with categories bitmap will obtain the bitmap shown in Table 9.8.

Now, one can easily compute the frequency for each new binary value, defined CONFIDENCE. After filtration based on minimum support and minimum confidence, influential association rules can be obtained. Aggregation can also be efficiently computed through the category bitmap, whose positions point to the corresponding positions in relation view *R*.

As can be seen from the previous section, bitmap index technology is widely used in data warehouses. In data mining, one can take advantage of the inherent efficiency of bit manipulations supported in underlying hardware. Bitmap indexing provides algorithm design space for discovery of

Table 9.8 Dimensions Bitmap Shift Left 3 Bits OR Category Bitmap

RID	Dimensions–Categories
1	010 001
2	101 101
3	001 110
4	010 011
5	110 100
6	011 111
7	101 110
8	100 001
9	010 010
10	111 101

influential association rules. A new algorithm, influential association rule mining using bitmap (IARMBM), has been developed for discovery of influential association rules in the data warehouse environment. The IARMBM constructs one bitmap for all dimension attributes and one bitmap for all measure attributes; then, the two bitmaps are merged into one. From this merged bitmap, there is a set of all possible candidate influential association rules in binary format. Minimum support and minimum confidence are then applied to filter this set of rules to obtain candidate influential association rules, which can then further be refined to discover final desired influential association rules. For details, see Zhang et al. (2001).

9.9   Summary

Since the algorithms described in this chapter cover a wide range of issues discussed earlier, to wrap up this chapter, as well as this book, calls for only the following brief remarks. It has been shown that intelligent data warehousing is a dynamic and complex phenomenon. Of course, data warehousing means integration of data, but, more importantly, it is concerned with integrated use of various methods developed in database management systems, artificial intelligence, and mathematics, as well as many other fields of science. In this book, due to space limitation, it has been possible to examin only a small number of selected issues; nevertheless, they demonstrate the diversity of problems that exist and methods that can be used to address them. Data warehousing is thus a typical showcase of integration of methodologies. It has been motivated in business applications, and intelligent data warehousing should be developed to deal with important issues in business intelligence. In addition, although not much attention is paid to data warehousing applications outside the business world, it is believed that the data warehouse can play an important role in other fields as well. Many challenging issues remain, but the future is bright.

References

Agrawal, R., C. Faloutsos, and A. Swami, Efficient similarity in sequence databases, *Proc. 4th Int. Conf. Found. Data Organ. Algoritnms*, 1993, 69–84.

Agrawal, R. and R. Srikant, Fast algorithms for mining association Rules, presented at *Proc. 21st Int. Conf. Very Large Databases*, Santiago, Chile, 1994, 487–499.

Chan, C.-Y. and Y. E. Ioannidis, Bitmap index design and evaluation, presented at *Proc. ACM SIGMOD Int. Conf. Manage. Data*, Seattle, WA, 355–366, 1998.

Chen, Z., An integrated architecture for OLAP and data mining, in *Knowledge Discovery and Data Mining*, M. Bramer (Ed.), 1998, 114–136.

Chen, X., Z. Chen, and Q. Zhu, From OLAP to data mining: an analytical influential association approach, *J. Comput. Sci. Inf. Manage.*, 1–8, June, 1999.

Parsaye, K., OLAP and data mining: bridging the gap, *Database Programming Design*, 10(2), 30–37, 1997.

Winter, R. , Indexing goes a new direction, *Intell. Enterp.*, 2(2), 70–73, 1999.

Wu, M-C. and A. P. Buchmann, Encoded bitmap indexing for data warehouses, *Proc. IEEE Int. Conf. Data Eng.*, Orlando, FL, 1998.

Zhang, X., Z. Chen, and Q. Zhu, Mining influential association rule using bitmap indexing, Department of Computer Science, University of Nebraska at Omaha, 2001.

Zhang, X., Z. Chen, and Q. Zhu, Mining influential association rule using bitmap indexing, Technical Report, Department of Computer Science, University of Nebraska at Omaha, 2001.

Index

A

A* algorithm, 23
Access analysis tools, 12
Action List (AL), 161
Active databases, 163, 164
Active rules, 42
ActiveX controls, 19
ADMS project, *see* Architecture for Database
        Management Systems project
Agent(s)
    -based AI techniques, 26
    -based computing, 21
    goal-oriented, 28
    intelligent, 21
    interactional, 21
    remote, 28
    (semi)autonomous, 21
    situated, 21
    software, 21
    technology
        integration of ontologies and, 21
        Java and, 28
    transfer protocol (atp), 28
Aggregation
    functions, 127
    operations, defined on data cubes, 128
    value, 219
Aglet, 28
AI, *see* Artificial intelligence
AIS algorithm, 214
AL, *see* Action List
Algorithm(s)
    A*, 23

AIS, 214
Apriori, 192, 193, 194, 214
AprioriTid, 215, 224
BIRCH, 206
clustering, 74, 206
duplicate detection, 81
eager compensating, 159, 160
efficiency of, 167
genetic, 6, 25
    implementation, 139
    parameters, 140
greedy, 149
heuristic, 132, 135, 149
IARM, 216, 217, 219
k-means, 74
MAUVE, 169
optimization, 125
randomized, 136
reviews of for discovery of conventional
    association rules, 214
Strobe family of, 161
union-find, 81
ANNs, *see* Artificial neural networks
AOL, 194
API, *see* Application programming interface
Application(s)
    decision support, 126, 148
    developers, end-user, 18
    DSS, 118
    mobile client-server database, 175
    servers, 16
Application programming interface (API),
    16, 17, 76
    middleware, 76

OLAP, 119
Apriori algorithm, 192, 193, 194, 214
AprioriTid algorithm, 215, 224
Architecture for Database Management
        Systems (ADMS) project, 147
Artificial intelligence (AI), 3, 11, 21, *see also*
        Enterprise intelligence and
        artificial intelligence
    definition of, 21, 22
    early history of, 24
    integration of database management
        techniques and, 27
    machine learning in, 24
    symbol in context of, 22
    techniques
        agent-based, 26
        incorporation of into business
            intelligence, 6
        integration of into data warehousing,
            6
        use of for view selection, 150
Artificial neural networks (ANNs), 25
Association rule(s), 189
    computation, candidate, 211
    constraints in discovery of, 190
    conventional, 211
    discovery of, 190
    influential
        bitmap indexing and, 220
        discovery of, 212, 216
        mining of, 209
        significance of, 212
    mining, 187
    reviews of algorithms for discovery of
        conventional, 214
atp, *see* Agent transfer protocol

B

Back end tools, 54
Back-propagation neural network, 32
Bag-algebra operations, 154
Bankruptcy analysis, applying RSDA
        methodology for, 199
Basket data, 214
Benchmark, TPC-D decision-support, 119,
        120
BIRCH algorithm, 206
Bitmap
    categories, 225
    dimensions, 225
    indexing, 220
        algorithm design space provided by,
            225

binary encoded, 223
in data warehouses, 221
design space, 221
major advantage of, 220
time performance of, 222
Business
    community, different opinions on ER
        modeling by, 113
    -driven consultants, 4
    intelligence, 6, 14
    knowledge, 14
    warehouse, modeling of, 120
Bus structure, 107

C

Cache management, 118
Candidate association rule computation, 211
Cartesian product, 40
Catalog(s)
    DBMS, 44
    Web-based, 18
Categories bitmap, 225
CDWDM, *see* Data warehouse conceptual
        data model
Cell-address hashing scheme, 119
CGI, *see* Common gateway interface
Cisco Systems, 86, 93
Classification
    entities, 103
    rules, 204
Class libraries, for communicating with
        remote agents, 28
Clickstream, 29
    analysis, 33
    data mart, 33, 34
Client
    analysis tools, front-end, 54
    tools, front-end, 133
Client-server
    architecture, 48, 155
    databases, homogeneous, 155
Clustering algorithm, 74, 206
Common gateway interface (CGI), 16, 17
Common Object Request Broker Architecture
        (CORBA), 148
Complete view graph, 143
ConceptBase, 108
Conceptual data modeling, 97
Conceptual modeling, OLAP, 111
Concurrency control, 44, 45, 157
Condition part item set, support counting of,
        217
Conjunctive-query (CQ) views, 173

Connectionist networks, 25
Constellation schema, 104
Constraint mismatches, 73
Consultants, business-driven, 4
Consumer interests, Web trackers fine-tune
    mining of, 32
Convergence, occurrence of in GA, 136
Cookie(s)
    information, 30
    visitor identification, 30
CORBA, *see* Common Object Request Broker
    Architecture
COUNT, calculating, 129
CPU
    overhead, 62
    task parallelism at, 54
CQ views, *see* Conjunctive-query views
CRM, *see* Customer relationship
    management
CROQUE database, 174
Customer(s)
    association rules between products and,
        210
    bankruptcy, 204
    credit information, 200
    relationship management (CRM), 12, 17,
        29
Customization, data mart, 56

D

DAG, *see* Directed acyclic graph
Data
    analysis, *see also* Intelligent data analysis
        rough set, 195
        tool, 192
    auxiliary, 153
    basket, 214
    clarification, 191
    classification, 189, 191
    cleansing, 78, 79, 88
    clustering, 189
    denormalization, 61
    distribution, 147
    eliminating k sorts of, 83
    evolution and monitoring (DEMON), 206
    extraction, 79, 133
    generalization, 189
    inconsistency, 83, 84
    integration, 73, 74, 88
    maintenance-concurrent, 163
    management, multimedia, 59
    model, 133
        conceptual, 97

hierarchy, 39
    multidimensional, 171, 211, 213
preprocessing, 74
pumping, 75
quality, problems of, 77
raw, 51
reconciliation, multisource, 107
records with categorized, 201
reduction, 59, 84, 85, 89
requiring frequent refreshment, 149
semantics of, 21
source pipeline, 27
stock entry, 93
storage, relational database for, 53
structured, 40
transformation, 89
Webhouse, 17
Database (DB), 26
    active, 163, 164
    administrators (DBAs), 176
    applications, mobile client-server, 175
    client-server, 155
    connection to, 95
    conversion, 73
    CROQUE, 174
    data warehouses vs., 51
    deductive, 46, 173, 174
    design, 65
    distributed, 47
    extensional, 46
    food chain, 194
    IBM hierarchical, 133
    intensional, 46
    management (DBM), 27
    management systems (DBMS), 3, 5, 39, *see*
        also Data warehousing, from
        DBMS to
        advances in, 46
        architecture, popular distributed, 48
        basic knowledge about, 8
        catalog, 44
        physical implementation of, 43
    marketing, 17
    mobile, 175
    modification, deferred, 45
    object-oriented, 47, 174
    OLAP, 60
    operations, 154
    output created in, 95
    parallel, 47
    programming, using SQL, 8
    relational
        concepts related to keys in, 98
        for data storage, 53
    research community, 4

segmentation, 188
server
  OLAP, 66
  warehouse, 55
systems
  materialized views in advanced, 173
  object-oriented, 26
TPC-D benchmark, 123
updates, 153
Web as ultimate, 28
Data cube(s), 75, 120, 169
  aggregation operations defined on, 128
  calculating SUM on, 128
  cells of, 121
  dimensions of, 121
  dynamic OLAP, 172
  generation, automatic, 145
  materialization of, 118
  multidimensional, 170
  preconstructed data structures in, 127
Datalog model, 26
Data mart (DM), 15, 53, 54, 55, 68
  clickstream, 33, 34
  distributed, 35
  matrix approach for building, 100
  multiple, 57
  networked, 57
  performance, 65
  types of, 56
Data mining, *see also* OLAP and data mining,
        toward integrated
  categories of, 188
  dynamics of, 205
  incorporating OLAP considerations into,
        219
  integration of OLAP and, 209
  methods, predictive, 188
  predictive, 188
  recent progress of, 204
  relationship between OLAP operations
        and, 187
  spatial/temporal, 189
  tasks, 11
  tools, easy-to-use, 31
Data preparation and preprocessing, 73–96
  data cleansing, 78–83
    data cleansing methods, 79–83
    general aspects of data cleansing,
        78–79
  data preparation for stock food chain
        analysis, 85–93
    building of hierarchies, 91
    overview, 85–87
    preparation of data, 87–91
    resulting data, 91–93

data pumping, 75–76
data quality, 77–78
data reduction, 84–85
dealing with data inconsistency in
        multidatabase systems, 83–84
middleware, 76
overview, 73
schema and data integration, 73–75
Web log file preparation, 93–96
Data warehouse (DW), 68
  advantages of, 51
  architecture, 53
  aspects of building, 105
  bitmap indexing in, 221
  building of for grocery store, 101
  components, 53
  conceptual data model (CDWDM), 104
  databases vs., 51
  design, 54, 100
  future of, 34
  gestures, endowment of Web page user's
        interface with, 18
  human service, 130, 132
  kernel of, 118
  loading of, 107
  logical subset of complete, 15
  materialized views inside, 156
  mobile, 175
  optimal query benefit for, 144
  performance, measuring, 64
  prototyping of, 110
  quality, 78
  query, 64
  views, 134
  virtual, 50
  Web-enabled, 11, 19
Data warehouses, building of, 39, 97–115
  aspects of building data warehouses,
        105–110
    coherent management of warehouses
        for security, 110
    loading of warehouse, 107
    metadata management, 107–108
    operation phase, 108
    physical design, 105–106
    prototyping data warehouses, 110
    user behavior modeling for
        warehouse design, 109–110
    using data warehouse tools, 108–109
    using functional dependencies, 106
  conceptual data modeling, 97–100
    dimension modeling, 99–100
    entity-relationship modeling, 97–99
  data cubes, 111–112

data warehouse design using ER
approach, 100–105
example, 100–102
steps in using ER model for
warehousing conceptual
modeling, 102–104
research work on conceptual
modeling, 104–105
overview, 97
Data warehousing
historical development of, 12
importance of in industry today, 49
importance of to Web-enabling
techniques, 12
integrating artificial intelligence
techniques into, 6
intelligent, 4, 5
major milestones in, 13
meta issues related to, 4
motivations of, 48
real-time, 35
technique, godfather of, 49
transaction processing scenarios for, 161
Data warehousing, from DBMS to, 39–69
advances in DBMS, 46–52
basics of deductive databases, 46–47
distributed and parallel databases,
47–48
motivations of data warehousing,
48–52
object-relational and object-oriented
databases, 47
architecture and design of data
warehouses, 52–55
operational systems and warehouse
data, 52–53
data warehouse components, 53–54
data warehouse design, 54–55
data marts, 55–58
multiple data marts, 57
networked data marts, 57–58
types of data marts, 56–57
why data marts, 55–56
data warehouse performance, 64–66
measuring data warehouse
performance, 64–65
performance and warehousing
activities, 65–66
data warehousing and materialized
views, 60–64
materialized views, 60–62
indexing techniques, 62
indexing using metadata, 62–64
data warehousing and OLAP, 66–68
basics of OLAP, 66

relationship between data
warehousing and OLAP, 67–68
metadata, 58–60
overview of database management
systems, 39–46
basics of query processing, 43–44
basics of transaction processing, 44–46
data modeling, 39–40
integrity constraints, 42–43
normalization and normal forms, 43
overview, 39
relational data model, 40–41
DateOfIncident, 134, 135
DB, *see* Database
DBAs, *see* Database administrators
DBM, *see* Database management
DBMS, *see* Database management systems
Decision
class, 197
making, organizational, 3
matrix, 201
support
activities, 117
applications, 126, 148
benchmark, TPC-D, 119, 120
emergence of e-commerce as large
application of Internet in, 19, 50
queries, 6, 119
system (DSS), 3, 11, 27, 118
table, 196, 197, 198, 200
Deductive databases, 46, 173, 174
Deferred database modification, 45
Deferred view maintenance, 157
Deletion anomaly, example illustrating, 160
DEMON, *see* Data evolution and monitoring
Denormalization data, 61
Dependency lattice, 122
Dimension(s)
bitmap, 225
id, 129
modeling, 7, 97, 99
reduction, 85
Directed acyclic graph (DAG), 23, 167
Disk storage, 12
Distributed databases, 47
Distributed data marts, 35
DM, *see* Data mart
Domain
hierarchy, 99
-independent methods, 80
relevance, 79
Drill-down, 121
DSS, *see* Decision support system
Dumb e-catalog, 18
Duplicate detection algorithm, 81

Duplicate-eliminating projections, 155
DW, *see* Data warehouse
DynaMat, 157

E

Eager compensating algorithm (ECA), 159,
  160
E-BI, *see* E-business intelligence
E-business
  initiative, 11
  intelligence (E-BI), 34
ECA, *see* Eager compensating algorithm
E-catalog, dumb, 18
E-commerce, 17
  emergence of as large application of
    Internet in decision support, 19,
    50
  initiatives, 11
  World Wide Web and, 15
EDB, *see* Extensional database
Efficiency, data mart, 56
Electronic Industries Association, 58
Electronic retailing, 32
E-mail, 28
End-user application developers, 18
Enterprise intelligence and artificial
    intelligence, 11–37
  basic elements of data warehousing,
    14–15
  basics of artificial intelligence and
    machine learning, 21–26
    artificial intelligence as construction of
      intelligent agents, 21–22
    genetic algorithms, 25–26
    knowledge-based systems, 24
    state space search and knowledge
      representation, 22–24
    symbol-based machine learning,
      24–25
  databases and Web, 15–21
    data Webhouse, 17–20
    ontologies and semantic Web, 20–21
    World Wide Web and e-commerce,
      15–17
  data mining, CRM, Web mining, and
    clickstream, 29–34
    clickstream analysis, 33–34
    from data mining to Web mining,
      30–33
    what can be analyzed using intelligent
      data analysis, 29–30
  data warehousing and enterprise
    intelligence, 11–12

data warehousing with intelligent agents,
    26–29
    integration of database and
      knowledge-based systems, 26–27
    Java and agent technology, 28–29
    role of AI in warehousing, 27–28
  future of data warehouses, 34–35
  historical development of data
      warehousing, 12–14
    early 1990s, 13
    mid-1990s, 14
    prehistory, 12–13
    toward business intelligence, 14
  overview, 11
Entity sets, 97
Entity-relationship (ER), 7, 14, 39
  approach, data warehouse design using,
    100
  diagrams (ERDs), 97
    controversial role of, 99
    conversion of, 99
    retail chain, 101
  model, 14, 39, 61, 97
    different opinions on, 113
    hierarchy in, 103
    major constructs involved in, 98
    steps in use of for warehousing
      conceptual modeling, 102
  normalized school, 62
ER, *see* Entity-relationship
ERDs, *see* ER diagrams
ETL process, *see* Extraction, transformation
    and loading process
EVE, *see* Evolvable view environment
Event-entity-relationship model (EVER), 105
EVER, *see* Event-entity-relationship model
Evolvable view environment (EVE), 167
Exabyte, 87
Extensible markup language (XML), 16, 17
  metadata interchange format, 58
  pages, 16
  role of in describing metadata for Web
    documents, 60
Extensional database (EDB), 46
Extraction, transformation and loading (ETL)
    process, 79

F

Fact table record, 100
Find/Union processes, 83
Fitness function, 137
Flat schema, 104
Food chain database, 194

Foreign key, 98
Four-dimensional lattice, 111
Fragmentation, horizontal, 48
Frequently asked queries, 117
Front end
    client tools, 133
    server software, 133
    tools, 54
Full information, 151
Functional dependencies, 42, 106
Fuzzy set theory, 197

G

GA, *see* Genetic algorithm
Galaxy schema, 104
Gateways, server, accessing tabular data in
        relational databases from Web
        clients via, 20
Generalized projection, selection, and join
        (GPSJ) expressions, 108
Genetic algorithm (GA), 6, 25, 136
    convergence occurring in, 136
    implementation, 139
    parameters, 140
    results, 143, 144
    search space, 26
Geographical user interface (GUI), 31, 192,
        193
Goal-oriented agents, 28
GPSJ expressions, *see* Generalized projection,
        selection, and join expressions
Greedy algorithms, 149
GUI, *see* Geographical user interface

H

Hash-based methods, with optimization
        techniques, 170
Hash table, 124
Heuristic algorithms, 132, 135, 149
Heuristic search methods, 6
Hewlett-Packard Company (HWP), 91
Hierarchy(ies)
    building of, 91
    data model, 39
    dimensions, combining, 124
    domain, 99
HTML, *see* Hypertext markup language
HTTP protocol, 16
Human service data warehouse, 130, 132
HWP, *see* Hewlett-Packard Company
Hypertext markup language (HTML), 15, 16
    pages, 16

record of generated by single hit, 31
reports, static, 19

I

IARM, *see* Influential association rule mining
IARMBM, *see* Influential association rules
        using bitmap indexing
IBM, 87
    hierarchical database, 133
    mainframe
        data extraction occurring on, 133
        IDMS table on, 134
IC, *see* Integrity constraint
IDB, *see* Intensional database
Incremental maintenance, of SQL view, 153
Index
    structures, building of on materialized
        views, 61
    use of metadata as, 63, 64
Indexing
    bitmap, 220, 221, 222, 223, 225
    join, 68
    OLAP, 66
    techniques, 62, 168
Influential association rule(s), 209, 210
    bitmap indexing and, 220
    discovery of, 212, 216
    mining (IARM), 209, 217
        algorithm, 216, 217, 219
        candidate, 218
    pruning and refining candidate, 218
    significance of, 212
    using bitmap indexing (IARMBM), 223,
        226
Information
    collection of from Web, 91
    cookie, 30
    customer credit, 200
    dissemination
        on intranet, 20
        pull technology in, 21
    full, 151
    multidimensional visual presentation of,
        13
    partial, 152, 164
    retrieval (IR), 33
    semantic, 177
    time-stamped, 188
Informix Universal Server, 169
Inmon, William, 49
Integration paradigm, relational model as
        common, 165
Integrity constraint (IC), 42, 61, 163

Intelligence
    artificial, *see* Artificial intelligence;
            Enterprise intelligence and
            artificial intelligence
    business, 6, 14
    e-business, 34
    enterprise, *see* Enterprise intelligence and
            artificial intelligence
Intelligent agents, construction of, 21
Intelligent data analysis, 4, 187–207
    basics of data mining, 188–192
        association rule mining, 189–191
        categories of data mining, 188–189
        data classification and
            characterization, 191–192
        overview, 187–188
    recent progress of data mining, 204–206
        discovery of low-support rules, 205
        dynamics of data mining, 205–206
        mining of metadata, 205
        user expectations, 205
    rough set data analysis, 195–204
        applying RSDA methodology for
            bankruptcy analysis, 199–204
        basics, 195–198
    stock food chain analysis, 192–195
        analysis, 194–195
        graphical user interface, 193–194
        implementing Apriori algorithm,
            192–193
        overview, 192
Intelligent data warehousing, 4, 5
Intelligent software agent, 22
Intensional database (IDB), 46
Interactional agents, 21
Internet, 26
    -based, client-server architecture, 155
    emergence of e-commerce as large
            application of in decision
            support, 19, 50
    Engineering Task Force, 58
Intranets, 20, 26
IR, *see* Information retrieval
ISO Standard Committee, 58

J

Java, 28
    applets, 19
    Database Connection (JDBC), 16
    Server Pages (JSPs), 17
    servlets, 17
JDBC, *see* Java Database Connection

Join
    indexing, 68
    operation, 40
    queries, 62
JSPs, *see* Java Server Pages

K

KBSs, *see* Knowledge-based systems
KDD, *see* Knowledge discovery in databases
Kernel, data warehouse, 118
Key
    foreign, 98
    minimal super, 98
    primary, 98
Key performance indicators, 106
KM, *see* Knowledge management
k-means algorithm, 74
Knowledge
    -based systems (KBSs), 24, 26
    business, 14
    discovery, 7, 188
    discovery in databases (KDD), 29, 187
    management (KM), 17, 26
    pattern, 95
    representation, , 22
Korn shell scripting, 94
k views, optimization algorithm for selecting
            set of, 125
K-way sort
    concept, 83
    duplicate detection method, 82

L

Lattice(s)
    composite, 122
    dependency, 122
    four-dimensional, 111
    hierarchies in, 121, 126
    with selected materialized views, 127
Learning methods, 6
Legacy
    applications, growing level of discomfort
            with, 13
    systems, 117
Lineage tracing package, 150
Linear recursion, 174
Log files, redundant, 31
Loose coupling, 187
Lotus notes, 26
Low-support rules, discovery of, 205

M

Machine learning, 21, 191
  in artificial intelligence, 24
  relationship between knowledge-based
      approaches and, 25
  symbol-based, 24
Maintenance
  -concurrent data, 163
  cost calculation example, 139
  deferred, 158
  policies, 159
Management information systems (MIS), 3
Many-to-many relationships, 104
Mapping rules, 79
Market basket analysis (MBA), 189
Massively parallel processing (MPP), 29–30
Materialized views (MVs), 7, 60, 62, 68, 117
  in advanced database systems, 173
  building of index structures on, 61
  consequence of, 159
  examination of perspective of data
      warehousing as, 117
  externally, 155
  incremental maintenance of, with
      duplicates, 154
  inside data warehouse, 156
  maintaining thousands of in distributed
      framework, 75
  maintaining of using partial information,
      164
  model, 50
  in object-oriented databases, 174
  at warehouse, 160
Materialized views, advances in, 147–184
  consistency in view maintenance, 157–163
    concurrent updates in distributed
        environment, 162–163
    dealing with anomalies in view
        maintenance, 159–162
    immediate and deferred view
        maintenance, 157–159
  data cubes, 169–173
  data warehouse design through
      materialized views, 148–151
    data warehouse design, 148
    view data lineage problem, 150–151
    view selection problem, 148–150
  dynamic warehouse design, 165–168
    dynamicity of warehouse design, 165
    from static to dynamic warehouse
        design, 166–167
    view redefinition and adaptation,
        167–168
    warehouse evolution, 165–166

implementation issues and online
    updates, 168–169
  indexing techniques, 168
  online updates, 168–169
  physical implementation, 168
integrity constraints and active databases,
    163–165
  active databases, 164–165
  integrity constraints, 163–164
maintenance of materialized views,
    151–157
  dealing with irrelevant update, 154
  externally materialized views, 155
  incremental maintenance of
      materialized views with
      duplicates, 154–155
  other work, 157
  snapshot differential problem, 151
  unified view selection and
      maintenance, 156–157
  using auxiliary data and auxiliary
      views, 153–154
  using full and partial information for
      view maintenance, 151–152
  using incremental techniques, 152–153
  views and queries, 155–156
materialized views in advanced database
    systems, 173–174
  deductive databases, 173–174
  object-oriented databases, 174
other issues, 175–177
  materialized views in Oracle, 176–177
  real-time warehousing, 176
  temporal view self-maintenance,
      175–176
overview, 147–148
relationship with mobile databases, 175
Materialized views, basics of, 117–146
  aggregate calculation using
      preconstructed data structures in
      data cubes, 127–130
    aggregation operations defined on
        data cubes, 128–130
    preliminaries of aggregation
        functions, 127–128
  data cubes, 118–125
    materialization of data cubes, 118–121
    using lattice, 121–125
  overview, 117–118
  using simple optimization algorithm to
      select views, 125–127
  view selection for human service data
      warehouse, 130–145
    background information, 133
    data model, 133–134

development of OR view graph,
134–135
implementation, 135–139
overview of case study, 132–133
queries selected, 134
resulting views, 139–144
summary of case study, 144–145
Matrix table, 202
MAUVE algorithm, 169
Maxtor Corporation, 87
MBA, *see* Market basket analysis
MDDB, *see* Multidimensional database
Memory level capabilities, server, 54
Metadata, 35, 58, 68, 177
indexing using, 62
management, 107
mining of, 205
role of XML in description of for Web
documents, 60
syntax, 58
technical, 60
use of as index, 63, 64
Meta Data Coalition, 58
MHC, *see* Multidimensional hierarchical
clustering
Microsoft Corporation (MSFT), 91
Access, 87, 88, 143, 192
Money Central, 87
SQL server, 108
stock food chain, 86
Middleware, 29
application programming interface, 76
engine, 76
Minimal super key, 98
Minimum confidence, 190
Minimum support, 190
Mining path traversal patterns, 189
MIS, *see* Management information systems
Mobile databases, 175
Model
/algorithm training parameters, selection
of, 74
business warehouse, 120
conceptual data, 97
data, 133
hierarchy, 39
multidimensional, 171, 211, 213
relational, 40
Datalog, 26
dimensional, 7, 97, 99
entity-relationship, 14, 39, 61, 97
different opinions on, 113
hierarchy in, 103
major constructs involved in, 98

steps in use of for warehousing
conceptual modeling, 102
event-entity-relationship, 105
materialized view, 50
publish-and-subscribe, 28
relational, most important asset of, 60
starER, 105
structured entity relationship, 105
user query behavior, 109
virtual view, 50
MOLAP, *see* Multidimensional OLAP
Monitoring utilities, 54
MPP, *see* Massively parallel processing
MRE wrapper, *see* Multirelation
encapsulation wrapper
MSFT, *see* Microsoft Corporation
Multidatabase systems, dealing with
inconsistency in, 83
Multidimensional database (MDDB), 119
Multidimensional data model, 171
Multidimensional hierarchical clustering
(MHC), 172
Multidimensional OLAP (MOLAP), 66, 111
Multimedia data management, 59
Multi-pass sorted neighborhood duplicate
detection method, 80
Multiple view consistency (MVC), 162
Multirelation encapsulation (MRE) wrapper,
163
Multiway array aggregation, 111
Mutation, 137
MVC, *see* Multiple view consistency
MVPP, 166
MVs, *see* Materialized views

N

NASDAQ stocks, 87
Network(s)
bandwidth, 64
connectionist, 25
neural, 25, 32, 191
traffic, 34
wireless, 175
Neural network, 191
artificial, 25
back-propagation, 32
New-visitor click profile, 34
Nonflat tables, 47
NP-hard problem, 135
Numeric measure, categorization and
support counting of, 217

O

Object Management Group (OMG), 58
Object-oriented database (OODB), 47
  materialized views in, 174
  systems, 26
Object partitioning, 202
Object-relational data warehousing (ORDW),
    108
ODSs, *see* Operational data stores
OLAM, *see* On-Line Analytical Mining
OLAP, *see* On-line analytical processing
OLAP and data mining, toward integrated,
    209–227
  bitmap indexing and influential
      association rules, 220–223
    basic idea of bitmap indexing, 220–221
    bitmap indexing in data warehouses,
        221–223
  discovery of influential association rules,
      216–220
    ARM algorithm, 216–217
    categorization and support counting
        of numeric measure, 217–218
    mining candidate influential
        association rules, 218
    problems of IARM algorithm, 219–220
    pruning and refining candidate
        influential association rules,
        218–219
    support counting of condition part
        item set, 217
  influential association rules, 210–212
  integration of OLAP and data mining,
      209–210
  mining influential association rules using
      bitmap indexing, 223–226
  overview, 209
  reviews of algorithms for discovery of
      conventional association rules,
      214–216
  significance of influential association
      rules, 212–213
OLTP, *see* On-line transaction processing
OMG, *see* Object Management Group
On-Line Analytical Mining (OLAM), 210
On-line analytical processing (OLAP), 6, 11,
    39, 50, 54
  aggregation and, 210
  APIs for, 119
  broad deployment of, 19
  conceptual elements of, 99
  conceptual modeling for, 111
  database server, 66
  data cubes, dynamic, 172

decision support queries in, 41
  design, benefits of, 109
  engines, vendors of, 50
  implementation approaches facilitating,
      119
  indexing, 66
  integration of data mining and, 209
  multidimensional, 66
  operations, 55, 187
  physical dimensional design techniques
      for, 57
  popularity of data cubes in, 75
  query, 14, 111
  relational, 66
  relationship between data warehousing
      and, 67
  roll-up operations, 213
  system(s)
    commercial, 110
    dominant relational database for
        developing, 108
    most read environment of, 62
    support of data analysis by, 171
    two-step process in, 168
  tools
    advanced functionality provided by,
        27
    software companies producing, 13
On-line transaction processing (OLTP), 14,
    43, 52
  data mart design teams dealing with, 61
  queries, 14, 119
  systems, 49
Online updates, 168
Ontologies, 20, 21
OODB, *see* Object-oriented databases
Operational data stores (ODSs), 14, 52
Optimization
  algorithm, use of simple, 125
  techniques, hash-based methods with,
      170
ORACLE, 94
Oracle8*i*, 177
Oracle Materialized Views, 176
ORDW, *see* Object-relational data
    warehousing
Organizational decision making, 3
OR view graph(s)
  complete, 135, 142
  development of, 134
  GA results, 144
  large, 145
  parameters, complete, 143
  problem based on, 132
  small, 139, 140

Outer-join expressions, 152
Output, sample, 96

P

Parallel databases, 47
Parent table, 47
Partial information, 152, 164
Partitioning, based on decision, 203
Penalty function, 138
Perl, 16
Pivot, motivation behind operation of, 112
Polish Academy of Sciences, 196
Prediction
    methods, 85
    programs, 84
PRE_MAX tree, 130, 131
Primary key, 98
Probability theory, 197
Process-creation overhead, 16
Processor costs, 12
Product
    relation, 102
    table, 62
Product_class relation, 102
Promotion relation, 102
Proof-of-concepts, 110
Proxy servers, 20
PSWEEP, 163
Publish-and-subscribe model, 28
Pull technology, in information
    dissemination, 21

Q

Quality factor, reevaluated, 108
Query(ies)
    actual cost of, 124
    benefit, 137
        function, 138
        optimal, for data warehouse, 144
    costs, 138, 139, 141, 142
    data warehouse, 64
    decision support, 6, 41, 119
    direct ancestor view for answering, 124
    examples, SQL, 89
    frequently asked, 117
    interrelated, 170
    join, 62
    KDD, 187
    manager, 44
    nested SQL, 41
    OLAP, 14, 111
    OLTP, 14, 119

optimization, 44n, 61
    strategy, for decision-support
        applications, 126
    technique, powerful, 118
    optimizer, relational, 156
    performance, 119
    processing, 43, 166
    response time, 171
    results, 77
    rewrite, 169
    selection of, 134
    similar to SQL statements, 223
    SPJ, 156
    SQL, 43, 121
    time-stamped information, 188
    Web resources, 20
Querying
    engine, 50
    interface, 50
    operations, commonly used, 121

R

RA, *see* Relational algebra
Raw-data relation, 121
RDBMS, *see* Relational database management
    system
ReadRite Corporation, 87
Real-time data warehousing, 35
Record-to-record comparisons, 83
Referential-integrity constraint, 42
Refreshment process, propagation of changes
    during, 107
Relational algebra (RA), 40, 41
Relational database(s)
    concepts related to keys in, 98
    for data storage, 53
    management system (RDBMS), 13
    vendor, 29
Relational model, most important asset of, 60
Relational OLAP (ROLAP), 66
Relevance, data mart, 56
Remote agents, 28
Requirements analysis, importance of, 73
Resolution function, 84
Retail chain, ERD for, 101
Return on investment (ROI), 12
ROI, *see* Return on investment
ROLAP, *see* Relational OLAP
Roll-up, 112, 122
Rough set data analysis (RSDA), 195, 199
    application of on sample data, 203
    methodology, application of for
        bankruptcy analysis, 199

Rough set theory, 7, 187, 198, 204
RSDA, *see* Rough set data analysis
Run-time system optimization, 108, 109

S

Sale(s)
    relation, 102
    roll up, 112
    table, 63
Schema
    constellation, 104
    entities, semantic mismatches of, 73
    flat, 104
    formation, 40
    galaxy, 104
    relation in database with, 112
    snowflake, 103, 104
    star, 62, 67
    star cluster, 104
    terraced, 104
Search
    methods, heuristic, 6
    space, GA, 26
    state space, 21
    tool, 25
Search-and-scan performance, 61
Self-determination, data mart, 56
Semantic(s)
    issues, 73
    machine-processable, 21
Serializability, 45
SERM, *see* Structured entity relationship
        model
Server(s)
    application, 16
    gateways, accessing tabular data in
        relational databases from Web
        clients via, 20
    Informix Universal, 169
    memory level capabilities of, 54
    Microsoft SQL, 108
    OLAP database, 66
    proxy, 20
    software, front-end, 133
    warehouse database, 55
    Web, 16
Set
    difference, 40
    semantics, deductive databases using, 174
Situated agents, 21
Snapshot differential problem, 151
Snowflake schema, 103, 104
Software
    agent, intelligent, 22

availability of for access and analysis of
    data, 56
companies, OLAP tools produced by, 13
front-end server, 133
SOIF, 58
Solution encoding, 136
Sorted neighborhood method, 80, 82
Source data, 199
Spatial/temporal data mining, 189
SPJ queries, 156
SQL, *see* Structured query language
Star cluster schema, 104
StarER model, 105
Star schema, 62, 67
State space search, 21
Stock(s)
    data, collection of, 86
    entry data, 93
    food chain
        analysis, 85, 192
        Apriori algorithm, GUI for, 193
        Microsoft, 86
        relationships, 91, 92–93
    market, volatile nature of, 194
    NASDAQ, 87
    parent, 192
    prices, 88
Store relation, 102
Strobe family of algorithms, 161
Structured entity relationship model (SERM),
    105
Structured query language (SQL), 41, 151
    database programming using, 8
    query(ies), 43, 121
        data transfer implemented by, 109
        examples, 89
        nested, 41
    select expression, 164
    statement(s), 41
        queries similar to, 223
        series of, 88
    view
        materialized, 150
        problem of incremental maintenance
        of, 153
Summary-delta table method, 170
Summary tables, 168
Summation graph, 82, 83
Sun Microsystems, 87
Supply-chain relationships, transformation
    of, 18
Support
    counting
        of condition part item set, 217
        of numeric measure, 217

user-specified, 212
SWEEP, 162, 163
Sybase, 94
Symbol-based machine learning, 24
System optimization, run-time, 108, 109

T

Table(s)
    decision, 196, 197, 198, 200
    fact, 100
    hash, 124
    IDMS, 134
    matrix, 202
    nonflat, 47
    parent, 47
    product, 62
    sale, 62
    summary, 168
    summary-delta, 170
Technical metadata, 60
TeleChart 2000, 87
Temporal view self-maintenance, 175
Temporary update problem, 45
Terraced schema, 104
Text
    mining, 188
    strings, 80
3NF, *see* Third normal form
Third normal form (3NF), 43
Time
    attributes, hierarchy of, 122
    -stamped information, query of, 188
Total maintenance cost equation, 138
Toyota sales cross tabulation, 112
TPC-D benchmark database, 123
TPC-D decision-support benchmark, 119, 120
Transaction(s)
    entities, 102
    failure, 45
    processing scenarios, for data
        warehousing, 161
    small, 51
Transformation
    programs, 133
    workflow, 79
Transitive closure, 81
Triggers, 42
2PC, *see* Two-phase commit protocol
Two-phase commit protocol (2PC), 48
Two-phase locking (2PL), 45, 159
2PL, *see* Two-phase locking
Two version no locking (2VNL), 169
2VNL, *see* Two version no locking

U

Uncertainty reasoning, 191
Union, 40
Union-find algorithms, 81
Universal resource locator (URL), 15, 16, 29
University of Warsaw, 196
UNIX, 94
Updates
    concurrent, in distributed environment,
        162
    online, 168
URL, *see* Universal resource locator
User
    behavior, prediction of, 109
    -defined programs, data transfer
        implemented by, 109
    expectations, 205
    query behavior, model of, 109
    -specified support, 212

V

Vendor(s)
    OLAP engine, 50
    relational database, 29
View(s), *see also* Materialized views
    auxiliary, 164
    conjunctive-query, 173
    data
        lineage problem, 150
        warehouse, 134
    externally materialized, 155
    graph
        parameters, 137
        results from small, 141
    information retrieval, 33
    k, 125
    maintenance, 152
        consistency in, 157
        cost, 148
        dealing with anomalies in, 159
        deferred, 157
        problem, 107, 152
    redefinition, 167
    refreshment, 158
    selection
        problem, 135, 148
        unified, 156
        use of artificial intelligence techniques
           for, 150
    self-maintenance, temporal, 175
    SQL, 153

use of simple optimization algorithm to select, 125
virtual, 50
Virtual data warehouse, 50
Virtual view model, 50
Visitor identification cookies, 30
Visual Basic code, 192
Voluntary Inter-industry Commerce Standards Council, 58
VSAM files, 133

W

WANs, *see* Wide area networks
Warehouse(s), *see also* Data warehouse
   activities, 65
   coherent management of for security, 110
   database server, 55
   design
      dynamic, 165
      role of functional dependencies in conceptual, 106
      static to dynamic, 166
   evolution, 165
   materialized view at, 160
   real-time, 176
   refreshment, 168
   strategy, 4
WareHousing Information Project at Stanford University (WHIPS), 147
   data warehousing system prototype, 150–151
   prototype, 148
Web
   -based catalogs, 18
   browser, 16
   content mining, 33
   data, creating and enhancing, 31
   databases and, 15
   documents, role of XML in describing metadata for, 60
   -enabling techniques, 6, 12
   information collected from, 91
   log file preparation, 93
   marketing, 32
   mining, 29, 30, 33
   page development, 18
   resources, query and access, 20
   semantic, 20
   server, 16
   services, integration of agent technology and ontologies affecting use of, 21
   trackers, fine-tune mining of consumer interests, 32
   as ultimate database, 28
Webhouses, 17, 18, 30
WHIPS, *see* WareHousing Information Project at Stanford University
Wide area networks (WANs), 20
Window NT, 94
Wireless network, 175
World Wide Web (WWW), 16, 26, *see also* Web Consortium (W3C), 58
   e-commerce and, 15
W3C, *see* World Wide Web Consortium
WWW, *see* World Wide Web

X

XML, *see* Extensible markup language

Y

Yahoo!, 87

Z

ZIP code, 30

T - #0124 - 101024 - C0 - 234/156/14 [16] - CB - 9780849312045 - Gloss Lamination